MANAGING WATER CONFLICT

Asia, Africa and the Middle East

ASHOK SWAIN

Department of Peace and Conflict Research
Uppsala University, Sweden

Routledge
Taylor & Francis Group

LONDON AND NEW YORK

First published 2004
by Routledge
11 New Fetter Lane, London EC4P 4EE

Simultaneously published in the USA and Canada
by Routledge
29 West 35th Street, New York, NY 10001

Routledge is an imprint of the Taylor & Francis Group

© 2004 Ashok Swain

Typeset in Classical Garamond by
Frank Cass Books Ltd

Printed and bound in Great Britain by
Antony Rowe Ltd, Chippenham, Wiltshire

British Library Cataloguing in Publication Data
Swain, Ashok
Managing water conflict: Asia, Africa and the Middle East.
1. Water resources development 2. Water resources development
– Case studies 3. Water resources development –
International cooperation 4. Water resources development –
International cooperation – Case studies 5. Pacific
settlement of international disputes – Case studies
I. Title
333.9'1

Library of Congress Cataloging-in-Publication Data
Swain, Ashok
Managing water conflict: Asia, Africa, and the Middle East / Ashok
Swain
p.cm
Includes bibliographical references and index
ISBN 0-714-65566-X (hardback)
1. Water-supply–Asia–Management–International cooperation. 2.
Water-supply–Africa–Management–International cooperation. 3.
Water-supply–Middle East–Management–International cooperation.
4. Watershed management–Asia. 5. Watershed management–Africa. 6.
Watershed management–Middle East. 7. International rivers–Asia. 8.
International rivers–Africa 9. International rivers–Middle East. I. Title

TD299.S93 2004
363.6'1–dc22
2003062745

ISBN 0–714–65566–X

To the memory of B. N. Swain, my father

Contents

List of Maps, Tables and Figures   viii
Preface   x
Acknowledgements   xi

1 Water Scarcity: A Threat to Security or
   an Incentive to Cooperate?   1

2 South Asia and its Large Rivers:
   The Indus, the Mahakali and with Special Emphasis
   on the Ganges   43

3 Rivers in the Middle East and North Africa:
   The Jordan, the Euphrates-Tigris and with
   Special Emphasis on the Nile   79

4 Southeast Asia and the Mekong River   116

5 Southern Africa and its Shared Rivers:
   The Orange, the Limpopo, the Okavango and with
   Special Emphasis on the Zambezi   140

6 Sustaining Water Agreements and Maturing Cooperation   158

   Appendix: Convention on the Law of the Non-navigational
   Uses of International Watercourses, 1997   182
   Bibliography   199
   Index   217

List of Maps, Tables and Figures

MAPS

1	The Ganges River	55
2	The Nile River	92
3	The Mekong River	117
4	The Zambezi River	150

TABLES

1.1	Countries facing water scarcity	5/6
1.2	Countries failing to meet basic water requirement (BWR)	8/9
1.3	Regional distribution of international rivers	27
1.4	Countries heavily dependent on imported surface water	28
1.5	Selected fresh water basins and existing cooperative institutions	34/35
2.1	Basin area of Ganges-Brahmaputra-Meghna River system	57
3.1	Illustrative data for Nile basin countries	93
3.2	Comparing the Nile with other major river systems in Africa	94
4.1	The Mekong River basin and the riparian states	117

5.1 Sectoral water withdrawals by SADC states   141

5.2 Shared river basins in Southern Africa   142

5.3 Statewise share of the Zambezi River basin   150

6.1 Voting in the General Assembly for the Adoption of Convention on the Law of the Non-navigational Uses of International Watercourses   166

FIGURE

1.1 Increasing demand over water and creation of conflicting actors   20

Preface

There is a water crisis today. Water is not only a 'commodity', it is synonymous with life. All life on earth is dependent on water. If water is life, its possession bestows power. Water has crucial economic value, and it is a subsistence resource. Also, water has an emotional and symbolic value for certain countries and communities. The scarcity of water is increasing worldwide and its quality is continuously deteriorating. Water shortages reduce food production, aggrandize poverty, amplify disease and force people to migrate. The scarcity of water also undermines the state's capacity to govern. Nearly half of the world's population lives in international river basins. Sharing of the international rivers can therefore be a serious object of contention between riparian nations. For the last few years, 'water war' has been a topic of widespread debate. However, wars over river water are likely only under a narrow set of circumstances, as there are also more examples of water cooperation than water conflict among countries.

Nevertheless, the increasing scarcity of water raises doubt about the sustainability of these cooperative agreements over the international rivers. Water scarcity is particularly severe in Asia, Africa and the Middle East, owing to population growth, urbanization and industrialization. Whether the water crisis intensifies the dispute over the shared waters or whether it can be turned towards sustainable cooperative management of river resources, depends on many interacting processes. This book, after analysing the existing sharing mechanisms of the major international river systems in these regions, argues that the real solution lies in a comprehensive approach to river basin management.

Acknowledgements

This book would not have been possible without the accumulated help and support of several individuals in the last ten years. The Department of Peace and Conflict Research, Uppsala University, Sweden, is a perfect home for this work. My thanks go to all the Department colleagues who provided a stimulating research environment. Special thanks must go to Peter Wallensteen, who introduced me to this topic in the early 1990s and has remained as a source of constant support, motivation and inspiration. Ramses Amer, Hans Blomkvist, Gunnel Cederlöf, Birger Heldt, Kjell-Åke Nordquist, Margareta Sollenberg, Niklas Swanström, Sten Widmalm and Carl Johan Åsberg are other colleagues at Uppsala University to whom I am particularly grateful for their inputs and support.

Managing Water Conflict has resulted from the aggregated research findings that I have published, sometimes with co-authors, in journals, edited books, monographs and research reports since 1993. Materials that I co-authored with Elisabeth Corell, Jerome Riviere, Patrik Stålgren and Peter Wallensteen have been incorporated into the book in several chapters as mentioned in those chapters' endnotes. I am particularly grateful to Peter Holtsberg, who helped me to write the chapter on the Mekong River. Others who contributed valuable help and ideas were J. A. Allan, Kamrulzaman Askandar, Asit Biswas, J. S. A. Brichieri-Colombi, Anna Brismar, Gunilla Björklund, Manas Chatterji, Ken Conca, Geoffrey Dabelko, Ulf Ehlin, Sarif Elmusa, Malin Falkenmark, Sabil Francis, Krishna Ghimire, Jan Lundqvist, Nils Petter Gleditsch, Peter Gleick, Jesse Hamner, Björn Hettne, Thomas Homer-Dixon, Jim Lee, Steve Lonergan, Clovis Maksoud, Sam Moyo, E. Wayne Nafziger, Leif Ohlsson, Salman M. A. Salman, Rajinder Saxena, Brian Smith, Larry Swatuk, Daniel Tavera, Rajeev Thottappillil, Raimo Väyrynen, Aaron Wolf and Joakim Öjendal. Financial support for the research by SAREC, Sida, is also gratefully acknowledged.

Earlier versions of various portions of this book have been presented at different institutions, including American University (Washington DC), Copenhagen University, Dhaka University, Gothenburg University,

Harvard University, Linköping University, Lund University, Nordic Institute Asian Studies, Oslo University, SARIP – Harare, United Nations University, University of Chicago, University of Science, Malaysia, WIDER (Helsinki) and Woodrow Wilson Centre. I profited very much from the constructive and thoughtful comments from those attending the presentations. I would also like to thank my students, whose questions and comments in the classroom have brought clarity to the ideas and arguments in the book.

With loving gratitude, I thank my wife Ranjula, for her patience and generous support in all phases of this work. She not only read all the chapters and made useful suggestions, but also put up with me while I finished it. Our son contributed nothing to the manuscript except frequent distractions, but nonetheless he was the steady source of love and hope. Thank you Kabir. Thanks are also due to my mother, parents-in-law and family in India for their love and support. Finally, I would like to dedicate this book in memory of my father Baikunth Nath Swain, for, among so many other things, instilling in me the values of sharing. Rest in peace, Bapa!

Water Scarcity: A Threat to Security or an Incentive to Cooperate?[1]

Water is one of the most precious commodities for human beings. To some, it is the very lifeblood of the world. From time immemorial, the availability of water has determined the rhythms of daily life in many regions. The critical importance of water to the survival of the human race can be seen in the earliest civilizations whose growth and sustenance were closely tied to its water distribution systems. Many authors have located the importance of water in different religious observances. In Hindu and Buddhist traditions, the rivers of the earth, including the Indus, the Ganges and the Brahmaputra, originate from the mythical Mount Meru, the living place for the gods.[2] In the Christian tradition, the waters originate from the Garden of Eden, and that divides the world into greatest streams: the Nile, the Tigris, the Euphrates, the Indus and the Ganges.[3] Islam also gives water its due importance. The holy book Koran describes that every living thing is made from water.[4] As Caponera points out, it seems that in the Koran, the most precious creation after humankind is water.[5]

The planet earth is unique in the solar system in having water in liquid form. The other planets of the solar system are either too hot or too cold to maintain a water cycle, which can support life. However, water is also at the same time one of the most erratic objects on earth. The total volume of water available on our planet is 1.41 billion cubic kilometres. If evenly distributed, this amount of water is sufficient to cover a depth of nearly three kilometres over the earth's surface. However, 98 per cent of this amount is not usable since it is found in the saltwater of the oceans, inland seas and deep underground basins. Most of the remaining 2 per cent of fresh water is stored in ice caps, glaciers, underground, in the soil, in the atmosphere and in living beings. Excluding lakes, only about 2,000 cubic kilometres of fresh water, found mainly in rivers, is available for human consumption.[6] As Igor A. Shiklomanov estimates, 'Fresh water lakes and rivers, which are the main sources for human water consumption, contain on average about 90,000 cubic kilometres of water, or just 0.26 per cent of total global fresh water reserves.[7]

The surface runoff is the most important source of fresh water. The total global runoff average in annual basis is 44,500 cubic kilometres, which excludes the ice flow in Antarctica.[8] This runoff is highly capricious in nature among different parts of the world. Most of the total global runoff is converged in the temperate areas and equatorial regions, which host a relatively small population. In the continent of Europe, the per capita runoff is half of the global per capita average. But, the larger part of the continent is endowed with temperate climate and many small rivers with steady flows, which makes it possible to tap a high proportion of the runoff. According to Malin Falkenmark, the belief that fresh water abounds pervades the mindset of the developed world, which lives in the temperate zone.[9] Thus, the water development and management specialists of the temperate north show 'water blindness' or 'temperate bias'.[10]

In the tropical and arid areas, where most of the world population lives, the limited flowing water resources are very unevenly distributed. Almost all the developing countries are in the arid and semi-arid, tropical and subtropical regions and many of them are facing severe water shortages. The volume of the rivers, which is the major source of the fresh water, is also unequally distributed among the countries within these regions. The runoff from the Amazon River alone amounts to 80 per cent of South America's average runoff. Similarly, 30 per cent of the total runoff in Africa originates from a single river basin, the Congo/Zaire. Another major share among the African rivers is made up by the Nile system. In Asia, the Ganges-Brahmaputra and Mekong basins are the carriers of a significantly high proportion of the continent's runoff. River runoff in the temperate belt is not as disproportionate as it is in the tropical and arid regions. The runoff in the countries of tropical regions also suffers from high seasonal fluctuations. Many regions get nearly all of their yearly precipitation during a short, intense rainy season.

With increasing global population and mankind's pursuit for a higher standard of living, the demand for scarce water resource is continuing to increase. The water crisis is becoming widespread and more insidious, particularly in arid and tropical countries. Thus, the issue of management of international water systems demand serious attention, both nationally and internationally. With the help of several case studies in Asia, Africa and the Middle East, this book aspires to illustrate that the sharing of international rivers is not a zero-sum game, but properly conceived and executed management strategies for these water bodies to produce win-win situations for all the riparian countries.

2

GROWING WATER SCARCITY

Between 1940 and 1990, world population leaped from 2.3 billion to 5.3 billion human beings. At the same time, the per capita use of water also doubled from 400 to 800 cubic metres per person per year. As a result, the global human consumption of water increased more than four times in 50 years.[11] Present estimates indicate that the global population is likely to be doubled between 1990 and 2100 and most of this increase will probably occur by the year 2025. As the practical availability of usable renewable fresh water on a yearly basis is limited to between 9,000 and 14,000 cubic kilometres, it is unlikely that another quadrupling of world water use can happen again. As the population increases and the sum of available water resources remains fairly constant, the maximum per capita demand that a country can support decreases correspondingly. The population growth has reduced the specific per capita water supply. Owing to the current population projection, the per capita water supply is projected to decline at a much faster rate.

More than 90 million people add to the world's population every year, with 95 per cent of growth taking place in the developing countries of Africa, Asia and Latin America.[12] Some countries have already stabilized their population, while many others are expanding at 3 per cent or more per year. Continentwise, Africa is projected to witness the highest growth rate, while the population of Europe in 2100 is estimated to be less than it is at present.[13] Human life relies on continuous access to fresh water and food resources. Food production, however, is critically contingent upon the availability of water. The total agricultural water requirement has increased 6.5 times in the last century (1900–2000). Besides demand in the agricultural sector, with the rise in world population water requirements for the purpose of energy generation, domestic uses and industrial production have also increased.

Agriculture is accountable for 67 per cent of the total water withdrawal on the earth. Industry uses 19 per cent, whereas municipal and domestic water supply accounts for 9 per cent of the total water withdrawal.[14] Much of this water returns to the rivers or other water systems for the use of other consumers. If we calculate purely consumptive use of water, then agriculture consumes a staggering 86.9 per cent.[15] There is a high consumptive use of water in the agricultural sector.

The introduction of hybrid varieties of plantation is the major reason for rapidly increasing use of water in the agricultural sector. To meet the needs of growing population, irrigation has become the cornerstone of global food security. Across the world, nearly 17 per cent of the cropland is irrigated and provides one-third of global harvest. The amount of water used for irrigation networks has increased ten times in the last century, and elaborate plans are being carried out for further expansion.[16] In spite of rapid expansions of irrigation schemes, per capita availability of irrigated land is decreasing owing to massive population growth. In 1978, per capita irrigated land peaked at 48 hectares for every thousand people and since then it has started decreasing.[17] Irrigation is extremely important as 40 per cent of the world's grain is produced from the 17 per cent of the global cropland that is watered artificially.[18] Irrigated land provides over 60 per cent of the food grain in India and almost 70 per cent of the food grain in China.[19] As nearly all the easily available irrigation schemes have now been developed, the implementation of new projects is becoming politically, economically and environmentally hazardous.

Some sobering statistics illustrate that water scarcity has become a crucial issue. The 'water barrier' concept of Malin Falkenmark is frequently used to measure the water adequacy of different countries. This concept uses a simple index of annual per capita fresh water availability for each country. The countries having an index value of more than 1,700 cubic metres are treated as water sufficient. These countries face only occasional water problems of a localized nature. When the index lies between 1,000 and 1,700 cubic metres, the country confronts 'water stress'. In these countries proper water management is required to address widespread shortage problems. When the index falls below 1,000 cubic metres, the country reaches 'water scarcity'. In these countries, water scarcity threatens public health and affects socio-economic development. If the index drops to 500 cubic metres, the country reaches 'absolute water scarcity'. After crossing this red line, the country is almost certain to face inherent water deficit problems, with often outright shortages and acute scarcity.

The growing population is further shrinking the amount of water available per capita in many countries. The increase in population has reduced the global per capita water availability from 33,300 cubic metres per year in 1850 to 8,500 cubic metres per year in 1993.[20] With the current population growth projection, per capita water supply is projected to decline at a much faster rate than this. The amount of water available per person from the hydrological cycle will reduce by 73 per cent between 1950 and 2050.[21] It is anticipated that between 44 per cent and 65 per cent of the world's population will experience conditions of water scarcity or water stress by the middle of the twenty-first century.[22]

The 'water barrier' approach provides a simple and comprehensive global view of the water situation. However, it does not address the water availability to a country from trans-boundary sources. Besides, its emphasis is on population, while the per capita demand for water

Table 1.1 Countries Facing Water Scarcity

Country	Population 1995 (millions)	Water per capita (1995) in cubic metres per year	Population 2025 (millions)	Water per capita (2025) in cubic metres per year	Total fertility rate 1998	Per cent population growth rate 1998
Countries within 'Water scarcity' category						
Algeria	28.1	527	47.3	313	4.4	2.4
Bahrain	0.6	161	0.9	104	3.2	2.0
Barbados	0.3	192	0.9	169	1.7	0.5
Burundi	6.1	594	12.3	292	6.6	2.5
Cape Verde	0.4	777	0.7	442	5.3	2.9
Comoros	0.6	1,667	1.3	760	5.1	2.7
Cyprus	0.7	1,208	1.0	947	2.1	0.7
Egypt	62.1	936	95.8	607	3.6	2.2
Ethiopia	56.4	1,905	136.3	807	7.0	2.5
Haiti	7.1	1,544	12.5	879	4.8	2.1
Iran	68.4	1,719	128.5	916	3.0	1.8
Israel	5.5	389	8.0	270	2.9	1.5
Jordan	5.4	318	11.9	144	4.4	2.5
Kenya	27.2	1,112	50.2	602	4.5	2.0
Kuwait	1.7	95	2.9	55	3.2	2.3
Libya	5.4	111	12.9	47	6.3	3.7
Malawi	9.7	1,933	20.4	917	5.9	1.7
Malta	0.4	82	0.4	71	2.1	0.6
Morocco	26.5	1,131	39.9	751	3.3	1.8
Oman	2.2	874	6.5	295	7.1	3.9
Qatar	0.5	91	0.8	64	4.1	1.7
Rwanda	5.2	1,215	13.0	485	6.0	2.1
Saudi Arabia	18.3	249	42.4	107	6.4	3.1
Singapore	9.5	1,422	23.7	570	7.0	3.2
Somalia	9.5	1,422	23.7	570	7.0	3.2
South Africa	41.5	1,206	71.6	698	3.3	1.6
Tunisia	9.0	434	13.5	288	3.2	1.9
UAE	2.2	902	3.3	604	4.9	2.2
Yemen	15.0	346	39.6	131	7.3	3.3
Countries within 'Water stress' category						
Afghanistan	19.7	2,543	45.3	1,105	6.1	2.5
Belgium	10.1	1,234	10.3	1,217	1.6	0.1
Burkina Faso	10.5	2,672	23.5	1,194	6.9	2.9
Eritrea	3.2	2,775	6.5	1,353	6.1	3.0
Ghana	17.3	3,068	36.3	1,494	5.5	2.9
India	929.0	2,244	1,330.2	1,567	3.4	1.9
Lebanon	3.0	1,854	4.4	1,261	2.3	1.6
Lesotho	2.0	2,565	4.0	1,290	4.3	2.1
Mauritius	1.1	1,970	1.5	1,485	2.0	1.0
Niger	9.2	3,552	22.4	1,452	7.4	3.4
Nigeria	111.7	2,506	238.4	1,175	6.5	3.0
Peru	23.5	1,700	35.5	1,126	3.5	2.2
Poland	38.6	1,458	40.0	1,406	1.6	0.1
South Korea	44.9	1,472	52.5	1,258	1.7	1.0
Tanzania	30.7	2,964	62.4	1,425	5.7	2.5
Togo	4.1	2,938	8.8	1,370	6.8	3.6

(Continued)

Table 1.1 continued

Country	Population 1995 (millions)	Water per capita (1995) in cubic metres per year	Population 2025 (millions)	Water per capita (2025) in cubic metres per year	Total fertility rate 1998	Per cent population growth rate 1998
Uganda	19.7	3,352	45.0	1,467	6.9	2.7
UK	58.1	1,222	89.5	1,193	1.7	0.2
Zimbabwe	11.2	1,787	19.3	1,034	4.4	1.5

Source: D. Hinrichsen and H. Tacio, 'The Coming Freshwater Crisis is Already Here', in *Finding the Source: The Linkage Between Population and Water* (Washington DC: Woodrow Wilson International Centre for Scholars, ECSP Publication, 2002), pp. 22–3. Original source: T. Gardner-Outlaw and R. Engelman, *Sustaining Water, Easing Scarcity: A Second Update* (Washington DC: Population Action International, 1997); and Population Reference Bureau, *Population and Environment Dynamics* (Wall Chart) (Washington DC: Population Reference Bureau, 1998).

depends on economic activities, type of agriculture, livestock practices and lifestyle.[23] The approach also hides the seasonal and local nature of water scarcity. Moreover, the concept fails to capture the different forms of water use among the various regions of the world.

There are many countries that are not captured by the water barrier concept, but for various reasons have serious water shortages: difficult geographical terrain, seasonal precipitation, unequal water distribution within the country, lack of economic and technological infrastructure to tame the nature, and so forth. The most illuminating example of a seasonal water scarcity is Cherapunji in north-eastern India. This area holds the world record of annual precipitation (more than ten metres). After a few months of the heavy monsoon season, a severe water problem occurs in this region.[24] On a global scale the large variations in precipitation and evapotransportation produce large differences in the actual availability of water.

In this context, it may also be useful to look at the per capita water use rather than only its availability in various countries. As Gleick points out, the statistics on the per capita water use is 'more representative of actual human well-being'.[25] Moreover, with this approach we can more readily identify the regions which are vulnerable to problems caused by water scarcity. This is because: (1) this index helps to locate the regions which are going to undertake intensive water resource development in the future to meet the demand for water, and (2) reflects the capacity of the society to address various issues arising from water scarcity.

As water is a basic condition for life, a minimum amount of water is required for human survival. Although the availability of water in a country is important, how much water is being provided for the use of the people is even more important. World Bank and WHO recommend 20–40 litres per capita per day as a minimum for water and sanitation requirements.[26] In addition to the UN International Drinking Water Supply and Sanitation Decade, Agenda 21 of the Earth Summit also makes similar recommendation. Besides the most basic recommended needs (5 litres of water per person per day for drinking water and 20 litres of water per person per day for sanitation and hygiene), Peter Gleick adds an additional 15 litres of water per day for bathing and 10 litres of water per person for cooking. According to Gleick, 50 litres per person per day should be the basic water requirement standard for human needs: drinking water for survival, water for human hygiene, sanitation services and modest household needs for preparing foods.[27] As we can see in Table 1.2, there are 55 countries where 1990 per capita water withdrawal for domestic requirement falls below 50 litres.

Most countries that use less than 50 litres domestic daily water per capita are in Africa. The rest are in the developing regions of Asia and Latin America. Large numbers of people lack access to even basic water requirement, though not because of scarce water availability.[28] While many of these countries are not listed as those with water scarcity, in reality the people of these lands have too little water to meet basic needs. This has been primarily owing to geographical barriers, an underdeveloped economy, and the failure of the state and its institutions.

The increasing use of fertilizers and pesticides in order to achieve food security is contaminating the available water supply in many developing countries. Tables 1.1 and 1.2 do not indicate the quality of water. Not only do all these countries have fewer litres per person, but also much of this water is polluted or contaminated in other ways. In addition to water scarcity, water quality poses a serious problem.

WATER POLLUTION

The use of fertilizers and pesticides on a massive scale to increase agricultural production is contaminating the available water supply in many regions. It is true that the developed countries are much ahead in using the amount of fertilizer, but their developing counterparts are catching up. In 1980, fertilizer use per hectare in developing countries was 5.5 times less than in developed countries, but by 1986, this figure had dropped to only 2.2.[29] World fertilizer use increased from less than 14 million tonnes in 1950 to 145 million tonnes in 1988. However, by 1996, it had somewhat reduced to 135 million tonnes.[30] Fertilizer consumption is stable or declining in the North, while demand is still growing in the developing world.[31] Similarly, pesticide use has increased

Table 1.2 Countries Failing to Meet Basic Water Requirement (BWR)

Country	Population 1990 (millions)	Total domestic water use (litres/person/day)	Total domestic use as a percentage of the BWR
Gambia	0.86	4.5	9
Mali	9.21	8	16
Somalia	7.5	8.9	18
Mozambique	15.66	9.3	19
Uganda	18.79	9.3	19
Cambodia	8.25	9.5	19
Tanzania	27.32	10.1	20
Central African Republic	3.04	13.2	26
Ethiopia	49.24	13.3	27
Rwanda	7.24	13.6	27
Chad	5.68	13.9	28
Bhutan	1.52	14.8	30
Albania	3.25	15.5	31
Zaire	35.57	16.7	33
Nepal	19.14	17	34
Lesotho	1.77	17	34
Sierra Leone	4.15	17.1	34
Bangladesh	115.59	17.3	35
Burundi	5.47	18	36
Angola	10.02	18.3	37
Djibouti	0.41	18.7	37
Ghana	15.03	19.1	38
Benin	4.63	19.5	39
Solomon Islands	0.32	19.7	39
Myanmar	41.68	19.8	40
Papua New Guinea	3.87	19.9	40
Cape Verde	0.37	20	40
Fiji	0.76	20.3	41
Burkina Faso	9	22.2	44
Senegal	7.33	25.4	51
Oman	1.5	26.7	53
Sri Lanka	17.22	27.6	55
Niger	7.73	28.4	57
Nigeria	108.54	28.4	57
Guinea-Bissau	0.96	28.5	57
Vietnam	66.69	28.8	58
Malawi	8.75	29.7	59
Congo	2.27	29.9	60
Jamaica	2.46	30.1	60
Haiti	6.51	30.2	60
Indonesia	184.28	34.2	68
Guatemala	9.2	34.3	69
Guinea	5.76	35.2	70
Ivory Coast	12	35.6	71
Swaziland	0.79	36.4	73
Madagascar	12	37.2	74
Liberia	2.58	37.3	75
Afghanistan	16.56	39.3	79
Uruguay	3.09	39.6	79
Cameroon	11.83	42.6	85

(Continued)

TABLE 1.2 continued

Country	Population 1990 (million)	Total domestic water use (litres/person/day)	Total domestic use as a percentage of the BWR
Togo	3.53	43.5	87
Paraguay	4.28	45.6	91
Kenya	24.03	46	92
El Salvador	5.25	46.2	92
Zimbabwe	9.71	48.2	96

Source: P. H. Gleick, *The World's Water: The Biennial Report on Freshwater Resources 1998–1999* (Washington DC: Island Press, 1998), p. 45.

much more than fertilizer use. The first contemporary form of pesticides, organochlorine insecticides, such as DDT, was introduced in the 1940s. Since then the use of pesticide has multiplied in almost every part of the world as the foremost option for pest control. In the US, for example, pesticide use has jumped ten-fold from the 1940s to the 1990s. In many countries, governmental subsidies continue to encourage excessive fertilizer and pesticide use.[32] Until recently, irrigation contributed marginally to the pollution of water basins, but the widespread use of fertilizers and pesticides has started to heavily pollute irrigation return flows. Drainage and runoff from fertilized crops bring high concentrations of nitrogen and phosphorous nutrients, and the infusion of nitrates into drinking water lead to various human health hazards.

Change is also taking place in the pattern of water use. In the early years of the 1900s, agriculture was responsible for nearly 90 per cent of total water requirements. By the end of the century, this amount had reduced to 67 per cent.[33] But use in the industrial sector, whose share was only 6 per cent in 1900, has increased to 19 per cent.[34] Currently, the largest single industrial use of water is in the nuclear and fossil fuel power plants. In these cases, water comes back to its source after cooling the plants, so the concern is not about the increasing volume of water withdrawn, but the discharge of heated and polluted water back to the system.

The industrial use of water in Finland accounts for 85 per cent of the total water used. In the US, Canada and Poland, 40 per cent of total water use goes to power stations as cooling water.[35] The large-scale industrial use of water gives birth to severe problems of water quality. Water quality has already become one of the major environmental issues in many of the industrialized countries.

In Sweden, industrial water use quintupled between 1930 and 1965, but since then has shown a marked decline. Strict environmental protection requirements for the pulp and paper industries, which account for about 80 per cent of the country's industrial water withdrawal, fostered widespread adoption of recycling technology. Despite more than doubling of production between the early 1960s and late 1970s, the industry sector cut its total water use by half – a four-fold increase in water efficiency.[36] Similarly, in the former West Germany, total industrial water use in 1991 was at the same level as it was in 1975, while industrial output had risen 44 per cent.[37]

However, it has not been the same across the Baltic Sea. In Poland, the share of river water of highest quality for drinking has dropped from 32 per cent to less than 5 per cent during the 1970s and 1980s. In spite of recent improvements in the situation, owing to international assistance, some rivers are still too contaminated even for industrial use. In water-affluent Canada, which has 9 per cent of the world's available fresh water supply, there are water shortages at the local level and widespread contamination of both surface and ground water. The situation in the US, France and Russia is even worse. Europe and North America are the two regions that currently use more water in industry compared to agriculture. Water quality in the rivers of these regions suffers from many contaminants and chemical pollution is quite common.

If the present trend continues, water use in the industrial sector will be doubled by the year 2025. With it, there will be a four-fold increase in pollutant discharge to water bodies.[38] Industrial and chemical pollution of water resources is gradually spreading to the urban-industrial centres of industrializing countries in the South. China is projected to witness at least a five-fold increase to its industrial water use by the year 2030.[39] Industrial water pollution in neighbouring India has already reached an alarming proportion, and it is estimated that 70 per cent of India's rivers are polluted with industrial waste.[40] More than a hundred cities pour untreated sewage into India's most important river, the Ganges. Its Yamuna tributary picks up a daily 200 million litres of sewage and 20 million litres of industrial waste in Delhi alone. In the industrial city of Kanpur, only 3 factories out of 647 have treatment plants.

In most of the developed countries in the North, where the per capita water availability is fairly plentiful, much of the water supply is polluted by various human activities in conspicuous consumption. The flush toilets and private swimming pool facilities in the households of these countries have been responsible for exceeding the water consumption levels of 500 litres per capita per day. The richest state of the US – California – is now facing the problem of how to combine the conspicuous consumption habit of its population and vast irrigated farmlands in its semi-arid climate. As Victor D. Hanson describes his home state California's dilemma: 'Our apparent birthright of sprawling suburbs with rye lawns, pools, residential lakes, and golf courses cannot exist alongside millions of acres of irrigated agriculture – at least not in the Mediterranean climate and deserts of California.'[41] The average daily use of water per capita is much less in the developing countries compared to their industrialized counterparts. However, the affluent urban localities in the developing countries are rapidly getting caught in this 'Californian Syndrome'.[42]

The world is passing through an urban revolution. Nearly 3 billion people, about 45 per cent of the world's population, now lives in urban areas. According to FAO statistics, cities in the world added more than 2 billion people from 1950 to 2000, and they are estimated to add another 2 billion from 2000 to 2025.[43] While the urban population is growing by only 0.8 per cent per year in the developed countries, the growth rate in the developing regions is 3.6 per cent. Africa's annual urban growth rate is now 4 per cent, which is the highest in the world. In 1994, among ten largest mega-cities in the world, three cities were from the developed world. However, by 2015 only Tokyo is expected to remain on the list. This rapid growth of mega-cities in the developing world is posing serious planning and management challenges.[44] Most of the cities in developing countries are already surrounded by shanty suburbs, housing millions of inhabitants in mostly unauthorized slums without proper sanitation facilities. More than 600 million urban residents in Africa, Asia and Latin America already live in squatter settlements and shanty towns.[45]

The Thames River was full of salmon in the eighteenth century. Owing to dumping of industrial waste and untreated water from the sewage into the river, it became so polluted that it started stinking in the nineteenth century.[46] It was not until 1974 that two purification plants with the latest treatment equipment were used to alleviate the situation. In 1983, the first salmon in a century and a half was caught in the river.[47] Like the Thames, the Rhine was known as 'the sewer of Europe' in the 1950s. The Rhine Action Plan in 1987 has reduced the chemical contaminants to a level that now salmon are swimming in the river. Similar initiatives are being undertaken in the Baltic sea basin and Danube basin. This has also become possible due to impressive international assistance, particularly from the Nordic countries.

In the developed countries, sewage and wastewater treatment facilities have been put in place in recent years at considerable cost. However, the growing urban centres in the developing countries have not been able to use these treatment facilities. Domestic pollution from the untreated water sewage of these areas contaminates nearly all the available source of water, which is affecting the quality of water especially for domestic use. The Global Environment Monitoring System (GEMS), the network that monitors the global water quality, has assessed that the organic matter present in the domestic sewage is the most widespread water pollutant.[48] Polluted water and water shortages cause a number of illnesses such as cholera, amoebic dysentery, hepatitis A, dengue fevers, killing over 12 million people every year.[49] Water quantity and quality issues are linked to each other as minimal river flow levels are required to dilute polluted waters. According to traditional hydrological approach, 'the solution to pollution is dilution'. The GEMS Study estimates that all over the world, nearly 450 cubic kilometres of wastewater enter the river system. To dilute and transport this mounting pollution, 6,000 cubic kilometres of clean water are required.[50] This amount is nearly two-thirds of the world's available runoff, and if the ongoing trend continues soon the entire global river flow will be needed for pollutant transport and dilution.

ADOPTED STRATEGIES TO FACE WATER SCARCITY

Countries have been meeting growing water demand by building reservoirs for water storage, using a canal to divert water from one area to another, or extracting groundwater. These water projects have been the epitome of modernization, accounting for a large share of public investment in most countries. Unfortunately, a number of these water development projects create conflicts in the society over water ownership. There is, however, another side to the coin of water resource development projects: environmental destruction and population displacement.

Construction of Large Dams

In the twentieth century, there was a tremendous increase in the construction of dams to meet the growing water demand. By 1949, there were nearly 5,000 dams worldwide, out of which three-quarters were in industrialized countries. In 50 years, by the end of the century, there were over 45,000 large dams in more than 140 countries. In the last century, the world has spent more than 2 trillion dollars in constructing these large dams. Augmenting water storages and retaining floodwater for future use became the essential element of the water resource management. The requirement of hydro-energy and commercial fishing has also contributed towards human intervention in water. Dam building, which has already become out of fashion in North America and Western Europe, is still considered the panacea for water shortage problems in many developing countries. During the 1990s, the world was spending between 32 and 46 billion dollars annually on large dam construction, four-fifths of it by the developing countries. In Europe and North America, the construction of large dams peaked in the 1970s but now these regions are witnessing decommissioning of the dams. However, approximately 1,700 large dams are at present under construction in other parts of the world: India, with 40 per cent share of the total number, leads the list, followed by China, Turkey and South Korea.[51] Moreover, these newly built dams and their reservoirs are becoming larger.

In 1992, 60 per cent of the dams being constructed were more than 30 metres high, compared with only 21 per cent of existing dams in 1986. The construction of dams higher than 100 metres has also increased considerably. This new tendency is because of the increasing scarcity of water and the reduced availability of suitable dam sites. In the world today, there are more than 100 'super dams' with a height of more than 150 metres. Lake Mead, behind the Hoover Dam, was the largest dam reservoir in the world in 1936, with 38 billion cubic metres of water. By the 1970s, it was dwarfed by a series of dam reservoirs in developing countries: the Kariba Dam in Southern Africa with 160 billion cubic metres, Aswan's Lake Nasser with 157 billion cubic metres and Ghana's Akosombo with 148 billion cubic metres. Nearly 500,000 square kilometres of land area is covered by dam reservoirs worldwide, with the capacity of storing 6,000 cubic kilometres of water.[52]

Currently the largest dam in the world is the Itaipu Dam on the Parana River, which forms the border between Paraguay and Brazil.[53] However, China's Three Gorges Dam project (Sanxia), which is presently under construction, is going to break this record. This dam and associated construction projects are the biggest public works project in China since the Great Wall. It aims to be completed in 2009 and the 185 metres tall dam on the Yangtze River, just downstream from the scenic Three Gorges, will create 632 square kilometres of reservoir with a total storage capacity of nearly 40 billion cubic metres. This huge project aims to increase the discharge flow of the river in the dry seasons to meet the increasing need for water. Besides inundating vast areas of farmland, the project will adversely affect the aquatic life of the river. Moreover, it will cause direct displacement of more than a million people.[54] China tops the list of dam-building nations. It is now site for 22,000 large dams, which is almost half the world's total number. Before the communist revolution, China had only 22 of these dams.

Construction and operation of large dams and their reservoirs have led to many significant, social, human and environmental impacts. Besides triggering earthquakes, they build up soil salinity, change groundwater levels and create water logging. Dams extract a high human toll as well. The dam projects submerge vast areas of land and forest and displace their inhabitants. There are millions of people who have lost their homes and livelihoods due to these projects. According to the World Commission on Dams, the construction of large dams has forced the displacement of 40–80 million people worldwide. The construction of 300 large dams on an average each year has displaced 4 million people annually between 1986 and 1993. In the late 1980s, China officially admitted to have 10.2 million people as 'reservoir resettlers'. In India, one author estimates that the number of dam-related displaced people between 1951 and 1990 is 14 million.[55] Several movements have arisen in India recently to protest against these displacements. The dam-displaced people are gradually becoming organized and have taken their struggle to the streets.[56] A number of big dam projects were undertaken in India after independence in 1947 to meet the increasing demand for water for irrigation. In spite of popular protests, dam building and its consequent population displacement are still going on in a big way in India.

Because of increasing water scarcity there are very few rivers left in the world which run freely towards the sea. While the slow-flowing Amazon has been saved from dam construction until now, the Brazilian government in its 'Plan 2010' envisages 80 dams on its tributaries in order to meet future demand for water. The other important river basin of South America, the Rio de la Plata, is threatened with a series of dam constructions, which will displace many people. A number of large dams have been built in Africa in its post-colonial period for energy production and to increase food production to meet the growing demand. Water scarcity in the Euphrates-Tigris river basin has led to the construction of a series of dams on this river. After China, Turkey was next on the list of countries engaged in building a large number of big dams (+10 metres) in the 1990s. These dams, besides creating conflicts with downstream Syria and Iraq, have also displaced a large number of people from the submerged areas.

In the twentieth century, significant advances in the design and construction of dams were achieved. Factors of safety have been refined, human errors reduced and design criteria have found international consensus.[57] But the three most detrimental effects of the big dams are still haunting policy makers and engineers: (1) displacement and resettlement of the population; (2) salination and waterlogging; and (3) health issues resulting from water-related diseases. The range of such social and environmental effects is gradually becoming apparent. The dams are being built to store water to provide irrigation and electricity for people in distant locations and to supply water to the cities, but at the same time these dams displace substantial populations and threaten their livelihoods.

Diversion of River Systems

There are several forms of water diversion schemes being implemented throughout the world. Many long-distance water transfer projects have remained in the planning stage for a long time: one of the most ostentatious was the North American Water and Power Alliance (NAWAPA) which was proposed in 1960. It was planned to divert the water from the rivers of Alaska and British Columbia to mid-western US and northern Mexico. In the Soviet Union, a massive Siberian river scheme was proposed to divert the water from Siberia to the central Asian region, but it was shelved by Gorbachev in 1980. Recently Turkey has come up with a scheme to divert water from its GAP project to Gulf countries. Even a Canadian company in 1998 had managed to receive permission to export Great Lakes water via tanker to Asia, which was subsequently withdrawn owing to public uproar.[58] However, in July 2001, the US President George W. Bush publicly expressed his plan of persuading the Canadian Prime Minister about piping Canadian water to the parched American Southwest.[59]

Massive economic and environmental costs are the major deterrents for the execution of these long-distance water diversion proposals. Such schemes become more problematic when the diversion routes have to pass through several political units. Thus, water diversion projects are usually carried out within a single fresh water basin. By using dams and canals, the powerful region gets preference over the others and grabs the major supply of water. This mostly takes place when a river is shared by more than one country. The region whose water gets diverted faces many environmental, social and economic problems. Water diversion also frequently occurs within individual countries. Large numbers of urban centres in arid and tropical regions of Africa, Asia and Latin America have grown beyond the point where required water supplies can be drawn from local sources. The problem of these urban areas often stem from the fact that the rates of urbanization have exceeded the capacities of the state to effectively plan and manage. Poor management and inefficient distribution of water contribute to the problems of water scarcity in these urban centres. So, the authorities are following an easy but unsustainable solution, i.e. diverting water from distant rivers and lakes to feed these cities.[60] China has recently unveiled its massive plan to transfer up to 48 billion cubic metres of water annually via three channels from around the Yangtze River in the South to the urban and industrial areas in the North.[61]

Rural and urban areas have different priorities of water use. Owing to political and economic reasons, urban and industrial water demands usually get priority over rural and agricultural needs. These water transfers lead to water scarcity in the rural areas and economic hardship for the rural population. The diversion of water towards cities and industrial centres endangers fish habitats, creates loss of wetlands, erodes riverbanks and, moreover, pollutes the water source. Most importantly, it adversely affects agricultural production, which provides the source of survival for a large population.

The rising demand for urban and industrial water supplies poses a serious threat to irrigated agriculture. In 1900, irrigation represented 90 per cent of the total water demand, while industry and municipal water demand was very minimal. It is estimated that by 2000 the share of industry and municipal water has increased to 28 per cent compared to irrigation's share of 67 per cent. The future projection leads to further reduction in the share of the agricultural sector. This indicates the growing competition between various water demands, particularly in arid and semi-arid regions. In general, the agricultural areas need more water for irrigation for fibre and cash crops to be self-sufficient and alleviate the poverty.

To meet increasing water demand, many diversion canals are being constructed to transport water to cities, to farmland and from one region to another. By altering the natural watercourses, these diversion projects create conflict between water receivers and water contributors. The diversion of water from agriculture to other sectors is likely to undermine the livelihoods of a large number of people. Water diversion schemes also require dam and canal building, which directly contributes to population displacement. Moreover, the areas whose water is diverted by the projects suffer various adverse environmental effects. The water diversion may result in the gradual loss of livelihood of many people living in the affected areas and force them to migrate to other areas in the search for survival.

Exploitation of Groundwater

Of the earth's estimated 37 million cubic kilometres of fresh water, the share of groundwater storages is about 22 per cent. Excluding polar ice caps, groundwater constitutes nearly 97 per cent of all fresh water potentially available for human consumption.[62] Some aquifers can be recharged by precipitation while others may not have any or may have only minor recharge sources.[63] Throughout history, groundwater has been an important source of water for human consumption and agricultural production. Groundwater supports almost one-third of the world's population, and is the only source of water for rural people in many parts of the world.[64]

However, the excessive groundwater withdrawal in the arid and semi-arid areas to meet the increasing scarcity situation has become unsustainable. The water table has fallen by tens of metres in India,

China, Middle East, transition economies, Mexico and the US. For example, in the Indian state of Gujarat, the water table has dropped by 40 metres in some areas owing to extreme groundwater withdrawal. The extraction of water from the ground has two adverse effects: intensifying land subsidence because of the falling water table, and the salt water intrusion into groundwater in the coastal areas. Besides drying up fresh water sources, these effects lead to soil salinization.[65] Unsound waste disposal, inadequate sewage treatment and inefficient irrigation practices adversely affect the quality of groundwater.[66] However, the major threat to groundwater is its massive extraction to reduce the scarcity of water.

The difficulty ensuing from the use of groundwater is that most of it renews much more slowly than other water sources. As estimated, on average, while moisture in the atmosphere renews every 8 days, stream water in 16 days, soil moisture in 1 year, swamp water every 5 years and lakewater every 17 years, groundwater is renewed only once every 1,400 years.[67] Groundwater needs to be used in an environmentally sustainable manner. The rate of withdrawal should be equal or less than the rate of recharge. But when the extraction rate from underground basins exceeds renewal rate, which is known as groundwater 'mining', the result is a falling water table and surface level. The falling of the water tables of coastal aquifers increases the likelihood of the infiltration of saline water, making water unsuitable for human use. Away from coastal areas, over-consumption of the aquifers leads either to their drying up completely, or the water table is lowered so much that it greatly increases the cost of pumping.

Groundwater is an important source of drinking water. About 75 per cent of Europe's drinking water supplies come from groundwater sources. In the US groundwater provides approximately 50 per cent of all drinking water.[68] Groundwater also plays an equally significant role as a source of irrigation water. The development of small pumps has brought one of the greatest technical revolutions in irrigation. Millions of small pumps are used to withdraw water for cultivation. The yield is higher from pump irrigation as compared to canal irrigation, because it provides water on demand. In many parts of the world, underground water pumping is now being carried out on a massive scale. In India, 50 per cent of the irrigation water comes from underground. The same is the case with many other arid countries. Owing to this unsustainable withdrawal of groundwater, water tables are falling in South Asia by two to three metres a year.[69] The termination of underground water supply, which is a distinct possibility in the future, will affect agriculture and even pose a threat to human survival.

Israel's annual renewable fresh water supply is much less than its current demand. Population growth and intensified agriculture are further expanding its water demand.[70] This water scarcity has driven the country to overpump its aquifers. In the 1970s and 1980s, Israel overused the coastal aquifers to such an extent that the water table in some areas fell below sea level, which resulted in salt water intruding into the empty aquifers. After the dilapidation of coastal aquifers, the mountain aquifers now constitute Israel's primary source of drinking water. However, there are three main aquifer groups within the mountain aquifers. Only one of these is located in Israel proper while the other two originate in occupied areas.[71]

Many countries in the Middle East and North Africa rely heavily on non-renewable groundwater supplies to augment their meagre fresh water supplies and create new agricultural areas in their desert environment. Large-scale underground water withdrawal is being carried out in Saudi Arabia and Libya for domestic and agricultural use. Several other Arab countries are also using their fossil aquifers in their short-term strategy to meet the growing water scarcity and to increase their agricultural production. The non-renewable underground basins of these countries are predicted to dry up completely in another 40 to 60 years, depending on the amount of withdrawal. This creates a highly uncertain future for the economy of these countries, especially for the population which is dependent on the newly created farmlands.[72]

Expansive groundwater withdrawal has become a serious anxiety in many parts of South Asia. The spread of pumping technologies for irrigation has increased groundwater extraction in the region. In India, the number of diesel and electrical pumps leaped from a mere 87,000 in 1950 to 12.6 million in 1990.[73] The expansion in number of pumps has brought significant decline in the water table of the country, particularly in areas of low or zero recharge. In most areas of India's breadbasket, Punjab, groundwater tables are dropping alarmingly, thus threatening agriculture. In Pakistan and Bangladesh, groundwater withdrawal has also increased dramatically in the 1980s and 1990s. In the early 1990s, a large number of irrigation pumps became inoperative in Bangladesh due to the falling groundwater table as a result of overpumping, creating further problems for the people of this region.[74]

Historically, groundwater has been perceived as an infinite resource, and this has been the major obstacle to effective groundwater management. Moreover, groundwater is a hidden resource and thus not easy to estimate. Its exploitation or overuse does not provoke opposition or popular protest initially, which makes it easier for the authorities to overuse it. It also offers an inexpensive way of augmenting water resources. All these factors have led to excessive groundwater mining in many parts of the world. As Stephen Foster states: 'The fact that they are "out of the public sight" has caused them also to be "out of the political mind" and they are too often abandoned to chance.'[75] Thus, the international groundwater law is still in the infancy stage and a number of principles are still appearing.

In various ways, attempts are being made to increase the supply of water to meet the growing demand. But at the same time, the economic, social and environmental costs of these attempts have been very high. The massive dams and their reservoirs have displaced millions of the population. Rural poor people have been the major victims. Due to inferior political and economic strength, these poor have become early and easy targets. Those water diversion schemes that have been implemented have caused major economic and environmental problems, particularly in areas whose interest has been sacrificed. The unsustainable groundwater extraction has brought uncertainties about future water availability in many parts of the world.

Because of rapidly increasing demand, developing countries in the arid and tropical regions are especially vulnerable to water scarcity. Furthermore, many of these states are characterized by strong ethnic identities, inefficient administration and a weak economy. Thus, it is logical that many observers expect water to become a key issue in disputes, conflicts or even wars in the future. Such developments might mean that technical solutions are impeded by political problems, and the water situation deteriorates even further. This is one possible scenario for the future. Others might be more optimistic by pointing to the ability of finding solutions, which are both social and technical.

WATER AS THE SOURCE OF CONFLICT

The scarcity of water is increasing worldwide and the quality of the water is continually deteriorating. The growing global water stress poses a threat to the survival and prosperity of present and future generations. The gap between the needs of the growing population and the diminishing fresh water resources is widening every day. In the arid and tropical regions, where countries possess a very limited supply of water, it is not difficult to perceive the consequences. Water, a key necessity of life, can also cause friction between communities and countries, particularly in climatic zones where it is hard to come by.

As Figure 1.1 suggests, population growth combined with hasty industrialization, huge urbanization and increasing agricultural activities will add to the demand for water resources as well as pollute the supply of water. The over-exploitation of water resources might result in an acute shortage. From this perspective, it will be impossible for all the social actors to remain comfortable with the present or future prospects of the availability of the resource. These actors will work purposefully and consciously for their own interests. Increasing

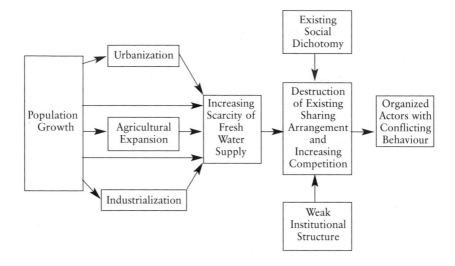

Figure 1.1 Increasing Demand Over Water and Creation of Conflicting Actors

competition can potentially destroy the existing social arrangements for water distribution in the society. Newly organized actors with conflict behaviours might emerge in the future or the incompatibilities between existing actors might grow in societies with a weak administrative structure and laden with ethnic and social dichotomies.

Internal Water Conflicts

Scarce water resources can potentially trigger conflicts between the state and its internal groups. The development of water resources by the state by building dams, irrigation infrastructures, or industries in a particular region might be perceived by the local population as exploitation for the interest of others. Regional parties may be activated or environmental groups may be formed to challenge the actions of the state. If a particular group is involved in exploiting more than its 'perceived' share of water with the backing of the state, then this inter-group conflict may escalate into conflict between the exploited group and the state itself.

As discussed earlier, the construction of large dams for the 'efficient' use of water resources has created tension between the state and a group of its own citizens in the past few years. The growing demand for irrigation and energy activates the state agencies to plan and build mega hydro-projects, which displace large population and inundate vast

20

areas. In many places, the project affected population take up of the struggle against the state. The list of mega dams that have witnessed this sort of protest is very long. The major ones include: Sanmenxia and Three Gorges in China; Madur Oya and Mahavali Project in Sri Lanka; Mangla, Nanela and Tarbela in Pakistan; Kaptai in Bangladesh; Arun in Nepal; Akasombo in Ghana; Kossou in Ivory Coast; Tana and Athi in Kenya; Itaparica and Tucurui in Brazil; Kainji and Niger Dams in Nigeria; Ataturk and Keban in Turkey; Lam Pao and Nam Pong in Thailand; Kedong Ombo and Batang Ai in Indonesia; Upper Pampanga in Philippines; Manantali in Mali; Savajina in Colombia; Brokopondo in Suriname; Caracol and Netzahualcoyotl in Mexico; and Nam Ngum in Laos. India, currently in the forefront of dam construction, deserves a separate list of its own. The Indian hydro-projects that have recently led to protest movements by the displaced people are: Pong Dam, Subarnarekha Project, Nagarjunsagar Project, Srisailam Project, Lower Manair Dam, Upper Krishna Projects, Tehri Dam, Narmada Projects and Ukai Reservoir Project.

Sometimes disagreement over the development and sharing of water resources may begin with competing groups inside a state, but the state's perceived favour of a particular group brings the state as a party to the conflict. Similarly, if the water source exploitation is perceived as the state's intentional act on a particular region or people, a group identity may form, leading to conflict with the state. The construction of dams for hydropower generations in the northern part of Sweden to provide energy to the industries and factories in the South has become an area of disagreement between the Sami people of the North and the Swedish state. The Samis, who live in the forests in the Arctic Circle, accuse the state of favouring city dwellers at the cost of their livelihood and welfare. Even though this dispute has not transformed into a violent separatist movement, the reactions to similar issues in South Asia have been quite different.

Disagreement over the sharing of river water from the Indus river system has been one of the major causes of violent secessionist movement in the Punjab province of India in the 1980s and 1990s. This Sikh-dominated province has been traditionally provided with a water supply from the Beas, Sutlej and Ravi Rivers. The demands of the downstream provinces of Rajasthan and Haryana persuaded the Indian government to construct canals and divert 60 per cent of Punjab's water and energy to those Hindu-majority regions. This became one of the major motivations for the Sikh Party (Akali Dal) to ask for autonomy in the 1970s, which subsequently transformed into an extreme violent secessionist movement in the 1980s and 1990s.[76] On the other side of the border, the dispute over the sharing of the same Indus river system water has also played a critical role in a major separatist movement in

Pakistan. The Pakistani part of Punjab, which is economically and politically the most powerful province in the country, takes advantage of its upstream location and consumes most of the waters of the Indus river system through the help of barrages and dams, ignoring the demand of the downstream Sind province. The perceived close tie of the federal government with the Punjab province has escalated this conflict between the Sind province and the Pakistani government. Similarly, the Mahaveli Project and the Kaptai Lake hydroelectric project have directly and significantly contributed to the Tamil revolt against the Singhlese-dominated government in Sri Lanka and the Chakma Buddhist insurgency against Bengali Muslim-dominated government in Bangladesh, respectively.[77]

One may argue that if the water project affected people belonging to an ethnic minority group, then the perceived discriminatory exploitation by the majority-governed state may further strain existing social dichotomies and play a role in the activation of conflictual actors. A historical, religious or cultural significance attached to the exploited water resources might raise the probability of group mobilization and an ensuing conflict with the state. In the absence of an early resolution, these conflicts can potentially lead to violent struggles for autonomy or even secession. A state structure weakened by strong ethnic identities, inefficient administration and a lack of water resources predisposes the countries in Asia, Africa and the Middle East to this development.

Conflicts are connected to groups in society with conflicting ideas or incompatibilities.[78] Control over the scarce water resource can be seen as an incompatibility among groups in a society. The perceived discrimination or exploitation of a shared water source by one group might help to mobilize new groups or to persuade the already existing groups to protect their interests. The formation of a new group might take place expeditiously in response to some acts by the perceived water exploiter, or it might come as a gradual rejoinder of the persisting resentment regarding water use.

In the 1960s, Arizona and California disputed each other's claim over the Colorado River water.[79] Ronald Reagan, the then Governor of California, threatened to use force against Arizona in order to protect their 'share' of water from the river. This prolonged dispute ended after a judicial verdict, which allocated shares for the conflicting parties. However, the resolution of this type of conflict has not been so peaceful in developing countries. Since the 1970s, Karnataka and Tamil Nadu, two southern Indian states, have been involved in a dispute over the sharing of the waters of the Cauvery River. This conflict has already resulted in political agitation and riots causing several deaths and displacing thousands of people. The decisions of the courts have been repeatedly challenged by mob violence in the state of Karnataka. There are several inter-state river disputes in India, prominent ones being conflict over sharing the Yamuna River water between Delhi and Haryana, and sharing of Krishna River water between Karnataka and Andhra Pradesh.[80]

There are also deep divisions between rural and urban population of a state, each holding sharply varying perceptions and priorities about the use of water. Most national policies accord highest priority to urban water supplies. One of the strategies adopted by the state for reconciling growing demands for urban water is to re-allocate water from the agricultural sector. Water sources near to urban areas are, in most cases, polluted. It is also politically prudent to provide water to urban dwellers at the expense of rural needs. Some argue that a small portion of water from the agricultural sector could meet most urban demands.[81] At an aggregate level, this may be true, but timing and location of this re-allocation can cause significant trouble. When rural people watch their water polluted, rivers depleted and their own needs rising, the emergence of conflict is inevitable. This type of rural–urban conflict is already prevalent and frequent. The grand Chinese scheme to divert the water of Yangtze from its southern part to more than 1,000 kilometres to the north to the vicinity of Beijing and Tianjin has caused tension between rural and urban water users. Reports of the falling water level of the river have further alarmed both sides.

In the 1920s, Native Americans blew up a pipeline which was meant to divert 'their' water from Owens Valley to the Los Angeles city.[82] Since the late 1970s, the residents of Adelaide and the farmers of the countryside have been in dispute over use of the water of the river Murray. The recent re-allocation of irrigation water of the Bhabani River system to the industrial establishment of the Coimbatore district of the Indian province of Tamil Nadu has also brought conflict between urban and rural population. The residents of Nairobi and Mombasa are in dispute over the use of Tana and Athi/Galana' Rivers water with their rural counterparts in Kenya. The same is the case in Angat basin in the Philippines. Extensive and rapid growth of the urban areas in the arid and tropical regions is gradually increasing the number of rural/urban water disputes.

Incompatibilities, either influenced or extracted by the fresh water scarcity, might form or energize a number of opposing groups in developing countries. Furthermore, the deliberate actions of these groups to confront or control the scarcity situation may be discerned correctly or incorrectly as designed conflict behaviour towards each other. This cognition may itself accelerate the conflict. These conflicts can be an immediate exhibition or a gradual escalation of hostility among the state or groups to appropriate or preserve the benefit of the same scarce water.

Conflicting groups in society emanate to preserve their portion of water or to acquire that of others. The activation of these conflicting groups takes place in consonance with existing religion, caste, class, linguistic, regional, cultural or other lines. In some cases, the scarce water resource itself brings the 'us/them' dichotomy into society. When segmental division in society is not so open, the elites sometimes also use water as an instrument to infuse group feelings. As discussed earlier, if one group rightly or wrongly apprehends the state as a collaborator with another, the inter-group conflict can transmute into a challenge against the state, subsequently leading to a violent separatist movement.

International Water Conflicts

The link between fresh water resources and international conflicts can be investigated at least in two different dimensions. First, in an inter-state conflict, the deliberate targeting of water storage facilities may be directly responsible for inducing water scarcity or reducing the water quality of the opponent. Thus, water scarcity becomes part of a military strategy and military behaviour. The British Royal Air Force damaged a few German dams in the bombing runs of 1943. Dams and dykes were destroyed during the Korean and Vietnam wars by the US bombing. Iran claimed to have hit a hydroelectric station in Iraq in July 1981, as part of the Iran–Iraq War. Dams, water storage and conveyance systems were targeted by the warring sides during the 1991 Gulf War. Allied forces even had thought of a plan to shut off the flow of water to Iraq by using the Ataturk Dam in Turkey.[83] Armies in Yemen (in the 1994 war) and former Yugoslavia (1991–95) used the water storage facilities as targets to create problems for their adversaries. In January 1993, the Serbian militia seriously damaged the Peruca Dam in Croatia.

These are cases where in fact a human population is held hostage to political and military leaders. Manipulation with such basic human supplies in times of war should be an urgent issue for international humanitarian law, and it certainly would be unacceptable under conditions of peace. However, the aim here is to concentrate on a second dimension of the relationship: the likelihood of changes in fresh water resource supply to cause or contribute to the emergence and/or escalation of conflicts among states.

As discussed before, there has been a general decline in the quantity and quality of global fresh water resource. This leads us to consider scarcity of resources as a cause of conflict, in conflict theory language: an incompatibility between already existing parties. A common starting point in the analysis of many inter-state conflicts has been sought in the desire of the leaders of states to acquire territory.[84] In the post-Second World War period, it has become unfashionable and immoral to

24

conquer territories of others. Nevertheless this has happened repeatedly, for instance, in the Middle East, in South and Southeast Asia and lately in Europe. Huth characterizes territorial dispute as 'one of the enduring features of international politics'.[85] But, why do states fight for each other's territory? As Toset, Gleditsch and Hegre explain, 'territory can be a symbol of self-determination and national identity, but it can also be a proxy for tangible resources found on the territory'.[86] Thus, access to water supply can be a motive of waging war.

Under special circumstances it is a possibility that scarcity of fresh water resources may give rise to serious armed conflict. Water is not transported across large distances, as is the case with oil or minerals, for instance. In the post-Second World War period, political actions are taking place more in order to satisfy the demands of the majorities of a country. This means that stronger nations might be more in need of natural resources on the territory of other states, to meet the growing needs and desires of the home population. In this way, 'development' might be seen to require the acquisition or exploitation of a larger share of jointly owned fresh water resource. Thus, the interests of other user states become affected. This then, might result in a spiral of events: subsequent actions by the affected states to protect their interests might escalate conflicts.

International River as the Source of Conflict

The water on the surface of the earth is naturally organized within river basins. The river basins are the fundamental units of the fresh water world and the central feature of the ecology of the planet. Moreover, the river runoff is the most important source of available fresh water for human consumption. However, the rivers do not follow the political boundaries; nearly 260 rivers flow from one country to another. More than 40 per cent of the world's population is directly dependent upon the fresh water from these international rivers and about two-thirds of these people live in developing countries. The use or misuse of water in the upstream countries affects its quantity and quality in the downstream countries. Downstream nations can affect the flow of water by building large-scale dams, with effects spilling over the borders. The International Water Management Institute in Colombo projects that in 2025, 3 billion people will be living in countries facing water stress. Water tables are increasingly falling in every continent. Many developing countries already face serious problems in meeting rapidly growing water demands. In order to meet such demands, further pressure is being placed on these 'blue' water resources, this over-exploitation resulting in acute shortages.[87] Faced with such scarcity, water has increasingly become a source of social tension, bringing further competition and creating conflict which, together, have the potential to destroy the existing arrangements for water distribution. Even though such tensions are omnipresent, they tend to be more complex and difficult where international rivers, lakes and aquifers are concerned.

The Centre for Natural Resources, Energy and Transport (CNRET), now a defunct UN unit, brought out a Register of International Rivers in 1978.[88] In that it listed 214 internationally shared rivers and lakes: 57 in Africa, 40 in Asia, 48 in Europe, 33 in North America and 36 in South America. The CNRET study has become dated because of significant changes in international geopolitical borders and names of countries and rivers in the last 25 years. The names of some countries and rivers have also changed in this period. The disintegration of the Soviet Union, Yugoslavia, Ethiopia and Czechoslovakia has helped to increase the number of internationally shared rivers and lakes, and also the number of basin countries. For example, the Volga River is now international, and the Aral Sea is shared by at least four independent states. The re-unification of Germany and Yemen has made the Weser basin and the Teban basin national, contributing to a decrease in the number of international fresh water resources.

Moreover, some do not accept the CNRET report as a definitive study on the grounds of its methodological and factual short-comings.[89] It was entirely a desk study, which drew its figures using only a polar planimetre on the then available maps in the UN Map Library. It is nearly impossible to locate all the international surface water systems from the small maps alone. The definition adopted by the CNRET only considers first-order river basins and does not include tributary or other outlet basins. However, sometimes second- or even third-order river basins are economically and politically more significant for the riparian states than first-order rivers. The total number of international river basins in the world is significantly higher than the number of the first-order rivers counted by the UN study. A good example would be the under-counting of international rivers between India and Bangladesh. While the UN study counts only one mega-basin, the Ganges-Brahmaputra (shared by India, Bangladesh, China, Nepal and Bhutan), the Indo-Bangladesh Joint River Commission identifies 54 river systems common to both countries.

The Transboundary Freshwater Database Project of Oregon State University has recently brought out a few new facts about international water. In 1999, this project reported 261 international rivers and lakes compared to the UN's 1978 list of 214.[90] Four reasons are attributed for the change to the numbers of international basins as compared to the 1978 CNRET Register: (1) political changes bringing break-up and unification of few countries; (2) availability of better digital and

Table 1.3 Regional Distribution of International Rivers

Region	Number of international river basins	Percentage of land area in international river basins	Number of countries in one or more international basins
Africa	60	62	47
Asia	53	39	34
Europe	71	54	42
North America	39	35	12
South America	38	60	13
Total	261	45	145

Source: A. T. Wolf, J. A. Natharius, J. J. Danielson, B. S. Ward and J. K. Pender, 'International River Basins of the World', *International Journal of Water Resources Development*, 15, 4 (1999). The total of 145 is correct because some countries overlap the continental boundaries.

hardcopy maps; (3) inclusion of some island nations; and, (4) consistent application of definition of 'international basins'.[91]

The international fresh water basins cover nearly 45.3 per cent of the earth's land surface area and account for approximately 60 per cent of global river flow: 145 countries have some share in international water systems and almost two-thirds (92 of 145) have more than half of their territories that come under the international basin. Only a few non-island states (including Denmark, Singapore and some Arab countries) are excluded from the list.[92]

The increasing scarcity of water resource combined with geographic facts, pave the way for a greater number of international river water disputes. Some commentators believe that the dependence of many developing countries on an external water supply may force them to re-orient their national security concerns in order to protect or preserve such availability. Several countries are currently in dispute over the sharing of their common water.

When multiple countries are jointly dependent on the same river systems, upstream withdrawal and pollution can potentially lead to 'upstream/downstream' conflicts. The origin of the English word rival is from the Latin term *rivalis*, which originally meant using the same stream (*rivus*). Not only does the prognostication of future water conflicts project a gloomy picture, but the present number of these conflicts has also become a matter of serious concern. The conflict between states may begin at diplomatic or economic levels, but failure to reach settlement can later culminate in the use of physical force. However, the 'non-armed' character of any dispute should not diminish its severity since other deterrent variables, e.g. difference in the size or strength of the actors, or perception of other actors' interference, might have hindered the use of force.

Table 1.4 Countries Heavily Dependent on Imported Surface Water

Country	Import component of renewable water resources (%)	Country	Import component of renewable water resources (%)
Turkmenistan	98	Paraguay	70
Egypt	97	Niger	68
Hungary	95	Iraq	66
Mauritania	95	Albania	53
Botswana	94	Uruguay	52
Bulgaria	91	Germany	51
Uzbekistan	91	Portugal	48
Netherlands	89	Bangladesh	42
Gambia	86	Thailand	39
Cambodia	82	Austria	38
Romania	82	Pakistan	36
Luxembourg	80	Jordan	36
Syria	80	Venezuela	35
Congo	77	Senegal	34
Sudan	77	Belgium	33

Sources: P. H. Gleick, 'Water and Conflict: Fresh Water Resources and International Security', *International Security*, 18, 1 (1993), pp. 79–112; D. R. Smith, 'Environmental Security and Shared Water Resources in Post-Soviet Central Asia', *Post-Soviet Geography*, 36 (1995).

The possibility for water induced conflict has brought global water issues into the arena of 'high politics' in the last decade. UN officials and World Bank analysts regularly proclaim that the previous war was about oil, the next war will be about water. In 1995 the World Bank's Vice-President for Environmentally Sustainable Development, Ismail Sergeldin, argued that 'The wars of next century will be over water.'[93] Similarly, in 1996, at the Habitat Conference in Istanbul, the Secretary General of the Conference stated that 'The scarcity of water is replacing oil as a flashpoint for conflict between nations in an increasingly urbanised world.'[94] The media has reported similar statements, by the leaders of Egypt, Jordan and Libya in the second half of the 1990s. Researchers investigating environmentally induced violent conflicts have also pointed to the international rivers as the source of inter-state hostilities.[95]

As Sadoff and Grey write, 'All international rivers, without exception, create some degree of tension among societies that they bind.'[96] Similarly, Gleditsch and Hamner conclude that 'the sharing of the international rivers does seem to be associated with conflict between nations'.[97] Conflicts among the riparian states can arise from the use of shared water resources. The arbitrary decision of the upper riparian country to undertake water storage and/or diversion project may lead to conflict as this construction has harmful consequences for the lower-lying states. The historical 'disparity' over the use of water among the riparian countries can also be challenged in the increasing scarcity situation when there simply is not enough water in the river to meet the needs, which may lead to conflict as well.[98]

The most publicized water conflict has centred on the control of the Jordan River basin among the riparian parties, Israel, Jordan, Lebanon, Syria and West Bank. The disagreement over the waters of the Jordan, Litani, Orontes, Yarmuk and other rivers was one of the reasons of the Arab–Israeli War in 1967, and it also partly influenced Israel's decision to invade Lebanon in 1982.[99] The peace agreements between Israel and Jordan in 1994 and Israel and the Palestinians in 1995 have recognized the water needs and rights of the riparians, but the implementation of these agreements faces a number of serious road blocks.

Since the 1920s, Egypt and Sudan have shared the Nile River water by mutual agreement between the two governments. Sudan now wants to revise the last agreement, which was signed in 1959, to acquire a larger share of the water. However, the major threat to Egypt's water supply comes from Ethiopia who contributes more than 80 per cent of the Nile's water entering Egypt. In the nearby region, Turkey is now implementing its plan to construct over 20 hydroelectric and irrigation facilities on the upper reaches of the Euphrates River. This huge 'GAP Project' has brought water shortages for downstream users, mainly in Syria. The GAP Project has not only strained relations between Turkey and Syria but also Syria's relations with Iraq. Population growth, increased agricultural activities and high rate of evaporation add to the increased demand for water in the basin. Lack of any existing legal water sharing agreements among the three major riparian countries and Turkey's offer to supply water to Israel increase the chances of deepening the conflict over the river water.

In recent years, Hungary and Slovakia have seriously disagreed over the construction and operation of the Gabcikovo/Nagymaros dam project on the Danube River. Hungary's unilateral withdrawal in 1992 from a 1977 treaty with Czechoslovakia concerning the construction of this project did not stop Slovakia from constructing the dam and diverting the Danube water via a canal. Massive public protest and military movement on the Hungarian side brought this conflict to the International Court of Justice (ICJ), which found both parties guilty. The construction of a large dam on the Han River by North Korea in the late 1980s has added another layer to the long-standing dispute between North and South Korea. The conflict over the distribution of the Ganges water between India and Bangladesh predates the creation of Bangladesh itself. Malaysia, which supplies about 50 per cent of Singapore's water, threatened to cut off that supply in 1997 after

Singapore criticized its government policies. Namibia's plan to construct a pipeline to divert water from the shared Okavango River to eastern Namibia has strained its relations with Botswana. The list of international water conflicts does not end here. There are reported disputes among the riparians over the Indus, Mahakali, Salween/Nu Jiang, Mekong, Parana, Lauca, Cenepa, Great Lakes, Colorado, Rio Grande, Lake Chad, Orange, Zambezi, Okavango, Senegal, Lake Victoria, Amu Dar'ya and Syr Dar'ya, Szamos. In some cases, there are existing agreements to regulate the water distribution among the riparian states, but the increasing scarcity is threatening their continuance.

Recently much has been written about international rivers being the source of 'water wars' in the near future. Some researchers challenge this supposition on the basis of lack of historical evidence of any war being fought over water. The only reported water war was 4,500 years back, in 2500 BC between the Sumerian city-states of Lagash and Umma over the Tigris River water.[100] According to Aaron Wolf 'the actual history of armed water conflict is somewhat less dramatic than the "water war" literature would lead one to believe'.[101] He finds only seven acute international water conflicts in the last century, in three of which there was no use of force.[102] However, Peter Gleick's list of violent water disputes both in ancient and recent history, is a much longer one.[103]

As the historical evidence suggests, water scarcity has caused a few minor skirmishes but no war has yet been fought. Wars are very rarely fought over one issue. So, establishing water as the sole incompatible factor to cause violent armed conflict between two nation-states is not that easy. Water might have played an indirect role in a war through its contribution to food scarcity, population displacement and ethnic alignment, which can lead to internal disturbances and political instability in the region. So, the real contribution of water to a war may not be properly examined through a conflict mapping data set. In-depth studies of individual wars might unfold the real contribution of water scarcity to the wars. In the last decade, the major inter-state wars are the Gulf War 1990–91, the Eritrea–Ethiopia war 1998–2000 and the peak in the India-Pakistan conflict in 1999. If we look at the immediate source of hostility of these warring parties, it is undoubtedly territory. However, if we travel to the history to trace the origin of these conflicts, we realise the significant contribution of a whole range of other factors. So, by just looking at the simple data sets, we should not dismiss the war causing potential of water scarcity.

There is also a need to take another close look at this 'water and war' discussion as the world has again started witnessing an increased number of inter-state armed conflicts in the last few years. After 11 September 2001, terrorism is being considered as the most significant threat to global peace and security. The US, with its allies, has already waged two wars, one against Taliban ruled Afghanistan and the other against Saddam ruled Iraq on the premise that these regimes were supporting global terrorism. Though the terrorism is being carried out by non-state actors, the wars are being fought against the states. The increasing number of wars against 'terrorist states' deserve serious attention of the international community to trace the origin and dynamics of these conflicts. If we move beyond the immediate factors contributing to group and agenda formation of the terrorist groups, then there is a greater possibility of finding the contribution of economic underdevelopment and deprivation. Recently, the chief of multinational Suez argued that there is a 'link between 11 September 2001 attacks and the rich–poor divide' and the 'access to water may be one of the most vital issues involved'.[104] If that is the case, the possible contribution of water to international violent conflicts cannot be ignored.

However, the river water issues have, thus far, not been the sole or immediate reasons for violent wars among the riparian states. Some may argue that war is too expensive a proposition for a state to acquire or control a low value commodity like water. For some others, it may be the resilience of existing large numbers of water treaties that thwarts the materialization of water wars. However, we think there are three possible reasons, which can explain why the so-called 'water war' has not taken place in the last decade, in spite of many threats and many predictions in this direction.

Time Factor
Threat of water diversion or storage by one riparian does not necessarily reduce water supply to the other users of the basin. To carry out the threat, a huge infrastructure has to be constructed, which takes a long period of time. A long interval between the 'expression of threat' and 'execution of threat' provides an opportunity for negotiated settlement among the riparian countries. The time factor can also help the parties to prepare themselves to face the possible water scarcity situation. As an example, in the Euphrates-Tigris basin, Syria seems to be adjusting itself with the reduced water availability from the Euphrates after the gradual realization of Turkey's South Anatolia Project.

Risk Factor
Many international rivers and lakes are the source of livelihood for a large number of people in the basin. Any violent conflict over the water issue might disrupt the water supply and bring damage to the water storage and distribution system. It is true that water projects, particularly dams (due to their size) are highly vulnerable to enemy attack. However, upstream riparian has no water related interest to attack the dams in the downstream. At the same time, the downstream country

will damage the dam in the upstream only at its own peril, as it would result in a wall of water rushing back to its own territory. The attack and destruction of water facilities for other strategic reasons can bring misery to a large number of civilian populations on both sides. The massive adverse consequences deter many disputing riparian states from attacking each other's water facilities. For example, India and Pakistan have fought several wars, but they refrain themselves from attacking any water infrastructures on the Indus River system.

Aid Factor

Most of the developing countries need financial and technical aid and assistance to undertake a large water project. Very few developing countries like Turkey (GAP Project), China (Three Gorges Project) and India (Narmada Project) can actually undertake expensive water projects on their own, but it comes with a heavy economic and political price tag. In recent years, particularly after the World Bank's change of policy in 1994 (OP 7.50), it is becoming increasingly difficult to receive external support for a disputed project in the international basin. The end of the Cold War has also stopped the alternative source of borrowing from the Eastern Bloc (e.g. Soviet assistance to the Aswan Dam Project in the 1950s and 1960s). In spite of increasing water demand, this new development restricts many upstream riparian countries (e.g. Ethiopia in the Nile basin, Kyrgyzstan and Tajikistan in Aral Sea basin) to undertake new projects, which might become the source of violent conflict in the basin.

Many conflicts are going on among users of international river basins in different parts of the world. With the possible exception of the Jordan basin, most such water conflicts have confined themselves to being non-armed in nature, though the threats of use of arms in these cases are not so uncommon. As early as the mid-1980s, US intelligence services estimated that there were at least ten places in the world where war could break out over the shortage of fresh water – the majority in the Middle East.[105] The study did not specify a time-frame, and so far serious conflicts have not arisen. In the early 1990s, several researchers predicted the Nile River would become the source of violent conflict in the near future.[106] It has not taken place; rather some basin- based cooperation is emerging among the Nilotic countries. Recently, Wolf and his associates have identified 17 international water basins which have the potential for creating political stress in the coming five to ten years.[107]

It raises the question of whether war or accommodation is the more likely outcome. There are conflicts on a lower level regularly reported from different parts of the world over international rivers. In some cases, there are agreements regulating the water distribution among the riparian states. Thus, the sharing of international rivers does seem to be associated with conflict between riparian states, as well as activities directed at conflict prevention and in some cases cooperation.

INTERNATIONAL RIVERS AND COOPERATION

Although Toset, Gleditsch and Hegre accept the possibility of armed conflict over water scarcity they nonetheless deny its inevitability.[108] In several cases, the competing riparian countries are moving towards sharing agreements rather than armed conflicts. Water in general and rivers in particular have also been seen as the source for state building in the past. Dynamic cultures have grown across river resources; Indus, Nile and Euphrates. Thus, water also brings people together. Better use of water, as well as the need to control water, is an important input in joint human construction. The shared water resource itself might not be the full explanation of inducing conflicts among the states; its various properties might have different contributions. So, it is necessary to analyse under what circumstances water-related issue conflict might take place among the riparians of an international river basin.

In the face of mutual dependence on the same fresh water resource, the withdrawal or pollution of one riparian state can potentially not only lead to disputes but also bring cooperation in the basin. In several cases, competing and disputing riparian countries are now moving towards cooperation. As Yoffe and Wolf point out, 145 water-related treaties have been signed in the last century.[109] Growing competition over the waters of the Mekong, Jordan, Ganges, Mahakali and Zambezi rivers have resulted in cooperative sharing arrangements in the 1990s. In spite of retaliatory nuclear tests and virtual war in the Kashmir Mountains, India and Pakistan are continuing their cooperative sharing of the Indus water since 1960. Within the Nile Basin Initiative, a Council of Ministers of Water Affairs of the Nile basin countries has paved the way for the establishment of a Nile River Commission. Even in the Euphrates-Tigris basin, a Technical Committee is in operation where all three major riparians are members.

Water can be an impetus for war or an impetus for peace. Sadoff and Grey argue that politics will govern whether the result is cooperation or conflict.[110] Similarly, Israeli hydrologist, Uri Shamir, highlights the importance of political factors in shaping the pattern of water use, 'If there is political will for peace, water will not be a hindrance. If you want reasons to fight, water will give you ample opportunities.'[111] Some others argue that the character of power distribution among the basin countries will determine the potential for conflict or cooperation over the shared water; i.e. power asymmetries in the basin are a major

Table 1.5 Selected Fresh Water Basins and Existing Cooperative Institutions

International fresh water basins	Disputing riparian countries	Incompatibility	Basin-based institutions
Jordan	Israel, Jordan, Syria, Lebanon, Palestine	Water scarcity and control	Yarmouk Commission (Jordan, Syria) Orontes & South Cebir Commission (Syria, Lebanon)
Euphrates-Tigris	Turkey, Syria, Iraq	Water scarcity and control of water	Tigris and Euphrates Joint Technical Committee
Amu Dar'ya & Syr Dar'ya	Uzbekistan, Krygyzstan, Kazakhstan	Water scarcity and storage	International Coordination Commission for Water-Supply (Concerning the Aral Sea and Tadschikistanian Rivers)
Minho, Douro, Tejo, Guadiana	Portugal, Spain	Water scarcity	International Commission between Portugal and Spain
Rhine	France, Germany, the Netherlands	Pollution	International Commission for the Protection of Rhine against Pollution (ICPR)
Danube	Hungary, Slovakia	Control (diversion) of water	Danube Commission; International Commission for the Protection of the Danube
Szamos	Hungary, Romania	Pollution	Romania-Hungary Hydrotechnical Commission
Mekong	China, Myanmar, Thailand, Laos, Cambodia, Vietnam	Scarcity and control of water	Mekong River Commission (Thailand, Laos, Cambodia, Vietnam)
Ganges	India, Bangladesh	Water scarcity, diversion	Indo-Bangladesh Joint River Commission
Indus	India, Pakistan	Scarcity of water	Joint Indus River Commission
Parana	Argentina, Brazil, Paraguay	Control of water	Programme Paraguay-Parana
Great Lakes	USA, Canada	Pollution	International Joint Commission (IJC)
Rio Grande	USA, Mexico	Pollution	International Boundary and Water Commission (IBWC) Rio Grande
Nile	Egypt, Sudan, Ethiopia	Water scarcity	Council of Ministers of Water Affairs of the Nile Basin Countries (COM)

Table 1.5 continued

International fresh water basins	Disputing riparian countries	Incompatibility	Basin-based institutions
Lake Chad	Nigeria, Chad, Cameroon	Water sharing	Lake Chad Basin Commission (LCBC)
Orange	South Africa, Lesotho	Water scarcity, diversion	SADC-Orange River Basin Commission
Zambezi	Zambia, Zimbabwe, Mozambique, South Africa	Water scarcity, diversion	SADC-Joint River Basin Commission: Zambezi River Authority (Zambia, Zimbabwe)
Okavango	Namibia, Botswana, Angola	Water scarcity	Okavango River basin Commission (OKACOM)
Senegal	Senegal, Mauritania	Water scarcity	Senegal River Development Organization
Lake Victoria	Uganda, Kenya, Tanzania	Water sharing	Lake Victoria Environmental Management Programme

Source: SIWI, *Water and Development: A Commissioned Study* (Stockholm: Stockholm International Water Institute for the European Parliament, 2000).

obstacle to the trans-boundary cooperation.[112] Involvement of non-basin actors may affect the existing power relationship among the riparian nations. It is because of the changing political will or shifting power relationship that water competition results, in most cases, in cooperative agreements. However, evidence suggests that cooperative arrangements among the riparian states cannot last if the latter do not interact with and gain support from such institutions for proper water management at the basin level. When the matter of contention is over the quantity of water, the challenge for long-term water sharing agreement is much higher. With the help of financial and technological resources, it is relatively easier to address the water quality problem.[113] The success of the 1972 Agreements between the US and Mexico over addressing the salinity problem in Colorado water and the 1976 (became operative in 1985) Agreement between France, Germany, Netherlands and Switzerland to reduce chloride pollution in the Rhine, testify to this fact. However, when the issue is quantity, the solution is not that easy. Bargaining over the volume of water further reinforces the differences between upstream and downstream riparian states, by demonstrating losses and gains. In some cases, owing to political or financial incentives, disputing riparian countries might reach some agreements. However, signing of a sharing agreement might diffuse the dispute for a short period of time, but it does not provide a long-term solution. The recent threats to the survival of the Indus River Agreement of 1960, Nile River Agreement of 1959, Euphrates River Agreement of 1987 and Ganges River Agreement of 1996 confirm this apprehension.

Allocated water in the sharing agreement is unable to meet the increasing demand. The scope of further augmentation of river water in many parts of the world is becoming limited owing to financial, technical and, more importantly, environmental reasons. There are very few international basins left, which can provide some hope for feasible further exploitation. Congo River basin is one of them. Its runoff is ten times more than Zambezi's and the Inga rapids alone have the potential of hydropower generating capacity of 45,000 megawatts. However, most of the international rivers have been exploited to a large extent. In many cases, the augmentation can be possible only at the cost of others. So, these schemes receive opposition from the affected people (e.g. Jonglei Project in the Nile basin). The time has come to realize the fact that addressing the supply side alone cannot find a lasting solution to the quantity question of the sharing of international rivers.

FUTURE CHALLENGES

Water is vital for the survival of human beings. The increasing demand for water from population growth, rapid industrialization, urbanization and expanding agriculture is so high that the present availability is not sufficient. This is especially serious for the countries in the arid, semi-arid and tropical regions. Unfortunately, most of these countries are weak states and lack the resources and administrative abilities to deal with problems arising from water scarcity. Lack of education and blind ethnic loyalties also easily lead to politicization of the water problem as well as ethnicization of the issue. Water scarcity is a current and future threat to the fragile security of the post-Cold War world. It is not prudent to overlook the problems caused by scarcity of water when making a security evaluation of a country or a region. In an interdependent and interconnected world, the conflicts, while mostly found in developing countries, might spill over to destroy the peace and tranquillity of the developed temperate regions.

It is predicted that between 44 and 65 per cent of the world's population will face some consequences of water scarcity or water stress by the middle of the next century. This situation can be attributed to several reasons. The massive population growth especially in the developing world, combined with rapid industrialization, massive urbanization and intensifying agricultural activities has contributed to this problem. As the demand for water for human and industrial use has increased, so has the competition for water used for irrigated agriculture. Many developing countries are already facing serious problems in meeting the rapidly increasing water demands. In order to meet the demands, they are exploiting the available water resource further. The over-exploitation of water resources can result in an acute shortage. In this scarcity situation, water increasingly has become a source of social tension as the users are worried about the present or future availability of the water resource. They may work purposefully and consciously to maximize the availability of water resource. Therefore, water scarcity has the potential to bring further competition and create conflict – and that can destroy the ongoing arrangements of water distribution.

NOTES

1. This chapter draws heavily from the author's earlier works: A. Swain, 'Water Scarcity: A Threat to Global Security', *Environment & Security*, 1, 1 (1996), pp. 156–72; P. Wallensteen and A. Swain, *International Fresh Water Resources: Source of Conflict or Cooperation* (Stockholm: Stockholm Environment Institute, 1997); A. Swain, 'Water Scarcity as a Source of Crises', in E. W. Nafziger, F. Stewart and R. Väyrynen (eds), *War, Hunger and Displacement: The Origins of Humanitarian Emergencies* (Oxford: Oxford University Press, 2000), pp. 179-205; A. Swain, 'Water Wars: Fact or Fiction', *Futurers*, 33, 8, 9 (2001), pp. 769–81.
2. According to M. A. Chitale, Stockholm water prize laureate of 1993, 'For Hindus, the river is a mother. Without water, there is no life.' See P. Hanneberg, *Our Struggle for Water* (Stockholm: SIWI, 2000), pp. 4–5.
3. See P. H. Gleick, 'An Introduction to Global Fresh Water Issues', in P. H. Gleick (ed.), *Water in Crisis: A Guide to the World's Fresh Water Resources* (New York: Oxford University Press, 1993), p. 3.
4. See M. Falkenmark, 'Living at the Mercy of the Water Cycle', in *Water Resources in the Next Century* (Stockholm: Proceedings of the Stockholm Water Symposium, 12–15 August 1991), p. 13.
5. D. A. Caponera, 'Ownership and Transfer of Water and Land in Islam', in N. I. Faruqui, A. K. Biswas and M. J. Bino (eds), *Water Management in Islam* (Tokyo: UNU Press, 2001), pp. 94–102.
6. World Resource Institute, *World Resources 1990–91* (New York: Oxford University Press, 1991), p. 166.
7. I. A. Shiklomanov, 'World Fresh Water Resources', in P. H. Gleick (ed.), *Water in Crisis: A Guide to the World's Fresh Water Resources* (New York: Oxford University Press, 1993), p. 13.
8. Ibid., p. 15.
9. M. Falkenmark, 'Global Water Issues Confronting Humanity', *Journal of Peace Research*, 27, 2 (1990), p. 17.
10. M. Falkenmark, 'Water Scarcity: Time for Realism', 20 (1993), pp. 11–12.
11. R. Engelman and P. LeRoy, *Sustaining Water: Population and the Future of Renewable Water Supplies* (Washington DC: Population and Environment Program, Population Action International, 1993), p. 10.
12. World Bank, *World Development Report 1992: Development and the Environment* (New York: Oxford University Press, 1992), p. 26.

13. See E. Bos, M. T. Vu, E. Massiah and R. A. Bulatao, *World Population Projection, 1994–1995* (Baltimore, MD: Johns Hopkins University Press, 1994).
14. D. Seckler, U. Amarasinghe, D. Mollen, R. de Silva and R. Baker, *World Water Demand and Supply, 1990 to 2025: Scenarios and Issues* (Colombo: IWMI Research Report 19, 1998).
15. See Shiklomanov, 'World Fresh Water Resources', p. 20.
16. S. Postel, *Last Oasis: Facing Water Scarcity* (New York: W.W. Norton & Co., 1992), p. 49.
17. After peaking in 1978, irrigation area per person fell more than 4% by 1988. Owing to expansion of irrigated area in Asia, particularly in India, the global average increased a bit around 1990, and was almost stable in the 1990s at 45.8 hectares per thousand people. See L. R. Brown, M. Renner and B. Halweil, *Vital Signs 1999* (New York: W.W. Norton & Co., 1999), pp. 44–5.
18. See FAO, 'Food Production: The Critical Role of Water', in *Technical Background Documents 6–11: Vol. 2* (Rome: FAO, 1996).
19. M. Rosegrant and C. Ringler, 'Impact on Food Security and Rural Development of Transferring Water out of Agriculture', *Water Policy*, 1 (1998), pp. 567–86.
20. See Shiklomanov, 'World Fresh Water Resources', p. 18.
21. L. R. Brown, G. Gardner and B. Halweil, *Beyond Malthus: Nineteen Dimensions of the Population Challenge* (New York: W.W. Norton & Co., 1999).
22. S. Lonergan, 'Water Resources and Conflict: Examples from the Middle East', Paper presented in the Conflict and the Environment, NATO Advanced Research Workshop, Bolkesjo, Norway, 12–16 June 1996.
23. P. Raskin, E. Hansen and R. Morgolis, *Water and Sustainability: A Global Outlook* (Stockholm: Stockholm Environment Institute, Polestar Series Report No. 4, 1995).
24. See J. Lundqvist, 'Water Scarcity in Abundance: Management and Policy Challenges', *Ecodecision*, 6 (1992), p. 41.
25. P. H. Gleick, 'Basic Water Requirements for Human Activities: Meeting Basic Needs', *Water International*, 21, 2 (1996), p. 88.
26. See World Bank, *Water Resource Management* (Washington DC: World Bank Policy Paper, 1993) and WHO, *Our Planet, Our Health: Report of the WHO Commission on Health and the Environment* (Geneva: World Health Organization, 1992).
27. See Gleick, 'Basic Water Requirements for Human Activities: Meeting Basic Needs', pp. 83–92.
28. P. H. Gleick, 'The Human Right to Water', *Water Policy*, 1 (1998), pp. 487–503.
29. UNEP, *Freshwater Pollution* (Nairobi: UNEP/GEMS Environment Library No. 6, 1991), p. 12.
30. FAOSTAT, *FAOSTAT Statistics Database* (Rome: FAO, 1997).
31. UNEP, *Global Environmental Outlook 2000* (London: Earthscan, 1999), p. 28.
32. See Brown, Renner and Halweil, *Vital Signs 1999.*
33. In Asia and Africa, the agriculture sector still accounts for 80 per cent of fresh water consumption.
34. Seckler et al., *World Water Demand and Supply, 1990 to 2025* (1998).
35. R. Clarke, *Water: The International Crisis* (London: Earthscan, 1991), p. 23.
36. See S. Postel, *Conserving Water: The Untapped Alternative* (Washington DC: Worldwatch Institute Paper No. 67, 1985).
37. R. Opie, 'Germany's Double Bill', *World Water and Environmental Engineer*, April (1991).
38. WMO et al., *Comprehensive Assessment of Freshwater Resources of the World* (Geneva: WMO, 1997).
39. L. Brown and B. Halweil, *China's Water Shortage* (Washington DC: Worldwatch Institute Press Release, 22 April 1998).
40. Clarke, *Water: The International Crisis*, p. 25.

41. *The Wall Street Journal Europe*, 23–24 March 2001.
42. D. Gyawali, 'Energizing Development and Sustaining the Environment – A Nepali's View', *Development*, 1 (1991).
43. http://apps.fao.org
44. See A. K. Biswas, 'Water for the Urban Areas of the Developing World in the Twenty-first Century', in J. I. Uitto and A. K. Biswas (eds), *Water for Urban Areas: Challenges and Perspectives* (Tokyo: UNU Press, 2000), pp. 1–23.
45. UNCHS, *An Urbanizing World: Global Report on Human Settlements 1996* (Oxford: Oxford University Press, 1996).
46. R. J. Mitchell and M. D. R. Leys, *A History of London Life* (London: Penguin, 1963), p. 273.
47. UNEP, *Technical Annexes to the State of the Marine Environment* (Nairobi: UNEP Regional Seas Reports and Studies No. 114, 1990), pp. 389–90.
48. UNEP, *Freshwater Pollution* (1991).
49. WHO, *Health and Environment in Sustainable Development: Five Years after the Earth Summit* (Geneva: WHO, 1997).
50. I. A. Shiklomanov, *Assessment of Water Resources and Water Availability in the World* (Stockholm: Stockholm Environment Institute, 1997).
51. See WCD, *Dams and Development: A New Framework for Decision Making* (The Report of the World Commission on Dams, 16 November 2000).
52. Shiklomanov, 'World Fresh Water Resources'.
53. F. Pearce, 'Tide of Opinion Turns Against Superdams', *Panscope*, 33 (1992), p. 3.
54. Official figure is that 1.3 million people will have to be resettled, which is the largest population displacement in the history of dam building. Researchers suggest that the displacement number will be as high as 1.9 million. A. Zich, 'Before the Flood: China's Three Georges', *National Geographic*, 192, 3 (1997), pp. 2–33. Also, see, G. Heggelund, *China's Environmental Crisis: The Battle of Sanxia* (Oslo: NUPI Research Report No. 170, 1993).
55. See W. Fernades, 'The Price of Development', *Seminar*, 412 (1993), pp. 19–24.
56. A. Swain, 'Democratic Consolidation: Environmental Movements in India', *Asian Survey*, 37, 9 (1997), pp. 818–32.
57. J. A. Veltrop, 'Importance of Dams for Water Supply and Hydropower', in A. K. Biswas et al. (eds), *Water for Sustainable Development in the Twenty-first Century* (Delhi: Oxford University Press, 1993), pp. 102–15.
58. *Financial Times*, 16 March 2000.
59. *International Rivers and Lakes*, 35 (2001), p. 6.
60. D. Satterthwaite, 'Securing Water for the Cities', *People & the Planet*, 2, 2 (1993), p. 13.
61. *Financial Times*, 8 March 2001.
62. S. Foster, 'Essential Concepts for Ground Water Regulators', in S. M. A. Salman (ed.), *Ground Water: Legal and Policy Perspectives* (Washington DC: World Bank Technical Paper No. 456, 1999).
63. An aquifer is 'the water bearing material in which groundwater is stored and through which it flows', R. Clarke et al., *Groundwater: A Threatened Resource* (Nairobi: UNEP Environment Library No. 15, 1996).
64. UNEP, *Global Environmental Outlook 2000*, p. 43.
65. A. Goudie, *The Human Impact on the Natural Environment* (Oxford: Basil Blackwell, 3rd edn, 1990), p. 179.
66. A. K. Biswas, 'Environmental Impact Assessment for Groundwater Management', *Water Resource Development*, 8, 2 (1992), pp. 113–17.
67. V. I. Korzoun and A. A. Sokolov, 'World Water Balance and Water Resources of the Earth', in United Nations, *Water Development and Management Proceedings of the United*

Nations Water Conference (London: Pergamon Press, 1978).

68. S. Burchi, 'National Regulations for Groundwater: Options, Issues and Best Practices', in S. M. A. Salman (ed.), *Ground Water: Legal and Policy Perspectives* (Washington DC: World Bank Technical Paper No. 456, 1999), p. 55.

69. IWMI, *Water Supply and Demand in 2025* (Colombo: International Water Management Institute, 2000).

70. T. Homer-Dixon and V. Percival, *Environmental Scarcity and Violent Conflict: Briefing Book* (The Project on Environment, Population and Security, American Association for the Advancement of Science & University College, University of Toronto, 1996), p. 50.

71. M. R. Lowi, 'Bridging the Divide: Transboundary Resource Disputes and the Case of West Bank Water', *International Security*, 18, 1 (1993), pp. 113–38.

72. A. Swain, 'A New Challenge: Water Scarcity in the Arab World', *Arab Studies Quarterly*, 20, 1 (1998), pp. 1–11.

73. CGWB, *Background Note: Colloquium on Strategy for Ground Water Development* (New Delhi: Central Ground Water Board, 1996).

74. M. K. Majumder, 'Bangladesh Keeps Priming the Pumps', *Panscope*, 31 (1992).

75. S. Foster, 'Ground for Concern', *Our Planet*, 8, 3 (1996), p. 13.

76. A. Swain, 'Fight for the Last Drop: Inter-state River Disputes in India', *Contemporary South Asia*, 7, 2 (1998), pp. 167–80.

77. A. Swain, *Environment and Conflict: Analysing the Developing World* (Uppsala: Department of Peace and Conflict Research, Report No. 37, 1993), p. 28.

78. P. Wallensteen (ed.), *Peace Research: Achievements and Challenges* (Boulder, CO: Westview Press, 1988).

79. The conflict between California and Arizona over the Colorado River goes back to the 1930s. In 1935, Arizona had even commissioned a navy (with only one ferry boat) and called out the National Guard and militia units to the Californian border to protest the construction of the Parker Dam and diversion on the Colorado River. See M. Reisner, *Cadillac Desert: The American West and its Disappearing Water* (New York: Penguin Books, 1986).

80. Swain, 'Fight for the Last Drop: Inter-state River Disputes in India'.

81. P. Rogers, H. Bouhia and J. Kalbermatten, 'Water for Big Cities: Big Problems, Easy Solutions?', in C. Rosan, B. A. Ruble and J. S. Tulchin (eds), *Urbanization, Population, Environment and Security: A Report of the Comparative Urban Studies Project* (Washington DC: Woodrow Wilson International Centre for Scholars, 2000).

82. Reisner, *Cadillac Desert: The American West and its Disappearing Water.*

83. However, there was no formal request from the allied coalition to Turkey to undertake this action. Dams are being perceived as offensive weapons in the Korean peninsula as well. In 1986, North Korea unveiled its plan to construct a major hydroelectric dam, just north of Seoul on the Han River. South Korea considers this proposed dam as a potential military weapon as the sudden release of water from its reservoir would destroy most of Seoul. The economic crisis of North Korea has held up the implementation of the dam construction, but South Korea has already built a number of check dams and levees above its capital to protect it against any such threat. See *Washington Post*, 30 September 1987.

84. K. J. Holsti, *Peace and War: Armed Conflicts and International Order 1649–1989* (Cambridge: Cambridge University Press, 1991); and J. A. Vasquez, *The War Puzzle* (Cambridge: Cambridge University Press, 1993).

85. P. K. Huth, *Standing your Ground: Territorial Disputes and International Conflict* (Ann Arbor, MI: University of Michigan Press, 1996), p. 5.

86. H. P. Toset, N. P. Gleditsch and H. Hegre, 'Shared Rivers and Interstate Conflict', *Political Geography*, 19 (2000), p. 973.

87. After hitting the ground, rainwater gets divided between the evaporating part, i.e. the *green water flow*, from wet surfaces and plant production processes and the liquid part,

i.e. the *blue water flow*, which flows through the landscapes via rivers, lakes and aquifers.

88. A 1958 United Nations panel of experts for the first time came up with the idea of bringing out a Register of International Rivers.

89. A. K. Biswas, 'Management of International Waters: Problems and Perspective, *Water Resource Development*, 9 (1993), pp. 167–88.

90. In 2003, the database revised the number of international watersheds to 263. Two from the original list have been merged as one (the Benito and Ntem) and three additional basins have been located: the Glama between Sweden and Norway, the Wiedau between Denmark and Germany and the Skagit between the US and Canada. See, A. T. Wolf, S. B. Yoffe, and M. Giordano, 'International Waters: Identifying Basins at Risk', *Water Policy*, 5 (2003), pp. 29–60.

91. A. T. Wolf, J. A. Natharius, J. J. Danielson, B. S. Ward and J. K. Pender, 'International River Basins of the World', *International Journal of Water Resources Development*, 15, 4 (1999).

92. K. Conca and F. Wu, 'Is there a Global River Regime', Paper presented at the 43rd Annual Meeting of the International Studies Association, New Orleans, 23–27 March 2002.

93. *New York Times*, 10 August 1995.

94. Cited from S. Lonergan, 'Water Resources and Conflict: Examples from the Middle East', in N. P. Gleditsch (ed.), *Conflict and the Environment* (Dordrecht: Kluwer Academic, 1997), p. 375.

95. T. F. Homer-Dixon, *Environment, Scarcity, and Violence* (Princeton, NJ: Princeton University Press, 1999).

96. C. W. Sadoff and D. Grey, 'Beyond the River: The Benefits of Cooperation on International Rivers', *Water Policy*, 4, 5 (2002), p. 391.

97. N. P. Gleditsch and J. Hamner, 'Shared Rivers, Conflict, and Cooperation', Paper presented at the 42nd Annual Meeting of the International Studies Association, Chicago, IL, 21–24 February 2001.

98. H. Haftendorn, 'Water and International Conflict', *Third World Quarterly*, 21, 1 (2000), pp. 51–68.

99. Libiszewski and Wolf argue that water was neither a cause nor a goal of 1967 or 1982 Arab-Israeli warfare. See S. Libiszewski, *Water Disputes in the Jordan Basin Region and their Role in the Resolution of the Arab-Israeli Conflict* (Zurich: Centre for Security Studies and Conflict Research Occasional Paper No. 13, 1995); A. T. Wolf, *Hydropolitics Along the Jordan River: Scarce Water and its Impact on the Arab-Israeli Conflict* (Tokyo: UNU Press, 1995).

100. J. Cooper, *Reconstructing History from Ancient Inscriptions: The Lagash-Umma Border Conflict* (Malibu, CA: Undena, 1983).

101. A. T. Wolf, 'Conflict and Cooperation along International Waterways, *Water Policy*, 1, 2 (1998), pp. 251–65.

102. Seven incidents are: (1) India and Pakistan over Indus River in 1948; (2) Syria and Israel over the Huleh basin from February 1951 to September 1953; (3) Sudan and Egypt over the Nile waters from January to April 1958; (4) Ethiopia and Somalia over the Ogaden desert, which includes important water resources from June 1963 to March 1964; (5) Israel and Syria over Jordan River waters from March 1965 to July 1966; (6) Syria and Iraq over the Euphrates water in 1975; and (7) Mauritania and Senegal over the Senegal River from April 1989 to July 1991. See ibid.

103. P. H. Gleick, *The World's Water: The Biennial Report on Freshwater Resources 1998–1999* (Washington DC: Island Press, 1998), pp. 125–30.

104. Quoted in *International Rivers and Lakes*, 36 (2001), pp. 7–8.

105. J. R. Starr, 'Water Wars', *Foreign Policy*, 82 (1991), p. 17.

106. T. F. Homer-Dixon, 'Environmental Scarcities and Violent Conflict: Evidence from

Cases', *International Security*, 191 (1994), pp. 5–40.
107. The basins at risk are: Ganges-Brahmaputra, Han, Incomati, Kunene, Kura-Araks, Lake Chad, La Plata, Lempa, Limpopo, Mekong, Ob (Ortis), Okavango, Orange, Salween, Senegal, Tumen and Zambezi. They have been identified on the basis of two sets of indicators: (1) basin management structure includes newly independent states; and, (2) unilateral development projects are being undertaken in the absence of cooperative regimes. See Wolf et al., 'International Waters: Identifying Basins at Risk'.
108. Toset et al., 'Shared Rivers and Interstate Conflict'.
109. S. B. Yoffe and A. T. Wolf, 'Water, Conflict and Cooperation: Geographical Perspectives', *Cambridge Review of International Affairs*, 12, 2 (1999), pp. 197–213. The UN Food and Agricultural Organization has even identified 3,600 international water related treaties from AD 805 to 1984.
110. Sadoff and Grey, 'Beyond the River: The Benefits of Cooperation on International Rivers', pp. 389–403.
111. Quoted in *International Rivers and Lakes*, 34 (2000), p. 7.
112. F. W. Frey, 'The Political Context of Conflict and Cooperation over International River Basins', *Water International*, 18, 1 (1993), pp. 54–68; R. E. Just and S. Netanyahu, 'International Water Resource Conflicts: Experience and Potential', in R. E. Just and S. Netanyahu (eds), *Conflict and Cooperation on Trans-boundary Water Resources* (Boston, MA: Kluwer Academic Publishers, 1998), pp. 1–26; A. T. Wolf, 'International Water Conflict Resolution: Lessons from Comparative Analysis', *International Journal of Water Resources Development*, 13, 3 (1997), pp. 333–65. However, Hamnar noticed that the basin level distribution of power does not significantly affect the water allocation in international agreements. J. Hamner, 'Weapons Won't Get You Water: State Power and Distribution of Benefits', Paper presented at the 43rd Annual Meeting of the International Studies Association, New Orleans, 23–27 March 2002.
113. See Wallensteen and Swain, *International Fresh Water Resources: Source of Conflict or Cooperation.*

South Asia and its Large Rivers: The Indus, the Mahakali and with Special Emphasis on the Ganges[1]

Fresh water is emerging as the most crucial resource issue facing South Asia. The countries in South Asia, primarily India, Pakistan, Bangladesh, Nepal and Bhutan,[2] are experiencing massive population growth, and also suffering from rampant poverty in both economic and human development terms. While the availability of fresh water is limited in the region, the demand for the resource continues to expand rapidly. High population density coupled with low per capita income and a predominantly agricultural economy necessitate the sustainable water management of shared rivers. South Asia has many great rivers, particularly the Indus and the Ganges-Brahmaputra, which have been the source of riparian dispute as well as cooperation for more than 50 years.

India's principal river, the Ganges, after rising in the Himalayas, flows across the Northern Plains and then Bangladesh to join the Brahmaputra before reaching the Bay of Bengal. A number of tributaries of this major river system originate in Nepal, one of them is the Mahakali River. In northern India, the major drainage basin is that of another Himalayan river, the Indus, though most of this basin lies in Pakistan. These major South Asian rivers are snow-fed. The Himalayas stores the largest quantity of ice outside the polar regions.[3] The melt-water from the Himalayan glaciers constitute the headwaters of South Asia's most important international river systems. Though perennial, the runoff from these rivers varies considerably from high season to dry season. Himalayan rivers experience two high water seasons, one in early summer originating from melting snow in the mountains, and the other in late summer caused by runoff from monsoon rains. However, there is a wide variation of precipitation from the eastern side of the Himalayas to the western side. Thus the monsoon flow of the Indus

River is relatively weak and of short duration compared to the Ganges system.

The countries of South Asia face challenges to their water security on several fronts. The first is the rise in the region's population, which is expected to reach 1.5 billion by AD 2020. Of this population, more than 50 per cent currently lives below the poverty line and lack of livelihood options. Despite substantial economic growth during the 1990s, the region has one of the lowest per capita incomes in the world. Growing subsistence needs impose larger demands on water, arable land, forests and coastal habitats.

In the nineteenth century, British colonial rule brought most parts of South Asia under a unitary state and centralized political unity, which was based on the notion of a singular and indivisible sovereignty through the practice of bureaucratic centralization.[4] One of the sectors that the colonial administration used to extract revenue was agriculture. To increase productivity, it pursued the path of building large-scale irrigation systems. Between 1800 and 1920 the colonial government built several such projects, whose construction was also guided by the objectives of protective irrigation and administrative control.[5] In its approach to water, the colonial state imposed technological options, but remained oblivious to the social and environmental complexity of the region and to traditional water management institutions.

Punjab province was the locus of the colonial water development scheme. The colonial administration constructed a vast network of irrigation canals, which were dug from rivers Ravi and Sutlej followed by rivers Chenab and Jhelum. These canals took water to villages in Western Punjab.[6] With the end of colonial rule and partition in 1947, most of the irrigated lands became part of Pakistan. The newly installed Congress government in India had to cope with the challenges of immigration caused by partition, a rising population and a growing food deficit. The government embarked upon a huge programme for developing large-scale surface water irrigation. In 1948 alone, 160 such projects were considered, investigated or executed. In the First Five-Year Plan (1951–1955), Indian state allocated 29 per cent of the budget for the purpose of large-scale irrigation development. The urgency of the food crisis at that time demanded this immediate and massive response.[7] The focus did bring about positive results; the annual growth rate of food grain production increased from 0.1 per cent of the pre-independence period to 3.1 per cent at the end of the plan period.

Encouraged by this success, the Indian leadership pursued the strategy of maximizing self-reliance by following a 'mixed' economy. In its Second Five-Year Plan India adopted a strategy of (1) restructuring an economy dependent on foreign capital into one which developed independently; (2) developing state capitalism and a capitalist form of development in the urban sector; and (3) transforming the feudalistic mode of agricultural production into capitalist farming. The result was the emergence of a dominant agricultural sector and a strong emerging industrial infrastructure. To meet the needs of industrialization, the government, in subsequent plan periods, accorded top priority not just to irrigation development but also to energy production and to mitigating hazards caused by floods. The end product was the proliferation of dams, surface irrigation systems and flood control embankments.

Other factors also led to making large-scale water development projects a top priority. One major objective of post-independence India was national integration; in fact, this cause dominated all other concerns of the time. Water projects were regarded as symbols of prestige with local pressure groups.[8] At a time of high expectations, development infrastructures were presented to the people as harbingers of a secure future; this claim allowed the political leadership to achieve a sense of legitimacy among the general public. The initiatives also helped the leadership in post-independence India to bring together some segments of the society that were outside the national mainstream. The strategy allowed the central government to mobilize external funds, which in turn enhanced its ability to distribute largesse and dispense patronage aimed at securing populist support.

Despite their benefits, the intensified development of large-scale water projects incurred high social and environmental costs, and growing dependency on external borrowing. The capital costs of beginning new projects, of providing resources for rehabilitation and of meeting recurrent expenditures for operation and maintenance have, however, increased the country's debt. Developing large-scale water projects also led to location-specific disruptions of the environment and to high social cost due to the displacement of native populations. The complications do not end there. Several Indian projects in the international water basins have adversely affected the downstream riparian countries.

No other geographical region is dominated by a single country as much as South Asia is by India. India is not only the largest and strongest, but it also constitutes the core of the region. India's population is three times more than the combined population of six other South Asian countries, it occupies 73 per cent of the total area of the region and its gross national product is three-fourths of the total in the region. There is a fear and suspicion of India in the perception of its smaller neighbours. The ongoing ambitious river water exploitation schemes of India further raises the mistrust and anxiety among the neighbouring countries, which has added another important dimension to the fragile security in South Asia.

The Indus River: India and Pakistan

The Indus River originates at 17,000 feet above sea level in Tibet. This 1,800 miles long river after flowing out of Tibet through the Himalayas enters Jammu and Kashmir in India and then moves into Pakistan before emptying into the Arabian Sea. The drainage area of the river is 450,000 square miles with an annual average inflow of 168 million acre feet (1 million acre feet is 1.2335 cubic kilometres of water). Five tributaries, the Chenab, the Jhelum, the Ravi, the Beas and the Sutlej, also originating from the Himalayas, join their waters with the Indus in Pakistan. The Indus River basin in British India constituted one of the oldest and largest irrigation systems in the world. Irrigation along the Indus River is as old as its civilization. It is now the largest contiguous irrigation system in the world with a command area of about 20 million hectares and annual irrigation capacity of over 12 million hectares.

A large investment was made by the colonial administration between 1860 and 1947 towards creation of the Indus basin irrigation system.[9] The partition of the Indian sub-continent in 1947 put the headwater of the basin in India; Pakistan received the lower part of the basin. Two important irrigation headworks, one at Madhopur on Ravi River and the other at Ferozepur on Sutlej River which were the source of supply to irrigation canals in Pakistan, were left in Indian territory. Over 90 per cent of Pakistan's agriculture was dependent on water of the Indus River system. Pakistani areas, which had been using the Indus water for centuries, after the partition suddenly found the water sources originating in another country.

India wishes to lay claim to a major portion of the Indus water for its own development. Increasing political unease, massive refugee movement and the issue of Kashmir further provoked the water sharing dispute between the two newly independent countries. The partition had not provided any agreed formula of how to share the Indus River system. Sir Cyril Redcliffe, Chairman of the British Partition Commission, had only expressed his hope that, 'some joint control and management of the irrigation system may be found'.[10] After the end of the 1947 monsoon season, Pakistan and India came up with a 'Standstill Agreement', which agreed not to disturb the existing position of water use in the East and West Punjab until 31 March 1948. Immediately after the expiry of this agreement, India stopped the water supplies to some Pakistani canals at the start of the summer irrigation season.[11] The water cut by India in 1948 affected 5.5 per cent of Pakistan's irrigated area and put tremendous strain on this new country. After some days of rancorous denunciation of each other, both countries started negotiating. Finally, a temporary agreement, known as the Inter-Dominion Accord, was reached in Delhi in May 1948, which required India to release sufficient waters to Pakistani regions in return for annual payments from the Pakistani government.

After the Accord, India claimed that the Pakistani acceptance of payment recognized India's sole claim over the Indus water. This was opposed by Pakistan, which claimed to enjoy the historic rights over the waters and its payment to India was only to cover the operation and maintenance costs.[12] In spite of conflicting claims, both countries signed the 'Delhi Agreement' in 1949, in which India assured Pakistan that it would not stop water supply without permitting time for Pakistan to develop alternative sources. This did not satisfy Pakistan, which proposed to refer the case to the World Court. India, on the other hand, was reluctant to refer the matter to a third party, instead it wanted to resolve the difference by the judges from both the countries. This deadlock continued through 1950.[13]

In February 1951, the US magazine *Collier's* sponsored David Lilienthal, former Chief of the Tennessee Valley Authority, to undertake a fact-finding tour in order to propose a solution to the problem.[14] Lilienthal visited the sub-continent, met the prime ministers of both the countries and concluded that while the two nations quarrelled over how much water each got, 80 per cent of the Indus flowed unused to the sea.[15] Lilienthal's article, 'Another "Korea" in the Making' in *Collier's* magazine's 4 August 1951 issue, argued for an early solution of the Indus water problem and urged that an extended canal system should be 'designed, built and operated as a unit' jointly financed by India, Pakistan and the World Bank. His friend, the then President of the World Bank, Eugene Black, read the article and welcomed the idea. He offered his good office to mediate. The World Bank, which had been withholding loan requests from both the countries until the progress on the water dispute had been made, informed both the prime ministers that it would like to mediate a settlement.

It was only when the World Bank, backed by its financial muscles, got into the negotiator's role, that India and Pakistan agreed on an important issue for the first time. The first meeting of the Working Party, which included engineers from India and Pakistan and also a consulting team from the World Bank, took place in Washington in May 1952. Subsequent meetings took place in Karachi and Delhi. In October 1953, both parties submitted their own plans for Indus water development, which were very different from each other on the allocation aspects. World Bank soon realized that the bilateral relationship between the two countries was not conducive for the integrated development of Indus water, as originally suggested by Lilienthal. In February 1954, it put forward its own proposal, which asked for the allocation of the entire flow of three eastern flowing rivers to India and all three western flowing rivers to Pakistan, except for a meagre amount from the Jhelum. India agreed immediately, but Pakistan was apprehensive that the western rivers alone would not be able to meet its water requirement. It was decided then that more storage would be built on western rivers. Finally, after eight long years of negotiation, the World Bank was able to bring both the riparian countries to see the 'water rationality'.[16]

The Indus Waters Treaty was signed on 19 September 1960 at Pakistani Port City of Karachi by India's Prime Minister Jawaharlal Nehru and Pakistan's President Mohammad Ayub Khan. The future prospect persuaded the two countries to share the quantity of the flow and agree to the following settlement: the partition of Indus basin waters by allocating the three eastern rivers – the Ravi, Beas and Sutlej – to India, and the three western rivers – the Indus, Jhelum and Chenab – to Pakistan. The average annual flow of eastern rivers is 33 million acre feet and of western rivers is 135 million acre feet. India was asked to pay £62,060,000 for the cost of replacement works. The World Bank and other international agencies (Australia, Canada, West Germany, New Zealand, UK and USA) constituted the Indus Basin Development Fund with India and Pakistan in 1960 and provided US$870 million to Pakistan and US$200 million to India to support their infrastructure cost.

Detailed provisions were made in the Treaty to allow Pakistan to construct a system of irrigation works on the western rivers, to compensate for the loss in irrigation supply from the eastern rivers. The Treaty also provided an elaborate system of mutual obligation by the two parties. The Treaty permitted India a limited aggregate storage capacity of all single-purpose and multi-purpose reservoirs to be constructed on western rivers. As per the provision of the Treaty, a Permanent Indus Commission was established, constituting two Commissioners for Indus Waters, one from India and the other from Pakistan. This Commission is entrusted to maintain a cooperative arrangement for the implementation of the Treaty. It undertakes periodical inspection of the river and meets regularly at least once a year, alternately in India and Pakistan before the 1 June and reports to the riparian governments.

The data of water projects and flood flows are regularly communicated between India and Pakistan.[17] The Indus Treaty had provisions for the construction of two major dams in Pakistan: the Mangla Dam on the Jhelum River and the Tarbela Dam on the Indus. Besides these two dams, Pakistan has also constructed several projects to divert water from its western rivers to replace reduced flows in the Sutlej Valley Project Region. Pakistan is currently constructing another dam on the Indus at Kalabagh, at the confluence of the Soan River. With the help of the Bhakra Nangal and Beas project and the partially completed Indira Gandhi Canal Project, India has been able to use 30 million acre feet of water from the eastern rivers. The Thein Dam on the Ravi River, parts of Indira Gandhi Canal Project and Sutlej-Yamuna Link Canal are under construction to harness the rest of the allocated water. India claims that it has not built any conservation storage facilities on western rivers. However, there have been disputes over a few projects on the western rivers between India and Pakistan. One of them is the issue of Tulbul Navigation Project/Wular Barrage being constructed by India on the Jhelum River to make the river navigable during the lean period.[18] Pakistan is opposed to this project on the ground that it has storage utility. Similarly, Pakistan has shown her reservation to India's construction of the Kishenganga hydropower project on the Neelam-Jhelum River and the proposed Baglihar hydroelectric dam on the Chenab River.

The Baglihar Project has become the recent source of tension between India and Pakistan. Pakistan has even threatened to go to the International Court of Justice on this matter.[19] Both India and Pakistan are in search of more water to meet their own demands. In Pakistan, Sindh and Punjab have been in dispute over their share of Indus water for years. In spite of an agreement in 1991, the issue is still simmering between these two powerful provinces in Pakistan. The Indus water has also been a source of conflict between Punjab, Haryana and Rajasthan on the Indian side. So, neither country is in a position to compromise over the waters allocated according to the 1960 Treaty.

However, the recent confrontation between India and Pakistan has brought serious doubts over the continuation of the Indus River Treaty. From December 2001 to June 2002, India was seriously considering pulling out of the Indus Treaty, as one of the steps of hitting back at Pakistan for its alleged support of terrorist outfits targeting India. The Indian state of Jammu and Kashmir has already made a public demand to review the Treaty.[20] Besides the legal obligation, the lack of storage facilities, the threat of Pakistani attacks on its irrigation facilities and disadvantageous natural hydraulic position have acted as deterrent for India to withdraw from the Treaty.[21] But, at the same time, since December 2001 the Indian Commissioner of Indus Basin has reduced contacts with his Pakistani counterparts to the barest minimum.

The Mahakali River: India and Nepal

The major rivers originating from the snow-capped Himalayas in Nepal are the Mahakali, the Gandak, the Karnali and the Saptakoshi. The Mahakali River begins its journey from the far western area of Nepal. The Kali River originating in the Taklakot area and the Kuthi-Yankti River beginning in the Zanskar range merge at Kawa Malla and become the Mahakali River. The Mahakali flows in a south-western direction and is joined by several tributaries. Then it moves on to become a western boundary for a long distance between Nepal and India, before moving southwards into Indian territory. In India, it is known as the Sarada River and after it joins the Ghaghra River assumes the latter's name and then flows in a south-easterly direction to join the Ganges River.

Nepal is a land-locked country, bordered by China to the north and India to the south, east and west. As the high Himalayan range forms the northern boundary with China, Nepal's most important neighbour for all practical purposes is India. Indo-Nepalese relations have been smooth and friendly in comparison to Indo-Pakistani or Indo-Bangladeshi relations in South Asia. However, water sharing of the major rivers originating in Nepal and flowing into India has strained the relationship between the two countries. Negotiations regarding projects on the shared river systems have been dominated by controversies owing to a lack of mutual trust.[22] Nepalese rivers have tremendous potential for the development of irrigation facilities and hydropower generation.

As Nepal is mostly mountainous, large-scale irrigation is only possible in its Terai plains. Out of its 1.77 million hectares of potential irrigable land, over 1.09 million hectares have already been covered under the irrigation infrastructure. However, Nepal is far behind in developing its hydropower potential, which is calculated at 83,000 megawatts of which 42,000 megawatts have already been identified as economically feasible. In spite of this vast potential, Nepal has developed only about 244 megawatts.[23] Nepal lacks the capital and technology required for large hydropower projects and also needs a buyer for its surplus hydropower. Owing to various factors, particularly thanks to the geographical location, India is the only country that could provide assistance. Thus, India's direct involvement in the utilization of the river water has been crucial.

Demand for water is increasing rapidly in India. Besides augmenting its water supply, India is also interested in developing river water resources in Nepal to absorb some of its hydropower. India's present power generation capacity is 90,000 megawatts, much less than the actual demand. The expected economic growth of the country will need much more power in the near future. India's efforts to exploit Himalayan river waters in Nepal started when India was still under British colonial administration. However, in general, the Nepalese feel that they have not been treated equitably under the various water-resource development agreements with India.[24]

The British government in India signed the Sarada Treaty with Nepal in 1920. The Sarada barrage was constructed by India on the Mahakali River after exchanging 4,000 acres of territory between India and Nepal. The Treaty also facilitated the construction of a power station

and the Sarada Canal Project. In return, Nepal was entitled to a speci-
fied supply of water for irrigation. However, Nepal was not satisfied
with the quantum of water (400 cusecs) allocated by the Treaty.
Moreover, the Sarada project also obstructed the construction of
Nepal's proposed Mahakali Irrigation Project, which was later called
the Pancheswar Project.

In the post-independence period, India and Nepal signed agreements
to construct Kosi Barrage in 1954 at Bhimnagar and Gandak Barrage in
1959 at Baisaltan. Both these projects were constructed on or near to
the Indo-Nepal border and were completely financed by India. Though
most of the benefits went to India, Nepal was entitled to receive a speci-
fied supply of water and power. All these projects were seen as a 'sell
out' of the national interest by most Nepalese. The massive popular
opposition in Nepal to these 'Indian' water projects has delayed the
implementation of several proposed dam projects, including Karnali
Project (Chisapani Dam) and Kosi high-dam project.

However, in the 1990s, construction of water projects on the
Mahakali River have raised a serious controversy between India and
Nepal. Downstream of Sarada Barrage, which was built after the 1920
Treaty, Mahakali River once again flows into Nepal, and then into India
where it joins the Ghagara. In 1983, exercising an upper riparian right,
National Hydro Power Corporation (NHPC) of India unilaterally built
a 120 megawatt dam in its own territory. The major construction activities of this Tanakpur power project were completed between 1983 and
1989.

Prior to 1989, the project was considered by both India and Nepal
to be an Indian project. The position of the Nepali government till 1989
was:

- since this was an Indian project (as claimed by India), the project
  should not in any way harm Nepali territory and

- discharge from the tail-race of the plant originally designed to be
  released into the Sarada Canal bypassing the Sarada Barrage would
  seriously deprive the Mahakali Irrigation Project in Nepal, and hence
  would have to be altered.

Resulting from Nepal's objection, India modified the design of the
power station to re-channel the tail-race water into the Mahakali River
upstream of the Sarada Barrage. Subsequently, the position of both
governments vis-à-vis the Tanakpur project went through a transformation. To ensure uninterrupted operation of the hydro-plant, the eastern
afflux bund (the retaining wall) was extended to the contiguous high
ground. Following the Indian request for the extension of the bund into
its territory, Nepal began to claim a share from the project for the

enhanced benefit that resulted from its contribution on making the barrage operational. In lieu of 2.9 hectares of land from Nepal, India agreed to provide free to Nepal from the Tanakpur project 150 cusecs of water through a head regulator of 1,000 cusecs capacity and 10 megawatts of electricity.[25] The possibilities of connecting the barrage with the East-West Highway in Nepal were also to be investigated. During the visit of Nepalese Prime Minister Girija Prasad Koirala to New Delhi in December 1991, the decision was formalized in a Memorandum of Understanding (MoU), which was commonly referred to as the Tanakpur Agreement.

This Agreement became extremely controversial in Nepal due to the internal political situation. The Nepalese opposition framed the issue in nationalist terms, by raising concern for Nepal's territorial sovereignty. They argued that while signing the Agreement, the government of G. P. Koirala had overlooked Nepal's interests to appease India. India, at the same time, resisted any change in the Agreement on Tanakpur. The controversy remained hotly disputed for five years. While the government of Nepal at the time attempted to frame the MoU as an 'understanding' and thus a non-constitutional issue, the opposition demanded parliamentary ratification of what was argued to be a 'treaty' involving the sharing of the country's natural resources.[26] The MoU seemed to imply that India had given Nepal electricity and water for irrigation as a gesture, but it was argued that these benefits were actually the country's rightful acquisition for conceding its territory to complete the project. Furthermore, Indian attempts to deny that any of the benefits of the project to Nepal for its contribution was seen as 'high-handedness' as well as unilateral imposition of solutions on resources having features of shared ownership.

When India's Prime Minister Narasimha Rao visited Nepal in 1992, some concessions were made from the Indian side. The Pancheswar project and other possible interventions were separated from the understanding reached on Tanakpur, allowing both countries freedom to negotiate on any other development in the Mahakali basin. India agreed to provide an additional 10 megawatts of electricity to Nepal, making a total of 20 megawatts.[27]

These Indian concessions were not enough to satisfy the opposition groups in Nepal. The 1991 MoU was challenged in the Nepalese Supreme Court. The petition sought the court's directive that the MoU be ratified in the Parliament in accordance with the country's constitutional provision. In December 1992, the Supreme Court gave a ruling that the MoU was in fact a treaty, necessitating ratification. The Supreme Court, however, permitted the government to determine whether the ratification was to be carried out by a two-thirds majority in the Joint Session of Parliament or by a simple majority of the Lower

House. Thereafter, the government constituted a committee to assess the impact of the project from social, political and diplomatic stand-points. The committee concluded that the impact of the treaty was not of a 'pervasive, long term and extensive' nature. Following this, the government wanted to ratify the treaty with the help of a simple major-ity vote. Due to substantial cross voting within the ruling Nepali Congress Party, the motion was rejected. An All Party Parliamentary Committee was subsequently formed to decide further course of action.

Political crisis brought the mid-term elections in December of 1994, which led to the defeat of the Nepali Congress Party. The Communist Party of Nepal (UML) formed a minority government. After nine months in office, the UML was voted out and replaced by a coalition led by the Nepali Congress Party, which brought an improvement in the bilateral relationship between India and Nepal. In December 1995, the Indian foreign minister came to Kathmandu and settled the Treaty on Integrated Development of the Mahakali River with his Nepali counterpart. On 12 February 1996, the prime ministers of India and Nepal signed the Mahakali Treaty.

The Treaty on the integrated development of the Mahakali River emerged in 1996 as a settlement to the series of disputes between Nepal and India over the Tanakpur Barrage project. The Treaty included three separate water development projects under its scope. In addition to endorsing the Tanakpur MoU of 1991, the Treaty has taken under its annex the regime established by the 1920 Sarada Treaty. It also paves the way for the construction of the 6,480 megawatt Pancheswar Hydropower project on a stretch of the Mahakali between the two countries.[28] This proposed 315 metre high rock-fill dam is going to be the second highest in the world after the Rogun Dam in the Ukraine. The reservoir of this dam will store 12 billion cubic metre flow of the Mahakali River to supply 885 cumecs discharge below the power house, of which there will be 3,240 megawatts capacity on each side of the river. In Nepal, the reservoir will flood 54 square kilometres of land and displace 15,000 people, and in India, it will inundate 80 square kilome-tres of land and displace 50,000 people.

The Mahakali Treaty was signed and ratified by the Nepali Parliament on 20 September 1996 as per the country's constitutional provisions. In June 1997, when Indian Prime Minister I. K. Gujral visited the Himalayan Kingdom, both countries exchanged the instru-ments of ratification of the treaty, which will remain valid for a period of 75 years.[29] According to Salman and Uprety:

> The Mahakali Treaty is a first in many ways. It lays down the principle that as a boundary river on large stretches, the Mahakali will be developed in an integrated way to maximize the total net

benefit from development. Both parties will, in theory, be entitled to equal benefits, and will share the costs in proportion to the share of benefits they actually receive.[30]

The 1996 Mahakali Treaty was undoubtedly a remarkable development towards the further bilateral cooperation on water resource development between India and Nepal. The Treaty has also stipulated the provisions for the establishment of the Mahakali River Commission with its relatively broad mandate. The comprehensive nature of the Treaty reflected the desire of political leadership in India and Nepal to move beyond the unilateral water development strategy to which they have adhered until now and instead promote and strengthen their bilateral cooperation in order to receive the maximum benefits out of jointly shared river water resources.[31] However, the Treaty has already faced several roadblocks. Both countries have failed to agree on a detailed project report,[32] particularly because of differences over the interpretation of certain provisions of the 1996 Treaty relating to how to share the river water. The water demands of the two countries are much higher than the proposed project's augmentation plan. There is also disagreement over the sharing of the capital cost of the Pancheswar project. Moreover, while India proposes phasing the power component in two stages for an assured supply of water to its Girjapur Barrage, Nepal prefers to maximize the power benefit.[33] The conflicting economic interest, lack of political trust and future water scarcity scenario have brought an impasse to the implementation of the Mahakali Treaty, which had offered an opportunity in 1996 to both India and Nepal to make a new start in re-conceptualizing their bilateral river water cooperation.

THE GANGES RIVER: INDIA AND BANGLADESH

The Ganges is an international river which flows through the territories of India and Bangladesh. In the Indian side, the Ganges is called the *Ganga*. This river originates on the southern slope of the Himalayan range, and on its way receives supplies from seven major tributaries.[34] Three of them – the Gandak, Karnali (Ghagara) and Kosi – pass through the Himalayan 'Hindu' Kingdom of Nepal, and they supply the major portion of the Ganges flow.[35] After leaving the Himalayas, the Ganges River flows in the south-easterly direction through the 'cow belt' of India to enter into 'Islamic' Bangladesh. India's *Ganga* then becomes *Padma* for a Bangladeshi. It forms the boundary between India and Bangladesh for about 112 kilometres and then turns south-east to join Brahmaputra River in the middle of Bangladesh. Then the Barak-

Map 1 The Ganges River

Meghna River consolidates the combined flow, which moves toward the Bay of Bengal. The major distributary, Bhagirathi-Hooghly, takes off from the south bank of the Ganges before the mainstream enters into Bangladesh.[36]

The Ganges is the holiest river for the Hindus, and it has been a symbol of the Indian culture and civilization for centuries. Described in the Hindu holy text *Rigveda*, the Ganges River is worshipped along its entire path in India. The diversity in Hinduism has not been able to affect the sanctity of this river. Vaishnavites (followers of Vishnu) believe that the Ganges originated from the big toe of Vishnu's left foot. For the Saivites (followers of Shiva), the river flows through their God's hair. However, both agree that the Ganges is the most sacred river on Earth.[37] Hindus from all over the world cherish the idea of a holy dip in it, under the faith that by doing so they will get rid of their sins of life. As the Indian epic *Mahabharata* describes, 'He who bathes in the Ganges purifies seven generations.' In this 'sin-eradication' ritual, a Hindu needs to take three dips in the Ganges water.

Moreover, for a devout Hindu, the gateway to heaven is to die on the banks of the Ganges. There are many burning ghats or funeral pyres along the river banks, where the last rites of thousands of people are performed every day. In some cases, Hindus throw the dead bodies in the Ganges water believing that the person will go straight to heaven. In spite of extreme pollution, a large number of religious Hindus drink only Ganges water and bathe in the river. In the distant villages, the waters from this river are sold as a medicine for the living and viaticum for the dying. There is a strong age-old belief that the Ganges water has some magical self-cleansing properties.[38]

Many sacred Hindu cities and places of pilgrimage are situated on the banks of the Ganges River. Allahabad, Varanasi, Kedarnath, Badrinath, Hardwar and Rishikesh are to name but a few. On its banks, the great Hindu festival 'Kumbh Mela' takes place every 12 years. Millions of Hindus take an early morning bath in its water on that occasion. Not only the mainstream Ganges, but its distributary Bhagirathi-Hooghly River is also considered sacred by the Hindus. Besides being holy, the Ganges River is also the economic life-line in the Gangetic plains of India. It supplies water for irrigation, creates rich alluvial soil, helps power generation and provides waterways for navigation. The importance of the Ganges can be judged from the fact that it is respectfully addressed as 'Ganga Mai' (Mother Ganges) by millions of Hindus in India.

The Ganges River bears significant importance not only for India but also for Bangladesh. The silt from the Ganges has built a large part of Bangladesh itself and this river has influenced the life and culture of Bangladeshis through centuries. Today, nearly one-third of the total area and about 40 million people of Bangladesh are directly dependent on the Ganges basin for their livelihood. The Ganges and its tributaries provide irrigation, navigation, fishing habitats and water for domestic and industrial use; their flow also resists salinity intrusion in Bangladesh. The water maintains the environment and ecology of the south-west region of Bangladesh.[39] This river system also has the potential to be the major source of future development of this underdeveloped region.[40]

India's relations with Bangladesh have experienced several turnabouts in the first 32 years of the latter's existence. Beginning with high cordiality immediately after the country's independence in 1971, relations soon began to dwindle.[41] There has been limited recovery at

Table 2.1 Basin Area of Ganges-Brahmaputra-Meghna River System

Country	Ganges basin area (million hectares)	Brahmaputra basin area (million hectares)	Meghna basin area (million hectares)	Total (million hectares)
India	86.14	19.5	4.2	109.84
Bangladesh	4.6	4.7	3.6	12.9
Bhutan	–	4.5	–	4.5
Nepal	14	–	–	14
Tibet (China)	4	29.3	–	33.3
Total	109.8	58	7.8	174.54

Source: B. G. Verghese and R. R. Iyer (eds), *Harnessing the Eastern Himalayan Rivers: Regional Cooperation in South Asia* (New Delhi: Konark Publishers, 1993), p. 6.

times, but on the whole relations suffer from mutual mistrust. There are several specific problems in the relations between India and Bangladesh, but perhaps the most prominent one is over the sharing of the Ganges River water.

Like other south flowing Himalayan river systems, the flow of the Ganges suffers from high seasonal fluctuations. Its monsoon runoff is not only more than sufficient to meet the needs of the basin, but also very often causes devastating floods in the region. However, the dry-season flow[42] is quite scanty to meet the growing needs of this highly populated area, which is dependent mostly on agricultural activities. To meet the present and future needs of their populations, both India and Bangladesh are interested in drawing the maximum amount possible from the dry-season flow of the river, and these 'resource grabbing' ventures have been the cause of bilateral dispute for some time.[43]

The Ganges water dispute goes back to 1951, when Bangladesh was still part of Pakistan. It began when India planned to build a barrage at Farakka, 18 kilometres upstream from the East Pakistan (Bangladesh) border on the ground of preservation and maintenance of the Calcutta port by improving the regime and navigability of the Bhagirathi-Hooghly River system. Calcutta is India's most important river port, which serves not only the eastern and north-eastern regions of India, but it is also vital to the overseas trade of land-locked Nepal and Bhutan. Because of reduced headwater supply of the Bhagirathi-Hooghly in the dry-season period, silting of the waterway was taking place at an intolerable speed. Gradually, it was becoming inaccessible to the bigger ships headed to the Calcutta port, which is situated about 200 kilometres from the coast. The Government of India's plan included a 38 kilometres canal to take off from the barrage in order to supplement the waters of the Bhagirathi-Hooghly tributary at the lower point that would make the water current strong enough to flush off the silt and make Calcutta port navigable, and also keep saltwater from infiltrating the city's water supply.[44]

When the Indian press reported on this proposal, Pakistan sent a note to India on 19 October 1951, pointing out that she should be consulted before any project likely to affect her vital interests be undertaken. To this, India responded that the barrage project was only at the stage of preliminary investigation and that Pakistan's apprehensions were therefore 'purely hypothetical'.[45] However, India continued her project planning at the same time. Owing to a lack of bilateral cooperation, in 1957 Pakistan suggested submitting the matter to the United Nations advisory and technical service, but India refused on the plea that bilateral discussions between experts would be sufficient. Pakistan accepted this and four meetings of experts were accordingly held, alternating in India and Pakistan from June 1960 to January 1962.[46] India's decision to commence the construction of the barrage in 1961,[47] and the bilateral tensions before and after the 1965 India–Pakistan War brought a pause to the negotiation for a few years.

In May 1967, the Government of Pakistan made an attempt to internationalize the issue – without much dividend. It raised the dispute in the International Water for Peace Conference held in Washington, in which 92 countries were present.[48] In the Conference, Pakistan submitted that the construction of the barrage at Farakka was a threat to her security and would also threaten the irrigation projects in its eastern province. India disregarded the Pakistani complaint and carried on the construction of the barrage.

After bringing up the issue in the Washington Conference, Pakistan's Foreign Minister Sharifudin Pirzada listed the following possible adverse consequences of the barrage on East Pakistan in a reply to the country's National Assembly:

1. The project would reduce East Pakistan's supply of water and deprive it of its share of water and further development.
2. The Ganga-Kobadak Scheme, which was intended to irrigate two million acres of land in Kushtia, Jessore and Khulna districts of East Pakistan and work on which had already reached an advanced stage, would be jeopardized.
3. The moisture content of the soil immediately after the monsoon season, which was vital for maturing summer crops, would be reduced drastically due to lowering of the existing water level. This would cause deterioration of agricultural conditions.
4. Navigation on the Ganga and its spill channels, especially the Gouri Madhumati beach, would be seriously affected.
5. The barrage would be a serious flood hazard to East Pakistan. India would be obliged to pour into East Pakistan the flood discharge of

the Ganga (about 1,000,000 cusecs) which used to spill into the Bhagirathi-Hooghly from the Ganga during the flood months.

6. India proposed to take silt free water to the Hooghly. This would mean that more silt would be discharged into East Pakistan, causing a rise in the riverbed and consequently an increase in the flood height. The existing flood problem would thus be increased.

7. The reduction of water flow would seriously affect the coastal areas of Khulna and Barisal. In that way, the saline water limit would creep up further and affect agriculture and the quality of the water supply in urban and industrial towns such as Khulna.

Responding to the Pakistani accusations, India's irrigation minister made a statement in the Indian Parliament on 24 June 1967, 'that the Government of India had no intention of giving up the project or modifying it in any way in response to Pakistan's objections'.[49] Several rounds of bilateral talks were held after this, but they did not deliver anything. India alleged that Pakistan was not interested in the negotiation in order to create mistrust between India and East Pakistan. In countering it, Pakistan argued that Indian tactics was to intensify bilateral hostilities by unilaterally proceeding with the building of the barrage at Farakka.[50]

The direct military intervention of India facilitated the independence of Bangladesh in 1971. The initial good relationship between the two neighbours helped to set up the Indo-Bangladesh Joint River Commission (JRC), 'to develop the waters of the rivers common to the two countries on a cooperative basis'.[51] Due to its sensitive nature, the issue of sharing Ganges water at Farakka Barrage was specifically excluded from negotiation. It was only taken up for the discussion by the prime ministers of the two countries at New Delhi in May 1974.[52]

The Farakka Barrage construction was completed in the beginning of 1975. This barrage complex constituted: (1) A barrage at Farakka on the Ganges with road-cum-rail bridge; (2) a head regulator on the right bank for the feeder canal; (3) feeder canal taking off from the head regulator; (4) a barrage at Jangipur across the Bhagirathi-Hooghly River; (5) four navigation locks; and (6) road-cum-rail and road bridges across the feeder canal.[53] After intensive negotiation, both countries came to an agreement on 18 April 1975 to share the Ganges water at Farakka for the last 40 days of the 1975 dry-season period. India and Bangladesh agreed to the limited trial operation of the barrage, with discharge varying between 11,000 and 16,000 cusecs in ten-day periods from 21 April to 31 May 1975, with the rest of the flow guaranteed to reach Bangladesh.

As per the 1975 Agreement, India received much less dry-season water than its original plan of withdrawal. However, the consent from

Bangladesh to operate the Farakka Barrage was a major diplomatic breakthrough for India. The Indian government praised the Agreement as a 'breakthrough' and 'an out-standing example of mutual under-standing and accommodation',[54] but it was not seen in the same spirit by many Indians and Bangladeshis. The Indian opposition parties complained that the share of 11,000–16,000 cusecs of water in the dry-season would not be able to flush the heavily silted Hooghly. At the same time, to the Bangladeshi opposition, it was another pro-Indian act of the Mujibur Rahman government overlooking the fundamental inter-ests of Bangladesh itself. On 15 August 1975, Mujibur was assassinated in a military coup, and some attribute the 'short-term agreement' as one of the reasons for his differences with the army.

A military regime came to power in Bangladesh after the death of Mujibur. India's Prime Minister, Indira Gandhi hardened her attitude towards the new regime. In the beginning of the 1976 dry-season, India unilaterally started to divert the Ganges dry-season flow (40,000 cusecs) at Farakka without any consultation with or concurrence by Bangladesh. The military rulers of Bangladesh raised this issue in inter-national forums without completely abandoning bilateralism. After lodging a formal protest with India on 15 January 1976 against the unilateral operation of the barrage, Bangladesh raised this issue at the Islamic Foreign Ministers' Conference at Istanbul in May 1976 and the Colombo Summit of non-aligned countries in August 1976. Only China and Pakistan openly supported the Bangladeshi cause. However, it did not deter Bangladesh from raising the issue at the 31st session of the United Nations in September 1976. India's successful opposition led to the withdrawal of the Bangladesh resolution. Instead, on 26 November 1976, the UN General Assembly adopted only a consensus statement, which encouraged both the riparian countries to meet urgently at ministerial level for negotiations.

Bangladesh's decision to raise the Farakka issue internationally was based on political consideration. Going to international forums like the United Nations, the Non-aligned Movement Summit and the Islamic Foreign Ministers Conference gave much needed international accep-tance to the new military leader. This public anti-Indian stance also gave the leadership support on the home front. However, considering India's power and posture, the reality of the situation forced the Bangladeshis to keep negotiations going at the bilateral level. As Ben Crow describes, 'Bangladesh returned to bilateral negotiations having tried a remedy of the last resort and found it wanting.'[55]

Maulana Bhasani, a political leader in Bangladesh, tried to mobilize public opinion against reduced flow of the Ganges. On 16 May 1976, he launched the 'Farakka Peace March' to demolish Farakka, but due to timely intervention of the Bangladeshi authorities it did not lead to any unpleasant incidents.[56] The Government of Bangladesh brought out a White Paper on the Ganges water dispute in September 1976 which stated that a grave crisis had arisen for Bangladesh due to India's unilateral action. In the beginning of 1977, the Bangladeshi government issued an Explanatory Memorandum, titled *Ganges Water: Crisis in Bangladesh*, which warned, 'Failure to resolve this (Farakka) issue expeditiously and satisfactorily carries with it potential threat of conflict affecting peace and security in the area and the region as a whole.'

In March 1977, India witnessed a significant political change and a newly formed Janata Party took over the reins of government by defeating Indira Gandhi's Congress Party. In the beginning, the new government was anxious to give fresh directions to foreign policy, particularly improving India's relations with its eastern and northern neighbours. At the same time, President Ziaur Rahman in Bangladesh was advocating in favour of forming an association for South Asian regional cooperation. Within a few months of the change of government in India, the two countries came to an agreement extending over a period of five years to share the Ganges water during the dry-seasons. They also promised to work towards finding a long-term solution to augment the dry-season flows of the Ganges. According to the agreement, which was signed on 5 November 1977, during the leanest ten days, 21 to 30 April, India was allowed to withdraw at Farakka 20,500 cusecs and Bangladesh 34,500 cusecs; the Indian share was 37.5 per cent of the total estimated flow of 55,000 cusecs and was to increase in the ensuing periods to 40 per cent of the total flow.

Crow and Lindquist divide the history of the 1977 negotiation into four phases.[57] From 1951 to 1971 the project was discussed and planned. From 1971 to 1977 the barrage was built and implemented, without international agreement. In 1977 the five-year agreement was signed between India and Bangladesh over the allocation of low season flows. It was envisioned that the negotiation of a full-scale treaty, setting the principles for the development of the Ganges and Brahmaputra basins would be completed, and taken for implementation in 1982. In the 1977 Agreement, both sides had made substantial concessions. But, there was something for each party to be happy about the arrangement. India's water share was still short of its requirement, but the volume had increased considerably in comparison to the 1975 Agreement. At the same time, Bangladesh was satisfied to get a deal for five years of water sharing and a commitment from the Indian side to work for augmenting the dry-season flow. The Agreement was described by the Indian government as an example that goodwill and readiness to compromise could solve even the thorniest issues between two countries. There was severe criticism against the Agreement in West Bengal. The Indian opposition groups were also very critical, which forced Prime Minister

Desai to give a long and detailed statement to the Parliament. In Bangladesh, the general reaction was 'wait and see'.[58] However, the welcome part of the 1977 Agreement was that both countries recognized the 'need for a solution to the long-term problem of augmenting the flows of the Ganges are in the mutual interests' realizing that the dry-season flow is not sufficient to satisfy the minimum needs of both the countries.

1978 Proposals for the Long-term Solutions

During the dry-season months, the average minimum discharge to Farakka was estimated to come below 55,000 cusecs, from which India wanted 40,000 cusecs and Bangladesh needed all the water to meet its growing demand. This reality persuaded both the countries to formally agree in 1977 that there was not enough water in the Ganges during the dry-season to meet their requirements. Negotiation within the Joint River Commission continued afterwards on augmentation. In March 1978, both the countries came forward with their definite proposals for augmenting the Ganges.

The Indian Proposal

The Indian plan proposed that the surplus waters of the Brahmaputra River, which flows from Tibet, through Arunachal Pradesh and Assam of India into Bangladesh should be used to augment the dry-season flow of the Ganges. India wanted to connect Brahmaputra with the Ganges through construction of a 320 kilometres long link-canal, 120 kilometres of which would run through Bangladesh. This 75 metres wide and 10 metres deep canal would have a carrying capacity of 100,000 cusecs and would be supplemented by three storage reservoirs on the Brahmaputra River. The proposal envisaged that the link-canal would take off from a barrage at Jogighope in Assam and terminate at a point above Farakka. In 1978, the estimated cost for the project was calculated in excess of 6 billion US dollars.

The Indian proposal was justified on the grounds that the waters of the Ganges were inadequate to meet the increasing demand, whereas Brahmaputra, which has four times more dry-season flow than Ganges, run down to the Bay of Bengal being unused. So, India argued, the augmentation of the Ganges water should be accomplished by diverting Brahmaputra waters to the Ganges. India claimed that the link-canal would provide irrigation to nearly 10 million acres of land in each country. Moreover, the water diversion scheme would help in the development of power and navigation in both the countries.

Bangladesh rejected the Indian blueprint as 'Legally unjustifiable, technically impractical, economically and ecologically disastrous and fraught with far-reaching human and sociological consequences.' There were several reasons which prevented Bangladesh from accepting the Indian scheme. Bangladesh did not receive any additional water by the Indian proposal as Brahmaputra already flowed through Bangladesh. Bangladesh was apprehensive about the ecological problems associated with the water division from a major river like Brahmaputra. Moreover, both the ends of the link-canal were proposed to be in Indian territory and that would limit the future prospects of manoeuvrability by Bangladesh. Bangladesh also feared that the link-canal might be instrumental to use Brahmaputra water in flushing out the silts from the Bhagirathi-Hooghly, and that would help India to divert all the Ganges waters for irrigation purposes. The proposed link-canal would add to Bangladesh's already existing communication problems by dividing the northern part of Bangladesh from the rest of the country. The project demanded huge financial resources, and moreover it was bound to displace millions of people in a highly populated country. The construction of the link-canal would take away 20,000 acres of fertile land from Bangladesh. Finally, China might demand to be a party to the arrangement as the Brahmaputra travels half of its route through Tibet and that may bring a legal problem. China might object to the link-canal as that would provide an excellent strategic advantage to India *vis-à-vis* China in their territorial dispute in the north-eastern part of India.

The Bangladeshi Proposal
Bangladesh, rejecting Indian proposals, proposed a tripartite partnership of herself, India and Nepal in seeking a solution to the augmentation problem. Bangladesh proposed storage dams in the Ganges, seven of those in its tributaries in Nepal. These dams would store monsoon flow, and yield a year round flow of about 176,400 cusecs of water. The Bangladeshi view of the best means of augmenting the Ganges dry-season flow lay within the Ganges system itself.

Bangladesh argued that the storage dams on the Nepalese tributaries would also help to control the downstreaming flooding in the Ganges during the monsoon seasons and, unlike the link-canal proposal, it would not affect the flow of another river. However, Bangladesh wanted to involve Nepal in the project since then it would be more difficult for India to break a trilateral commitment than a bilateral one. Bangladesh provided a couple of tempting offers for Nepal as well. Bangladesh claimed that its scheme would enable Nepal to export large amounts of hydropower to India and Bangladesh in return for precious foreign currency. In addition to that, Bangladesh also offered land-locked Nepal an alternative navigation route by digging a 30 kilometres canal across Indian territory to link the rivers of both countries that would give Nepal a direct outlet to the sea.

India rejected the proposal on the grounds that it was not based on necessary investigation, which could realistically provide for the extent of augmentation of flows at Farakka to meet the requirements of both India and Bangladesh. India also argued that there would be loss of water through seepage as the watercourse would be too long. But basically, India was averse to 'trilateralize' the issue. Nepal was also not enthusiastic about the Bangladesh proposal. The past disadvantageous experience over bilateral water development projects with India forced Nepal to think twice about the Bangladeshi proposal at that time. The prospects of a navigation route was not able to cut much ice because Nepal would remain at the mercy of India anyway, as the proposed canal would be in Indian territory.

There were serious difficulties in coming to an agreement in 1977. Consequently there were a number of ad-hoc extensions of the 1977 Agreement in the form of a Memorandum of Understanding (MoU) pending a new solution. When the 1977 Agreement expired in 1982, the political situation had changed in India. The Congress Party was back in power. The Congress Party in West Bengal, which was critical of the Janata Party government's action in 1977, started demanding revocation of the Agreement, arguing that it overlooked the interest of the state.[59] Despite pressures, the Indian and Bangladeshi leaders signed a MoU by extending for another 18 months the 1977 Agreement, but with changes. This new arrangement deleted the provision related to the reliability of the flow of the 1977 Agreement. The two countries also agreed to work for finding methods to augment the dry-season flow.

In the final review of the 1977 in 1982 Agreement, the delegates from both countries accepted their failure to reach any agreement on long-term augmentation and decided to refer the matter 'for decision between the two Governments at a high political level'.[60] The leaders of both the countries, while signing a MoU in 1983, directed the Joint River Commission (JRC) to complete the pre-feasibility study of the schemes for the augmentation of the dry-season flow of the Ganges at Farakka. This revived the negotiation on augmentation. In July 1983, the JRC decided to update the respective proposals of India and Bangladesh by taking into account the economic and implementation problems, not just the technical aspects. Both countries presented their 'Updated Proposals' followed by their comments on these in February 1984.[61] The updated proposals were essentially conforming to the earlier proposals of 1978 with some additional details, so the major differences persisted.

The MoU on the water sharing at Farakka, which was signed in October 1982 expired after 18 months. The failure of India and Bangladesh to reach an agreement on their respective dry-season augmentation schemes brought the deadlock to the further extension of the short-term arrangement. The refusal of the Indian government to renew the arrangement in 1984 and its unilateral diversion of water at Farakka were perceived in Bangladesh as a pressure tactic aimed to bring it to agreement on the link-canal proposal.[62]

Rajiv Gandhi became the Prime Minister of India after the assassination of his mother in November 1984. In the early days of his office, India's attitude towards her neighbours changed. A failed attempt of the Indian Minister of Irrigation to reach any water-sharing agreement with Bangladesh in his visit to Dhaka in June 1985 coincided with a severe cyclonic storm in Bangladesh. Rajiv Gandhi flew to Bangladesh to express a sense of solidarity and support, which generated much goodwill for him in that country. He was anxious to build upon that goodwill and to improve India's relations with its neighbour. This was reflected first in October 1985 when President Ershad and Prime Minister Gandhi reached an understanding on the sharing of river waters while they were both in Nassau (Bahamas) for the summit meeting of Commonwealth Heads of Government. In pursuance of this, talks took place between delegations from the two countries at New Delhi in November 1985, and a fresh MoU was signed for a three-year period.

In the new MoU, both countries pledged to make a joint study to find alternatives for sharing and augmenting the dry-season flow.[63] As a follow-up to this agreement, a new forum, Joint Committee of Experts (JCE) was created alongside the JRC, being headed by the Irrigation Secretaries of the two countries. The JCE met for the first time in Dhaka in January 1986, and there India deflected from her earlier stand by withholding her objection to the inclusion of Nepal in the water-sharing arrangement.[64] Several JCE meetings took place to find alternative ways of augmentation.[65] During the course of the JCE meetings, India agreed to make a joint approach along with Bangladesh to Nepal, while persuading the Bangladeshi side to take the Brahmaputra option on the agenda. According to Verghese and Iyer,[66] India hinted at three possibilities of using Brahmaputra water: (1) the old Indian proposal of a link canal from the Brahmaputra to the Ganges running through both countries; (2) a link canal entirely within Bangladesh, joining the Ganges below Hardinge Bridge; and (3) using the Brahmaputra waters not through a link canal but by diverting to the irrigational needs of Ganges dependent areas in Bangladesh. And from these alternatives, Bangladesh expressed her willingness to examine only the second possibilities, i.e. a link-canal within its own territory.

The JCE delegation, led by Indian and Bangladesh Water Resources Secretaries, accordingly visited Katmandu in November 1986. Nepal's response to it was one of caution and hesitancy, arising no doubt from her perception of 'the tangled history of past relations with India'.[67] A trilateral discussion among foreign ministers of India, Bangladesh and Nepal was held on the 17 January 1987. Though Nepal was demonstrating its intention to participate in the arrangement since 1977, it had never made any earnest endeavour to prepare a cost-benefit analysis. The realization of massive cost came only after India's acceptance of her inclusion, and then Nepal started to vacillate on the plea of studying the proposal.

Coinciding with Nepal's reluctance, Rajiv Gandhi started to harden his attitude towards the neighbours largely because of his trouble on the home front. The new initiatives for augmentation of the dry-season flow set in motion in the early days of Rajiv Gandhi's Prime Ministership ran out of steam due to domestic compulsions. After the failure of the joint approach to Nepal, the matter was not followed up seriously. In November 1987, the life of the Joint Committee of Experts expired without proceeding beyond its achievement reached in 1986. The MoU of 1985 expired in 1988 and after that, both the countries failed to sign a formal agreement to share the dry-season flow on a short-term basis, and leave aside the work for the augmentations of the dry-season flow.

In August and September 1988, Bangladesh suffered from a catastrophic flood. This was so devastating that three-fourths of the country went under water. President Ershad of Bangladesh, describing the flood as 'a catastrophe of an unprecedented dimension' and at the same time 'a man-made curse', appealed for international assistance. He refused to accept any assistance from India, whom he did not hesitate to describe as the main culprit for the misery. The failure of the government machinery to cope with the disaster turned public opinion against the government. So to save his regime from the public wrath, Ershad used the anti-India card vigorously. India got especially annoyed when Bangladesh returned the helicopters sent to help flood victims.

After the flood and when tensions began to recede, President Ershad, on his own initiative, flew to New Delhi on 29 September 1988, but India refused to extend the 1985 water-sharing agreement. However, an Indo-Bangladesh Task Force of Experts was set up to study the Ganges and Brahmaputra waters jointly for flood management and for water flows in both short-term and long-term bases. In the Task Force meetings, India insisted that Bangladesh should accept her 1978 augmentation proposal, while Bangladesh emphasized non-structural measures such as flood-forecasting and warning, etc. In the 1989 dry-season period, India started to withdraw water at Farakka at its own will. Bangladesh's renewed attempt to internationalize the water management issue by bringing it to the UN, the Commonwealth and the South Asian Association for Regional Cooperation (SAARC) ended in worsening the bilateral relationship further.

After three years of intermission, the Joint River Commission met again in April 1990 after the change of the regime in India, but made little progress. In the final months of 1990, a popular movement against President Ershad of Bangladesh swept him out of power. In a democratic election in February 1991, Begum Khaleda Zia came to power. The political turmoil at that time was similarly severe in India owing to the frequent change of governments and the assassination of Rajiv Gandhi in May 1991. After achieving some sort of stability at home, Prime Minister Rao of India and Prime Minister Zia of Bangladesh met in New Delhi in the last week of May 1992. In that meeting, they agreed to make 'renewed endeavours for achieving an acceptable long-term and comprehensive arrangement' and in the meantime they decided to deliver an interim arrangement for sharing the dry-season flows at Farakka.[68] To follow up, a ministerial meeting was held in Dhaka on 26–27 August 1992, which was followed by two Secretary level meetings in New Delhi and Dhaka successively, none achieving any progress.[69]

The failure to reach any agreement with India over the water sharing and the simultaneous falling water level in their part of the Ganges infuriated the political parties in Bangladesh. Several political organizations observed the 'Farakka Day'[70] on 16 March 1993, by burning an effigy of Indian Prime Minister Rao and taking out processions towards the Indian Mission in Dhaka.[71] In the middle of increasing domestic pressure, Bangladesh Prime Minister Khaleda Zia met her Indian counterpart in the Non-aligned Movement Summit in Jakarta, Indonesia, in September 1993. She pleaded for a short-term arrangement for the water sharing, while waiting to agree on the long-term augmentation measures.[72] But India insisted on Bangladesh's acceptance of the link-canal proposal. Finding no hope from the Indian side even in terms of short-term agreements, Bangladesh again started to internationalize the Ganges water dispute.

Prime Minister Zia in her speech to the 48th session of the United Nations General Assembly, on 1 October 1993 alleged: 'The unilateral withdrawal of the Ganges water by India has created unimaginable adverse effects on the economy and environment of Bangladesh.'[73] In spite of India's sharp reaction,[74] Bangladesh continued its effort to mobilize international attention to the Farakka withdrawal. In the Commonwealth Heads of Governments Meeting at Limassol, Cyprus, in the later part of October 1993, the Prime Minister of Bangladesh described her country's misery due to the Farakka withdrawal. Prime Minister Zia also discussed the problem with Nepal during her visit to Katmandu in November 1994 where she urged for a 'tripartite framework' to solve the water crisis.[75]

Bangladeshi attempts to internationalize the issue further worsened the already complicated relationship between India and Bangladesh.

The bilateral negotiation on water sharing came to a standstill. Having failed to receive any substantial international support to its cause *vis-à-vis* India, Bangladesh was forced again to pursue the bilateral negotiation track. The process of bilateral initiative again started in May 1995 after a meeting between the prime ministers of the two countries in New Delhi.[76] In its follow-up, their foreign secretaries met in Dhaka in June 1995, where they decided to convene a meeting of the JRC after a gap of nearly four years.[77] In this meeting, the Foreign Secretary of India stressed the need to permanently solve the Farakka issue while completely ruling out the involvement of Nepal. The Indian position was not favourable to a short-term arrangement to share at Farakka, and at the same time India kept up pressure on Bangladesh to accept its Brahmaputra link-canal proposal.

THE 1996 GANGES AGREEMENT

The change of governments in both India and Bangladesh in the summer of 1996 recreated new hope of getting a sharing agreement. The election of Sheikh Hasina, the daughter of Mujibur Rehman, as the Prime Minister of Bangladesh, provided the reason for her country's desire to strengthen the bilateral relationship with India. The discussion for water sharing started at the foreign secretary level. Then the Chief Minister of West Bengal, Jyoti Basu, became the chief negotiator from the Indian side. In his six-day visit to Bangladesh in the latter part of 1996, the draft of the Ganges water-sharing treaty was formalized. Sheikh Hasina flew to New Delhi and signed the Treaty on 12 December 1996 for a period of 30 years. The main features of the 1996 treaty are that the dry-season sharing is based on close to a 50:50 formula and three guaranteed ten-day periods for both countries when each will get 35,000 cusecs of water. The Treaty recognized not only the need for augmentation but also the importance of sharing all common rivers.[78]

With the signing of the Treaty, most observers of the South Asian region thought that the most outstanding problem in the Indo-Bangladeshi relationship was now over. But they all forgot to examine the agreement properly. It was basically a political agreement, which had not taken the real hydrological flow of the river into account. The agreement had been based on the flow average of 1949 to 1988, but the real flow at Farakka in the 1990s was much less than that. The flows reaching Farakka in the period since 1988 clearly show a decline in average flow for all the dry-season months.[79] To get a dependable figure, the water experts should have taken the average flow of the last ten years, rather than building on the history to protect the interest of their political masters. The Foreign Minister of Bangladesh had commented a few months before the signing of the agreement: 'Ice has started melting now, let us see where it reaches.' This melting of ice between the leaders of the two countries brought an agreement, but there is not enough snow in the *Gongotri* to melt in the dry-seasons to satisfy both the parties.

The Bangladeshi experts were very much aware of the flow at Farakka in the dry-seasons. In 1993, when they had complained of receiving only 9,000 cusecs of supply at Hardinge Bridge, they could have easily calculated the flow at Farakka to 49,000 cusecs, as the Farakka diversion canal's maximum carrying capacity is 40,000 cusecs. In the following years, Bangladesh gave the figures of water available at Hardinge Bridge as close to 10,000 cusecs. The basic arithmetic was overlooked when the political leaders of both the countries signed agreement on the basis of an illusory minimum figure of 60,000 cusecs.

For Hasina's new government, it would have been suicidal to accept any short-term arrangement in which the Bangladeshi share falls below the amount it was given as per the 1977 Agreement. The Leader of the Bangladeshi opposition, Begum Khaleda Zia, had given a warning to this effect after losing power: 'We want due share of Ganges water, we will not accept less than what we got on the agreement signed during the government of President Ziaur Rahman (1977 Agreement).'[80] India realized this, but at the same time it had its own political compulsions. The then Indian government was dependent upon the CPI(M) for its survival, and that party headed the government in West Bengal. Any agreement with less water to Calcutta would have never been acceptable to CPI(M) leaders. Moreover, any agreement with perceived advantage to Islamic Bangladesh on holy *Ganga* was bound to infuriate the then opposition Hindu fundamentalist, Bharatiya Janata Party (BJP). The constitutional conversion of Bangladesh from secularism to Islamic ideals in the 1980s has provided grounds to the powerful BJP to project the conflict as a struggle between Hindus and Muslims.

To get a face-saving formula, India tried to persuade Bangladesh to provide transit facilities at its Chittagong port in exchange for the water sharing at Farakka. India had serious problems in transporting goods and commodities to its seven north-eastern states which were only connected with the mainland by a 'chicken neck'. Extending transit facilities to India would have been a major source of revenue for Bangladesh, and at the same time, it would have helped the Indian authorities to counter internal oppositions to the water-sharing arrangement. In order to persuade Bangladesh on this front, India even offered to provide trade concessions to Bangladesh to bridge the trade imbalances.[81] But the Bangladeshi government was not prepared to go in for offering transit facilities because it had realized the political reverberation in the country.

However, at the same time, both regimes were under political compulsion to reach an agreement on Ganges water sharing. To get the fair share of Ganges water from India was the electoral promise of the Awami League Government of Bangladesh. The United Front Government in India and its then foreign minister was also interested to live up to their earlier image of friendly policy with the neighbours. But their precarious political survival did not allow them to reduce the share of water at Farakka on pen and paper. However, the 'game with the statistics' helped them to reach an agreement without receiving immediate internal opposition.

Unfortunately for both parties, the very first year of the Treaty witnessed a severely low dry-season runoff in the Ganges River. In the 1997 dry-season, the actual flow reaching Farakka fell much below that what had been assumed in the 1996 Treaty. Particularly, in the 21–31 March ten-day period, the actual flow reaching Farakka was only 48,487 cusecs compared to the Treaty's assumption of 64,688 cusecs.[82] The Government of Bangladesh came under serious threat from the opposition because of less water flow in the Ganges compared to previous years. To avoid political embarrassment, the regime tried to protect the water flow data, branding it as a national secret. But ultimately the Minister of Water Resources was forced to admit in the Parliament that Bangladesh did not get the water as per the agreement.[83] This gave a lot of ammunition to the opposition, the Bangladesh National Party (BNP) which was looking for any reason to bring down the Awami League government. On the Indian side, the BJP and Congress Party also openly criticized the agreement.

With the help of political support, the 1996 Agreement withstood the dramatic decrease in the 1997 annual rainfall at the upstream. However, the rainfall situation has improved since then. The 1996 Treaty has not covered extreme weather events. The Treaty asks for 'immediate consultation' in the event of flows falling below 50,000 cusecs, but does not offer any specific mechanism such as the 80 per cent guarantee clause prescribed by the 1977 Agreement. The seasonal and annual fluctuations in water flow have persuaded both Indian and Bangladeshi authorities to engage in serious negotiation to augment the dry-season runoff of the Ganges River. The Treaty also excludes the other major riparian country, notably Nepal. The Ganges system is an integral part of the Ganges-Brahmaputra-Meghna system.[84] Thus, the Treaty also fails to take two other major riparian countries, China and Bhutan, on board. However, the most important outcome of the 1996 Treaty is that it has created a conducive atmosphere for discussing and deliberating on a number of other outstanding issues between India and Bangladesh. This treaty also refers to some water-related issues like flood management, irrigation, river basin development and hydro-power generation for the mutual benefit of the two countries. The signing of this treaty has certainly provided both the riparian countries with an opportunity for meaningful cooperation.

The 1996 Ganges River Water Sharing Agreement has certainly helped the bilateral relation between India and Bangladesh to take a turn for the better. The successful signing of the Ganges water treaty encouraged Bangladesh to propose for the comprehensive agreement with India on the other rivers that flow between the two countries. As a follow-up to the 1996 Treaty, the JRC meeting took place in July 1997. In that meeting, both India and Bangladesh decided to form a Joint Committee of Experts (JCE) to work out long-term arrangements for sharing their common rivers. The JCE was asked to focus on seven small and medium sized rivers, with special emphasis to the Teesta.[85] In April 1999, the Joint River Commission discussed embankment of 54 common rivers, sharing of the Teesta waters and improving flood forecasting and warning. The signing of the 1996 Treaty also helped Bangladesh to revive its old proposal to build a barrage on the Ganges at Pangsha, downstream of Farakka in Bangladesh. India has welcomed the proposal and has formally offered technical assistance. India–Bangladesh relations gained significant momentum as long as Sheikh Hasina was in power.

The Khaleda Zia government came to power in the second half of 2001. Her party, BNP, projects the anti-India position. But, she has till now shown her eagerness to move positively in her country's relations with India and not to spoil the momentum which has been set by the 1996 Ganges sharing treaty. The two countries have also agreed to restore the multimodal communication link, in spite of Bangladeshi opposition to the transit issue.[86] India has even released more water to Bangladesh than its share in the 2002 dry-season.[87] The Ganges Treaty of 1996 has helped India and Bangladesh to build mutual trust in order to address some other traditional dispute areas. After the agreement, both countries are trying to sort out their differences over the territory, trade and transit. However, there is still a sharp difference over the augmentation plans for the Ganges River.

Obstacles to a Lasting Solution

Indian desire to divert the Brahmaputra water to its mainland and the Bangladeshi opposition to it, is the major obstacle to finding a lasting solution on the Ganges water-sharing issue. India has always justified the Farakka withdrawal to keep Calcutta port navigable. However, Calcutta is no longer the only major port at the head of the Bay of Bengal. The recent creation of another port facility at Haldia,[88] further downstream of the Bhagirathi-Hooghly River, and submission of much of the activities of the Calcutta port to the new one, creates doubt about it. The Haldia port has already become a major partner in the twin-dock Calcutta port system. The port facility at Paradip is also handling some of the bulk cargo freights in the region. If India is really serious about Calcutta port, the inadequate depth of the river for navigation can be corrected also by regular and more intensive dredging. Moreover, through the Upper Ganga Canal, Lower Ganga Canal and numerous pumped canals, India is withdrawing much of the Ganges' dry-season flow for its agriculture and industries before it even reaches Farakka, which could have been used to flush out the silts from the Bhagirathi-Hooghly. Thus, it raises doubt about India's real intention.

In contrast to the decreasing dry-season flow of the Ganges, dry-season flows of the Brahmaputra River are increasing.[89] India's Farakka withdrawal is perceived by Bangladesh as a pressure aimed at her to accept the link-canal proposals through which the waters of Brahmaputra would be diverted for Calcutta and also for the irrigation purposes in the state of West Bengal. Since 1982, India has carried out detailed studies for inter-linking of its major rivers. In December 2002, the Indian government appointed a task force to complete feasibility studies for linking of the rivers and implementation of the projects by the end of 2016. According to an Indian press report, India contemplates transferring some of the Brahmaputra water to the Peninsular rivers such as Mahanadi in Orissa and Godavari and Krishna in Andhra Pradesh. India's insistence to work bilaterally with Nepal for the augmentation of the Ganges water is perceived by Bangladesh as India's desire to utilize the increased water supply to meet the growing demand in her highly populated northern states. Moreover, India also needs increased supply in the Ganges for her proposed Ganga-Cauvery link.[90] India's interest for the Ganges-Brahmaputra Link-Canal multiplies owing to its potential of being an excellent navigable connection with her troubled north-eastern states.

SOUTH ASIAN RIVERS: SOURCES FOR PEACE?

The challenge before South Asian states is to provide their growing populations with access to clean drinking water, reliable irrigation, cheaper energy resources and flood protection. There is a sign of growing bilateral cooperation among governments in South Asia to share and develop common river water resources. This cooperation has been achieved in spite of strongly opposing historical, ethnic and political factors. The growing demand for water has helped the countries to put aside extremely politicized and highly emotional issues and start negotiating on their shared rivers. The cooperation on rivers sometimes spills-over to help the riparian countries in the region to build the mutual trust, which is necessary to address other traditional issues of contention. The contribution of the 1996 Ganges River Agreement between India and Bangladesh is a good example of this. Following the Agreement, both countries are working to sort out their differences over territory, trade and transit in a negotiation conducive atmosphere. Similarly, the 1996 Mahakali Treaty has also brought several positive developments in the bilateral relationship between India and Nepal. Immediately after the Agreement over the Mahakali River water, the Treaty of Trade was renewed for a further period of five years with the provision for automatic renewal of the treaty every five years. In spite of several political changes in Nepal and India, recent years have witnessed bilateral contacts at practically all levels. However, the improved bilateral relations between India and Bangladesh, and India and Nepal have not yet been able to find long-term solutions to the river water management issue.

Cooperative sharing of the Indus water since 1960 has not been able to influence India and Pakistan to improve their bilateral relationship. But, the functioning of the Indus Treaty for the last 43 years shows that even under the most problematic conditions, water can bring cooperation. Increasing water scarcity and its adverse effect on the agricultural sector has forced the countries in the South Asia to adopt and maintain a somewhat cooperative approach in sharing their international rivers. However, several factors raise doubts about the long-term sustainability of these river sharing agreements.

Most of these river sharing arrangements put strong emphasis on large-scale water infrastructure projects. These massive projects fail to satisfy the environmentalists, as they have not sincerely addressed the associated social and environmental factors. Moreover, the agreements do not involve ordinary people in the management of a shared water resource. To be lasting, water agreements must be bold, innovative and look beyond the conventional path of development. South Asian policy makers should realize that the water scarcity issue cannot be addressed adequately on the supply side only. Management of regions' shared river systems needs to be addressed at the regional level to achieve the best possible use of available water.

NOTES

1. This chapter has borrowed liberally from the author's earlier works: A. Swain, 'Conflicts over Water: The Ganges Water Dispute', *Security Dialogue*, 24, 4 (1993), pp. 429–39; A. Swain, 'Displacing the Conflict: Environmental Destruction in Bangladesh and Ethnic Conflict in India', *Journal of Peace Research*, 33, 2 (1996), pp. 189–204; A. Swain, *The Environmental Trap: The Ganges River Diversion,*

Bangladeshi Migration and Conflicts in India (Uppsala: Department of Peace and Conflict Research, 1996); A. Swain, 'Reconciling Disputes and Treaties: Water Development and Management in Ganga Basin', *Water Nepal*, 6, 1 (1998), pp. 43–65; A. Swain, 'Fight for the Last Drop: Inter-state River Disputes in India', *Contemporary South Asia*, 7, 2 (1998), pp. 167–80; A. Swain, 'Sharing the Ganges: Ugly Conflict over Holy Water', in F. Abbaszadegan and F. Wennberg (eds), *Hydropolitik och Demokrati* (Uppsala: Asiatic Society, 1998), pp. 7–19; and A. Swain, 'Environmental Cooperation in South Asia', in K. Conca and G. D. Dabelko (eds), *Environmental Peacemaking* (Baltimore: Johns Hopkins University Press, 2002), pp. 61–85. Both metric and imperial measurements have been used in this chapter, in correspondence with the systems in prevailing practice in the countries concerned in the region.

2. The other two countries of South Asia are Sri Lanka and the Maldives. The two small island nations are separated from the mainland.

3. See L. G. Thompson, Y. Tao, E. Mosley-Thompson, M. E. Davis, K. A. Henderson,and P. N. Lin, 'A High-Resolution Millennial Record of the South Asian Monsoon from Himalayan Ice Cores', *Science*, 289 (2000), pp. 1916–19.

4. N. C. Behera, 'State Formation Processes Weak States and Sustainable Development in South Asia', in D. D. Khanna (ed.), *Sustainable Development Environmental, Security and Disarmament Interface in South Asia* (New Delhi: Macmillan, 1997).

5. See A. Botrall, 'Fits and Misfits Over Time and Space: Technologies and Institutions of Water Development for South Asian Agriculture', *Contemporary South Asia*, 1, 2, (1992).

6. I. J. Singh, 'Agricultural Situation in India and Pakistan', *Economic and Political Weekly*, 32, 26 (1997).

7. A. H. Hansen, *The Process of Planning: A Study of India's Five Year Plans 1950–1964* (Oxford: Oxford University Press, 1966); G. Blyn, *Agriculture Trends in India, 1891–1957: Output, Availability, and Productivity* (Philadelphia, PA: University of Pennsylvania Press, 1966).

8. S. R. Sen, *The Strategy for Agricultural Development and Other Essays on Economic Policy and Planning* (New York: Asia Publishing House, 1962), p. 17.

9. S. N. A. Gillani and M. Azam, 'Indus River: Past, Present and Future', in A. M. Shady et al. (eds), *Management and Development of Major Rivers* (Calcutta: Oxford University Press, 1996), pp. 84–103.

10. J. S. Mehta, 'The Indus Water Treaty: A Case Study in the Resolution of an International River Basin Conflict', *Natural Resources Forum*, 12, 1 (1988), p. 74.

11. G. T. K. Pitman, 'The Role of the World Bank in Enhancing Cooperation and Resolving Conflict on International Watercourses: The Case of the Indus Basin', in S. M. A. Salman and L. B. de Chazournes (eds), *International Watercourses: Enhancing Cooperation and Managing Conflict* (Washington DC: World Bank Technical Paper No. 414, 1998).

12. A. K. Biswas, 'Indus Water Treaty: The Negotiating Process', *Water International*, 17 (1992), pp. 201–9.

13. H. L. Beach, J. Hamner, J. J. Hewitt, E. Kaufman, A. Kurki, J. A. Oppenheimer and A. T. Wolf, *Transboundary Freshwater Dispute Resolution: Theory, Practice, and Annotated References* (Tokyo: UNU Press, 2000), pp. 101–6.

14. David Lilienthal, after his famous stint as the chief of the Tennessee Valley Authority, became the head of the US Atomic Energy Commission. He resigned from this post, after the US decision to develop the hydrogen bomb. See D. R. Ward, *Water Wars: Drought, Flood, Folly, and the Politics of Thirst* (New York: Riverhead Books, 2002), p. 80.

15. D. A. Caponera, 'International Water Resources Law in the Indus Basin', Paper

presented at the Regional Symposium on *Water Resources Policy in Agro-Socio-Economic Development*, 4–8 August 1985, Dhaka, Bangladesh.

16. U. Alam, 'Water Rationality: Mediating the Indus Waters Treaty' (University of Durham: Unpublished PhD dissertation, 1998).

17. According to the Indus Waters Treaty, India is bound to inform Pakistan on a daily basis about the amount of water being released in the rivers flowing into Pakistan from the Indian side. Indus Water Commission of Pakistan receives this information daily and also closely monitors the data with the help of its own radar systems. However, in the flood seasons, that does not stop the spread of misinformation in Pakistan that India releases excessive amount of water in rivers to create problems in the downstream.

18. India refers to this project as the Tulbul Navigation Project, while Pakistan calls it the Wular Barrage.

19. After the Wular Barrage, this is the second time when Pakistan brought up this issue at the diplomatic level instead of dealing with it at the Permanent Indus Commission level.

20. *The Hindu*, 21 February 2002.

21. Probably these reasons had prompted India to allow the mandatory annual meeting of the Permanent Indus Commission to take place in Delhi in June 2002, even though the bilateral tension with Pakistan was at its height. *The Times of India*, 25 June 2002.

22. S. M. A. Salman and K. Uprety, 'Hydro-Politics in South Asia: A Comparative Analysis of the Mahakali and the Ganges Treaties', *Natural Resources Journal*, 39, 2 (1999), pp. 295–343.

23. See I. R. Onta, 'Harnessing the Himalayan Waters of Nepal: A Case for Partnership for the Ganges Basin', in A. K. Biswas and J. I. Uitto (eds), *Sustainable Development of the Ganges-Brahmaputra-Meghna Basins* (Tokyo: UNU Press, 2001), pp. 100–21.

24. B. C. Upreti, *Politics of Himalayan River Waters: An Analysis of the River Water Issues of Nepal, India and Bangladesh* (Jaipur: Nirala, 1993).

25. Salman and Uprety, 'Hydro-Politics in South Asia', p. 302.

26. The Nepali Constitution, in its article 126, stipulates that any agreement on sharing of the country's natural resources that has 'long term, pervasive and serious' impacts to the country needs ratification of the Parliament.

27. The 1996 Agreement on the Integrated Development of Mahakali provided to Nepal an additional 50 megawatts of electricity, making a total of 70 megawatts.

28. Swain, 'Reconciling Disputes and Treaties: Water Development and Management in Ganga Basin'.

29. *Deccan Herald*, 6 June 1997.

30. Salman and Uprety, 'Hydro-Politics in South Asia', p. 312.

31. B. G. Verghese, 'Give the Gujral Doctrine A Chance', *The Rediff Special in the Rediff on the Net* (1997).

32. Since December 1999, India and Nepal have established a Joint Project Office – Pancheswar Investigation (JPO–PI) to carry out field investigation and further studies to prepare a detailed project report on the Pancheswar multi-purpose dam project.

33. B. G. Verghese, 'From Dispute to Dialogue to Doing', in A. K. Biswas and J. I. Uitto (eds), *Sustainable Development of the Ganges-Brahmaputra-Meghna Basins* (Tokyo: UNU Press, 2001), pp. 163–89.

34. Seven major tributaries of the Ganges are: Yamuna, Ramganga, Gomti, Gandak, Karnali (Ghagara), Kosi and Bagmati.

35. These three tributaries contribute about 41 per cent of the annual flow and nearly 71 per cent of the dry-season flow of the Ganges. B. M. Abbas A T, *The Ganges Water Dispute* (Dhaka: University Press Ltd, 1982), pp. 9–10.

36. The Ganges-Brahmaputra-Meghna basin covers approximately 1.65 million square

kilometres. However, the total area of the Ganges-Brahmaputra-Meghna delta is 63,000 square kilometres. The three main rivers and the network of distributary channels linking them constitute this delta.

37. See B. N. Banerjee, *Can the Ganga be Cleaned?* (Delhi: B. R. Publishing Corporation, 1989).
38. D. D'Monte, 'Filthy Flows the Ganga', *People & the Planet*, 5, 3 (1996), pp. 20–2.
39. A. Swain, *The Environmental Trap*.
40. See B. G. Verghese, *Waters of Hope: Himalaya-Ganga Development and Cooperation of Billion People* (Oxford/New Delhi: IBH Publishing, 1990); B. G. Verghese and R. R. Iyer (eds), *Harnessing the Eastern Himalayan Rivers: Regional Cooperation in South Asia* (New Delhi: Konark Publishers, 1993); B. G. Verghese and R. R. Iyer (eds), *Converting Water into Wealth* (New Delhi: Konark Publishers, 1994); G. B. Chapman and M. Thompson (eds), *Water and the Quest for Sustainable Development in the Ganges Valley* (London: Cassell, 1995); A. K. Biswas and J. I. Uitto (eds), *Sustainable Development of the Ganges-Brahmaputra-Meghna Basins* (Tokyo: UNU Press, 2001); J. S. A. Brichieri-Colombi and R. W. Bradnock, 'Geopolitics, Water and Development in South Asia: Cooperative Development on the Ganges-Brahmaputra Delta', *The Geographical Journal*, 169, 1 (2003), pp. 43–64.
41. A. R. Khan, *India, Pakistan and Bangladesh: Conflict or Cooperation?* (Dacca: Sindabad, 1976).
42. All the South Asian rivers, which have originated from the Himalayas, face the 'lean season' or 'dry season' period from the beginning of January to the end of May every year. The short supply of water starts in January due to transformation of rainwater into snow in the Himalayan catchment area and the situation continues for the five months. The arrival of the summer in May helps to melt the snow and increases the flow in the river. The melting snow supplies water until the arrival of the monsoon in August.
43. M. R. Islam, *Ganges Water Dispute: Its International Legal Aspects* (Dhaka: University Press Limited, 1987).
44. C. N. Vakil and G. R. Rao, *Economic Relations between India and Pakistan* (Bombay: 1966).
45. H. R. Külz, 'Further Water Disputes Between India and Pakistan', *The International and Comparative Law Quarterly*, 18 (1969), p. 721.
46. The timing and location of these four meetings were: 28 June to 3 July 1960 in New Delhi; 1 to 3 October 1960 in Dhaka; 28 to 30 April 1961 in Calcutta; and 27 December 1961 to 8 January 1962 in Dhaka.
47. On 30 January 1961, the leader of the Indian experts' team informed his Pakistani counterpart about the start of the construction work of the Farakka barrage. Abbas A T, *The Ganges Water Dispute*, p. 20.
48. S. S. Bindra, *Indo-Bangladesh Relations* (New Delhi: Deep & Deep Publications, 1982), p. 75.
49. Külz, 'Further Water Disputes Between India and Pakistan', p. 724.
50. However, B. M. Abbas A T, who was a leading negotiator from the Pakistani side and later on became the Minister of Power, Flood Control and Water Resources of Bangladesh, gives a different account: 'To the Government of Pakistan, the Kashmir question was more important than the Farakka Problem ... The Indian side wanted a step by step approach in dealing with the various problems but Pakistan insisted on discussing the Kashmir question first. So the Farakka or any other problem could not be considered at all.' Abbas A T, *The Ganges Water Dispute*, p. 27.
51. There are 54 common rivers between India and Bangladesh.
52. K. P. Misra, 'The Farakka Accord', *The World Today*, 34, 2 (1978).
53. Abbas A T, *The Ganges Water Dispute*, pp. 14–15.
54. *Lok Sabha Debates*, 21 April 1975.

55. B. Crow, *Sharing the Ganges: The Politics and Technology of River Development* (New Delhi: Sage Publications, 1995), p. 111.
56. C. J. Gulati, *Bangladesh: Liberation to Fundamentalism: A Study of Volatile Indo-Bangladesh Relations* (New Delhi: Commonwealth Publishers, 1988), pp. 111–12.
57. B. Crow and A. Lindquist, *Development of the Rivers Ganges and Brahmaputra: The Difficulty of Negotiating a New Line* (Milton Keynes: Development Policy and Practice Research Group, 1990).
58. M. Rashiduzzaman, 'Bangladesh in 1977: Dilemmas of the Military Rulers', *Asian Survey*, 18, 2 (1978), p. 132.
59. An all-party delegation from West Bengal called upon Prime Minister Indira Gandhi on the eve of the visit by the new President of Bangladesh, H. M. Ershad to New Delhi in October 1982. They demanded that their state be assured a minimum of a 40,000 cusecs flow during the lean months. *Far Eastern Economic Review*, 15 October 1982, p. 28.
60. Verghese and Iyer, *Harnessing the Eastern Himalayan Rivers: Regional Cooperation in South Asia*, p. 181.
61. Verghese, *Waters of Hope: Himalaya-Ganga Development and Cooperation of Billion People*, p. 362.
62. P. J. Bertocci, 'Bangladesh in 1985: Resolute Against the Storms', *Asian Survey*, 26, 2 (1986), p. 233.
63. Crow, *Sharing the Ganges: The Politics and Technology of River Development*, p. 200.
64. Gulati, *Bangladesh: Liberation to Fundamentalism: A Study of Volatile Indo-Bangladesh Relations*, p. 127.
65. The JCE held seven meetings in all from January to November 1986, with a Ministerial review meeting in August 1986 and a visit to Nepal in October 1986.
66. Verghese and Iyer, *Harnessing the Eastern Himalayan Rivers: Regional Cooperation in South Asia*.
67. Ibid., p. 192.
68. While talking to Indian journalists after her meeting with the Indian Prime Minister, Prime Minister Zia completely ruled out the possibility of linking the rivers as an option for the augmentation (*The Statesman* (New Delhi), 28 May 1992).
69. While the Secretary level meeting was taking place in Dhaka in March 1993, the Indian delegation disputed the Bangladesh statistics showing all time low availability of water in the Ganges due to greater diversions at the upstream. In response to that, the Bangladesh team invited them to visit Hardinge Bridge which was declined by the Indian counterparts on the plea that 'the visit would spoil a day' (*The Bangladesh Observer* (Dhaka), 31 March 1993). The talk eventually ended without any result (*The Hindu* (Madras), 1 April 1993).
70. 'Farakka Day' was observed in Bangladesh to commemorate the long march towards Farakka led by late leader Maulana Bhasani in 1976.
71. Reacting to it, an Indian diplomat said, 'This sort of thing will not give pleasure to the Indian Government. Rather these would hurt New Delhi' (*The Pioneer* (New Delhi), 20 May 1993).
72. *The Daily Star* (Dhaka), 3 September 1993.
73. Ibid., 3 October 1993.
74. India taking strong exceptions to the Bangladesh effort to bring this issue in the UN, advised her to 'overcome temptation to play politics with the important river water issue' (*The Bangladesh Observer* (Dhaka), 18 October 1993). Reacting to it, the Foreign Secretary of Bangladesh, Reaz Rahman said, 'The raising of the Farakka issue in the UN is not a solution but a move towards a solution' (*The Times of India* (Bangalore), 18 October 1993).
75. The Prime Minister of Nepal, though welcoming the Bangladesh proposal, at the

same time wanted to discuss the matter with India before any commitment (*The Telegraph* (Dhaka), 27 November 1993).

76. *The Telegraph* (Calcutta), 4 May 1995.
77. *Times of India* (New Delhi), 26 June 1995.
78. A. Nishat, 'Development and Management of Water Resources in Bangladesh: Post-1996 Treaty Opportunities', in A. K. Biswas and J. I. Uitto (eds), *Sustainable Development of the Ganges-Brahmaputra-Meghna Basins* (Tokyo: UNU Press, 2001), p. 85.
79. Bangladesh Joint River Commission is the source of this river flow data. Brichieri-Colombi and Bradnock, 'Geopolitics, Water and Development in South Asia: Cooperative Development on the Ganges-Brahmaputra Delta'.
80. *The Daily Star* (Dhaka), 9 July 1996.
81. India exports to Bangladesh about 1 billion US dollars worth a year, while it imports only 50 million US dollars worth of Bangladeshi goods.
82. Nishat, 'Development and Management of Water Resources in Bangladesh: Post-1996 Treaty Opportunities', p. 86.
83. *The Daily Star* (Dhaka), 15 May 1997.
84. According to A. D. Mohile, 'The Ganges, the Brahmaputra, and the Barak-Meghna are separate subsystems in the combined river system, but they have a common delta system providing a common terminus into the sea and have considerable potential for spatial integration, both through possible physical links between the subsystems and in the possibility of shifting the water demand of the common delta to the water-rich subsystem in order to support larger development in other areas.' A. D. Mohile, 'Brahmaputra: Issues in Development', in A. K. Biswas and J. I. Uitto (eds), *Sustainable Development of the Ganges-Brahmaputra-Meghna Basins* (Tokyo: UNU Press, 2001), pp. 58–9.
85. I. M. Faisal, 'Managing Common Waters in the Ganges-Brahmaputra-Meghna Region', *SAIS Review*, 22, 2 (2002), pp. 309–27.
86. Realizing Bangladeshi strong sentiment against the transit facilities, India is trying to develop a joint port at Sittwe in Myanmar. If this project materializes, India can send goods easily to its north-eastern states from its Calcutta port.
87. *The Daily Star* (Dhaka), 7 February 2002.
88. The new Haldia port is situated 56.5 nautical miles downstream of Calcutta. It is on the north of the outfall of the river Haldia in the Hooghly. See K. Begum, *Tension Over the Farakka Barrage: A Techno-Political Tangle in South-Asia* (Dhaka: University Press Limited, 1987), p. 50.
89. Brichieri-Colombi and Bradnock, 'Geopolitics, Water and Development in South Asia: Cooperative Development on the Ganges-Brahmaputra Delta'.
90. The Government of India, for a long time, has been contemplating a big water resources project, which is known as the Ganga-Cauvery link. The proposed 2,500 kilometres long canal would link the Ganges River in the north (from a point near Patna in the state of Bihar) with the Cauvery River (this river has been the cause of a serious conflict between two Indian states, Tamilnadu and Karnataka for some years) in the south.

3

Rivers in the Middle East and North Africa: The Jordan, the Euphrates-Tigris and with Special Emphasis on the Nile[1]

The Middle East and North African region is poorly endowed with natural fresh water supplies, making it the driest region in the world. The countries in this region are home to 5 per cent of the world's people, but possess less than 1 per cent of the world's fresh water. The expected population growth in the region is likely to worsen the water problem further. Besides the growing population number, increasing agricultural and industrial activities also adversely affect the region's limited per capita water availability.[2] Several countries of the region have already exploited more than 100 per cent of their natural water procurement levels. In spite of this, almost 20 per cent of the region's population do not receive an adequate potable water supply, and nearly 35 per cent lack appropriate sanitation.

In the mid-1980s, the Central Intelligence Agency (CIA) had forewarned that there were at least ten places in the world where war could break out over the shortage of a supply of fresh water – the majority of them were in the Middle East and North Africa.[3] These water wars have not taken place yet, but the threat does exist. Many of the countries in this water-scarce region depend heavily on imported surface water, which comes through internationally shared river systems.[4] In a situation of increasing water demand, international rivers may become the battleground for conflicts among the riparian states. Many river conflicts are already active among the countries of the Middle East and North Africa. The water conflicts in this volatile region have the real potential of turning violent and causing large-scale human deaths and suffering.

Besides disputes over international river waters, there is also growing tension in the region over the use of underground water. Israel's annual renewable fresh water supply is about 1,950 million cubic metres (mcm), while the current demand (including Palestinian territories) is about 2,150 mcm. Thanks to population growth and water intensive agriculture, Israel's water demand is projected to exceed 2,600 mcm by 2020.[5] Israeli agriculture has become increasingly dependent on recycled sewerage effluents and other types of low quality water unsuitable for drinking use.[6] However, the demand for water in the non-agricultural sector is also quite high and growing. To meet this demand, Israel is overpumping the aquifers. During the 1970s and 1980s, the Coastal Aquifer was overused to such an extent that the water table fell to less than one metre above sea level, and in some areas it was below sea level. This led to the severe deterioration of quality and quantity of water in the aquifer. The increased level of salting and other pollutants reduced the quality of water to below the permissible level for drinking water. Thus, the Mountain Aquifer is now being used as the country's primary source of drinking water.

The Mountain Aquifer of the West Bank consists of three main aquifer groups, but only one of these is located in Israel proper, under the coastal plain. The remaining two originate in occupied areas, which are the source of 40 per cent of Israel's groundwater supply.[7] These western and north-eastern sections of the Mountain Aquifers reached their productive limits by the mid-1970s. In these areas, the groundwater table has been falling alarmingly since 1969.[8] The over-extraction of water from the aquifers has also deteriorated the quality of the water. The eastern aquifer is located under the slopes of the Judean and Samaria highlands towards the Jordan Valley and these areas have been designated for transfer to Palestinian control by Oslo Agreements.[9] The Palestinians blame Israeli settlers for unsustainably overpumping from a large section of these aquifers. The Israeli authority, while restricting the drilling of wells for the Arabs, has allowed the Jewish settlers to over-exploit the groundwater. The control of groundwater sources has been one of the major constraints to peace in this region. Furthermore, the drying of the Mountain Aquifer now poses a serious threat to the agricultural sector and thus to the economic prospects of the Palestinians.

The problem is not limited to the West Bank; the Gaza area is also very much affected. Gaza's limited underground water supply has been over-exploited, especially since the early 1970s. The aquifer system underlying the Gaza Strip is an extension of Israel's Coastal Aquifer. This narrow aquifer is fed primarily by direct local rainfall. The growing settlements in the area have hindered the recharge of the groundwater. The overpumping of the aquifer by the Jewish settlers has also reduced the water table in many places to below sea level. The situation has been further worsened following self-rule, as Palestinians have been digging more wells and drawing more water. Towards the end of 1995, the Water Commissioner of Israel warned that the Palestinian drilling operations were 'liable to cause heavy damage to

Israeli ground water supplies'.[10] The infiltration of saltwater from the Mediterranean Sea has already made the Gaza aquifer water unsuitable for agricultural use and Gaza's farmers are already experiencing declining crop yields.[11] It is not difficult to predict the total salinization of the aquifer in the near future, which will certainly aggravate the water supply situation.

The most important complication in the use of groundwater is that it renews much more slowly than other water sources. Thus groundwater has to be used in an environmentally sustainable manner. This means that the rate of withdrawal should be equal or less than the rate of recharge. Groundwater withdrawal in an unsustainable manner is not confined to Israel, the West Bank and the Gaza Strip. Many Arab regimes are using their fossil aquifers in their short-term strategy to meet the water scarcity and to increase agricultural production to meet growing food demand.

Saudi Arabia withdraws large amounts of underground water for its domestic and agricultural use. Nearly 2,000 billion cubic metres of water are deposited in the aquifers beneath Saudi Arabia, which provides 88 per cent of the country's water needs. The rest of the water supply comes mainly through its desalinization plants.[12] Saudi regime's fascination for the country's increased wheat production in recent years threatens to drain the country's underground water resources completely in 20 or 30 years. Saudi Arabia is mining its fossil water almost 1 billion cubic metres of water per annum for agricultural use. Like Saudi Arabia's oil resources, the fossil water deposit is also finite, and its complete drying up is not hard to imagine. Moreover, Saudi Arabia shares one of its major aquifers, *Qa Disi* aquifer with Jordan, which is the source of another complication. Jordan is also using 45 million cubic metres of fossil water every year for irrigation.

Groundwater resources throughout the region are over-exploited. In Jordan, groundwater is being used at about 200 per cent of its sustainable capability.[13] The conditions in Syria and Yemen are not any better. In North Africa, Libya provides another example of unsustainable underground water withdrawal. Libya's major fossil aquifers are located far from the country's agricultural area. So, Libya withdraws water from the underground basin in the southern desert and diverts it to the northern part near the Mediterranean coast for agricultural purposes. The water is transported through a long and expensive pipeline link. Libya shares this vast aquifer partly with Egypt, Sudan and Chad. This massive water withdrawal has brought Libya into conflict with the other riparian countries. The underground non-renewable basin is predicted to be completely dried up in 40 to 60 years depending upon the amount of withdrawal. This creates a highly uncertain future for the people who are living on these newly created farmlands.

Many Arab countries increasingly are relying on non-renewable groundwater supplies to augment their scarce water supply in order to respond to the growing demand. As groundwater is a hidden resource it provides the state an easier and cheaper form of supplementing water resources. This has led to senseless groundwater mining in the Arab world. Many of these countries are very vulnerable to the drying up of the aquifers in the near future. This creates a highly uncertain future for the people who are dependent on the waters of these underground sources and also the economy of these countries. Though over-exploitation of groundwater can potentially bring large-scale human suffering and migration, it is less likely to lead to a direct violent conflict among states. On the other hand, disagreement over the sharing of international river waters can potentially bring violent inter-state conflict to the Arab world.

THE JORDAN RIVER SYSTEM

The struggle over control of the Jordan River basin is one of the most discussed subjects in the 'water conflicts' literature. The riparian states of the Jordan River basin are Israel, Jordan, Lebanon and Syria. The Jordan River rises on the slopes of Mount Hermon in Syria and Lebanon, and moves to the south and passes through Lake Tiberias (Sea of Galilee) to empty into the Dead Sea. The Jordan River receives water from its major tributary, the Yarmuk River, whose catchment area lies in the Huran Plain and the Golan Heights as well as in some parts of Jordan. There are also other smaller tributaries to the Jordan River that originate in Jordan, Israel and the West Bank. From its origin to the entry of Lake Tiberias, the Jordan River is called 'upper Jordan' and the stretch between the Lake and the Dead Sea is called 'lower Jordan'.

The Jordan River is the largest and longest river that flows in Israel. Moreover, it is the only river within Israel that has a permanent flow year round. The other major rivers in Israel are contaminated with agricultural and industrial sewage, which makes Jordan River the only natural and clean river in the country. In spite of its relative large size in Israel, Jordan River is actually one of the smaller rivers in regional terms. With only 1,400 million cubic metres of usable annual flow, the Jordan River is the smallest major watershed in the region, compared to the Nile with 74,000 million cubic metres per year or the Euphrates at 32,000 million cubic metres per year.[14] The amount of water carried by the river has been decreasing over recent years, owing to exploitation of the fresh water of the Sea of Galilee and Yarmuk River of Syria. The Jordan River supplies Israel and Jordan with the majority of their water. As such, Israel mostly depends on water, which is either supplied from rivers that originate outside the border, or from disputed lands. For the State of Jordan, the Jordan River supplies about 75 per cent of its needs.

The need for water and the continuing hostility between Israel and the surrounding Arab states, has placed the Jordan River as a central bargaining chip since Israel's creation. The Israeli War of Independence was rooted in the fact that the Arab countries considered the State of Israel to be illegitimate. The Arab states have regularly denounced the unilateral diversion of the Jordan River by Israel. The Israeli response has been that the surrounding Arab nations were never willing to let Israel exist in peace. These historical disagreements intertwine with the dispute between Israel and Jordan in which the Jordan River plays a main role. In order to understand the core of the conflict between Israel and Jordan around the Jordan River, it is important to note the different perceptions of water between the two countries. Jordan, as part of the Arab world, perceived the water problem as part of the Arab–Israeli conflict. Therefore, for the Jordanians, water was always a matter of Arab national pride. For Israel, as a young country, water seemed to be an integral part of its territory and a necessary resource for development.[15]

The conflict over the Jordan River basin surfaced immediately after the establishment of Israel. In February 1947, with the end of its mandate, Great Britain turned the fate of Palestine over to the United Nations. The UN divided Palestine into Jewish and Arab states. Immediately after the withdrawal of British troops, Arab states waged a war against Israel. In the war, Israel lost three strategic locations along waterways in the Galilee region, causing reverberations until 1967.[16] From 1948 to 1967, Israel was primarily a mid-stream riparian of the Jordan River: Syria and Lebanon were the upper riparian countries and Jordan was the lower riparian. Israeli schemes to divert water out of the basin area brought several rounds of conflicts with its Arab neighbours in this period.[17] In 1951 the Israeli plan to drain the Huleh swamp and lake to reduce evaporation and reclaim agricultural land was opposed by Syria.[18] The next confrontation took place in 1953 when Israel attempted to divert water from the Jordan River in the demilitarized zone. Syria mobilized its armed forces and the issue came up to the Security Council.[19] The fear of more water-induced confrontations in the region led to the decision in October 1953 of US President Eisenhower to send his special envoy Eric Johnston to resolve the Jordan water issue.

Johnston made four trips to the region from 1953 to 1955 to formulate the Unified Plan (later known as the Johnston Plan) with Israel, Jordan, Syria and Lebanon. According to Lowi, the objective of the Johnston Plan was to use technical collaboration to inspire political settlement.[20] Though the plan failed to be ratified by the Arab states, Israel and Jordan began adhering to the plan and all the basin countries continued their unilateral water development projects. In 1964, Israel began to divert 320 million cubic metres of water per year through its National Water Carrier. Syria and Lebanon decided in 1965 to build canals to divert the Jordan's headwater, upstream of the National Water Carrier. Using armed forces, Israel destroyed the canal building equipment and forced Lebanon to stop the construction of the project. In a series of attacks, Israel also stopped the Syrian project in July 1966. Though the Six-Day War started a year later, the contribution of water to the growing tension which led to the war cannot be dismissed.

In the 1967 War, Israel occupied the Golan Heights and brought under its domination all the headwaters of the Jordan River and a larger stretch of the Yarmuk River. The occupation of the West Bank also gave control of the lower Jordan basin to Israel. This shift in power balance and hydro-strategic situation gave Israel almost a free hand to use most of the Jordan River's water. Further control over the water bodies was also probably influenced by Israel's decision to invade Lebanon in 1982. The invasion of Lebanon and the creation of the 'security zone' in the South gave Israel greater control of the Jordan and Litani Rivers.[21] Taking advantage of its new hydro-strategic position, Israel was withdrawing more water for its own use from the Jordan basin. By the early 1990s, Israeli utilization of the basin's total discharge had reached more than 60 per cent.[22]

In the past decades, Israel and Jordan have searched for new ways to maximize the use of Jordan River water. In Jordan, the effort has been geared towards the rehabilitation of the East Gohr Canal, the repair of the Yarmouk main canal tunnel and the constructions of the King Talal Dam on the Zarqa River. Israel, on the other hand, in recent years has sought solutions to its water problems by applying advanced technology and environmental research to increase its water supply. Besides drip irrigation systems and recycling of sewerage effluents, Israel was also desalinizing Mediterranean Sea water. However, gradually they discovered that unilateral initiatives were not enough to address the water scarcity issue. In the beginning of the 1990s, water for both countries became a source of cooperation.

On 26 October 1994, the prime ministers of Jordan and Israel signed a peace treaty, which brought an end to the state of war that had existed for almost 50 years between the two countries. Article 6 and Annex II of this comprehensive agreement deal with the water issues. This water part of the agreement covers two areas: the northern area contains the Jordan River and the southern region deals with their shared groundwater. Both countries, after the agreement, started to build storage facilities to hold excess water from rain floods and dams for river flow management. The construction of a dam across Yarmouk began in 1998, to provide water to both the riparians. Jordan commits to provide additional water to Israel in winter and, in return, Israel concedes the same to Jordan in the summer months.[23] In terms of environmental conservation, Jordan and Israel have agreed to protect the river from pollution, contamination, or industrial disposal. Furthermore, the Treaty brought forward a provision for establishment of a joint water committee to oversee issues regarding the quality of the water. However, this treaty was only the beginning of a wider regional agreement, which has aimed to include Palestine, Syria and Lebanon. There was a certain hope for a set of basin-wide water agreements in the mid-1990s, when the Israel–Jordan Peace Agreement was followed by the Oslo Accord in 1995, and then the backroom negotiations between Israel and Syria. But, the disagreement on water became a serious block in the peace negotiations between Israel and Syria in the late 1990s. The negotiations between Israel and Lebanon could not progress to deal with water issues.

Israeli failure to completely honour the water sharing with Jordan in the drought year of 1999, brought further tension in the region. In the mid-1980s, Israel had undertaken various precautionary measures to reduce water use in the agricultural sector and formulate a sustainable water management policy. This was possible owing to the demand of domestic environmental groups and US pressure. However, to improve its bargaining position in the peace negotiation, Israel changed its water use policy in 1993 from a cautious to a self-seeking approach.[24] According to Allan, 'Levels of water withdrawal, which had fallen from two billion cubic metres per year in 1985 to 1.6 billion cubic metres in 1992, rose within three years to the 1985 levels.'[25] This rapid transformation of Israeli water policy confirms the political importance attached to water sharing in the region.

The situation in the Middle East has again become very volatile after the new Palestinian uprising in the occupied territories of Israel and failure of the July 2000 Camp David meeting. The present hydro-political situation in the Jordan River basin is one of the intricate problems. Israel currently consumes almost all of its available water supplies. Occupation of the Golan Heights has given Israel near total control over the headwaters of the Jordan River and its tributaries and that has helped to increase the country's available water supply. The integration of this 'occupied' water into the Israeli economy has brought complications to find an understanding among the riparian countries over the sharing of the Jordan River water. A recent positive development brings some hope for finding alternative water supply in the basin. Since November 2001, Israel, realizing that manufacturing water is easier than negotiating it, has started building several desalination facilities. Through intensive desalination, the basin can potentially increase its water supply by 50 per cent. Thus, at present, the danger of water conflict in the region is growing *vis-à-vis* the opportunities for cooperation.

THE EUPHRATES-TIGRIS RIVERS

The Euphrates and the Tigris are the two largest rivers in the Middle East. Both rivers originate from the Anatolian highland regions in Turkey and flow through the Mesopotamian desert plain in Syria and Iraq. Both the rivers unite in Iraq at Qurna to form the Shatt al-Arab, which runs into the Gulf. Turkey contributes at least 95 per cent of the water flow for the Euphrates River and 44 per cent for the Tigris River. All the major tributaries of the Euphrates are in the extreme upper part of the basin. In contrast, the mainstream of the Tigris receives the flow from a number of larger tributaries: the Greater Zab, the Lesser Zab, the Adhaim and the Diyala.

In the lower part of the Euphrates-Tigris basin, there is evidence of water management activities dating back over six millennia. However, only around a hundred years back, major irrigation schemes developed in the region, what is now the country of Iraq, to manipulate the snow-melt flood waters of the two rivers from April to June. These activities were using a small proportion of the river water and most of the runoff was flowing unused into the Persian Gulf. However, since the 1950s, there has been a dramatic increase in water demand on this river system. The three major riparian countries of the Tigris-Euphrates,[26] Turkey, Syria and Iraq have rapidly growing populations and at the same time are pursuing development strategies that are heavily dependent on water resources.[27] With this, the emphasis of water management activities has shifted from downstream diversion projects to upstream water storage schemes. Syria and Iraq are also dependent upon external supply of water in their river systems: 80 per cent of Syria's and 66 per cent of Iraq's river flow originates outside of their borders. In this situation, Turkey embarked upon building a large number of dams in the upstream, which brings serious threat to the downstream flow to Iraq and Syria. Between 1923 and 1950, Turkey constructed three dams, in the 1950s six more, but by the mid-1990s it housed 140 dams.[28] After China, Turkey was second on the list of countries in building large numbers of big dams (higher than ten metres) in the 1990s.

The risk of water shortages constitutes one of the most strategically important security issues of the three Euphrates-Tigris basin states.[29] Though Turkey has comparatively more water resources, they are unevenly distributed among its regions. The Tigris and Euphrates Rivers carry one-third of the total surface water available in Turkey. The growing agricultural sector and booming urban areas have put tremendous stress on the country's water supply. Nearly 60 per cent of the Turks live in urban areas and the local water supply system is failing to meet their growing needs.

Under the 1923 Treaty of Lausanne, Turkey was under obligation to consult Iraq before undertaking any water exploitation in the upstream. The 1930 Treaty of Aleppo mentioned Syrian rights over the Tigris River. In 1946, Turkey and Iraq signed the Treaty of Friendship and Good Neighbourliness at Ankara. This agreement reiterated the provisions of the 1923 Treaty of Lausanne.[30] Syria and Iraq had also established a Joint Technical Committee in 1962 to facilitate sharing of the Euphrates-Tigris water. In the early 1970s, both countries made a few unsuccessful attempts to reach an understanding over water sharing. But, the operation of hydro-projects in Syria and Turkey from 1973 brought serious friction among the riparian countries.

In the 1960s, Turkey and Syria began planning several large-scale water projects over the Tigris-Euphrates. In 1974, Turkey completed its Keban Dam over the Euphrates while the first Syrian dam (Tabqa Dam) on the same river came into operation one year earlier. Construction of Keban Dam received strong official protest from the Syrian side. Keban Dam was not an irrigation project, but was meant for hydropower generation. So, the water availability was not the problem, but Syria was anxious about Turkey's control of river flow. The building of these projects in the upstream locations brought serious worries to Iraq about the reduction in the availability of water since it depends primarily on the Tigris-Euphrates system for the irrigation of its agricultural fields. In 1974, Iraq came very close to declaring war against Syria because of Syria's filling of Lake Assad behind the Tabqa (Ath-Thawrah) Dam, which affected 3 million Iraqi farmers. Iraq even started threatening to bomb the dams in Syria.[31] In 1975, the filling up of the storage in the upstream again revived this conflict. Iraq asked the Arab League to intervene. Syria, blaming Turkey for the decreased water in its rivers, closed in airspace for Iraqi flights. This was followed up with aggressive troop movements by both the countries on their mutual border.[32] With the Saudi Arabian and Soviet intervention, the crisis was averted.

In the early 1980s, Syria raised strong objection to the filling up of a second major Turkish dam on the Euphrates at Karakaya. In 1986, Turkey claimed to have uncovered a Syrian plot to blow up the Ataturk Dam. In early 1987, even Turkey threatened to cut the water supply to Syria because of its alleged help to the Kurdish insurgent group, PKK. However, in spite of the tense situation, Turkey and Syria signed a bilateral agreement in 1987, which allocated 500 cumecs of water to Syria. But, the relationship between Syria and Turkey took a downward turn again after the completion of the Ataturk Dam in 1990, which is part of the greater Turkish south-eastern Anatolia 'GAP' project and the ninth largest dam on the globe. The filling up of the lake behind this massive dam caused a 75 per cent drop in the downstream water supply for an entire month. This not only strained relations between Turkey and Syria but also Syria's relations with Iraq.[33] Both Syria and Iraq sent their ministers to Ankara to lodge protest about the reduced river flow. While Turkey insisted that the water flow issue was a technical one, this was not accepted by the downstream riparian countries. This incident was immediately followed up by the Kuwait War, and Turkey refused to go on with the reported encouragement of the Allies to stop the water supply to punish Iraq.[34] However, this comfort was not lasting for the downstream Iraq or Syria. In 1992, Turkey's Prime Minister argued: 'Water resources are Turkey's and oil is theirs (Syria's and Iraq's). Since we do not tell them, "Look, we have a right to half your oil", they cannot claim to what is ours.'[35]

The importance of hydropower provided the initial incentive for Turkey to undertake the GAP.[36] Moreover, nearly 40 per cent of Turkey's agricultural land is in its south-eastern Anatolia part. This region suffers from massive water scarcity. Poverty has already forced more than half of this region's population to cities such as Istanbul. The region houses a large number of Kurdish people. In order to address the water scarcity, reduce the poverty and check the population migration, Turkey initiated the GAP project in 1983. GAP is made up of 13 sub-projects, which aim to construct 22 dams, including the massive Ataturk Dam, 19 hydroelectric power plants and 17 irrigation schemes. Seven of these sub-projects are being undertaken on the Euphrates River, while Tigris will provide the sites for the other six. Turkey is now building other dams of this huge project. About 330 villages and 200,000 people are or will be directly affected by the GAP project. The latest major project of Turkey, which is going on within the GAP, is Ilisu Dam on the Tigris. This 135 metres high rockfill dam is being built about 60 kilometres upstream of the Syrian-Iraq border, in the heart of the Kurdish area.

When the GAP project is completed, it will bring further water shortages to the downstream riparian countries.[37] Through the help of GAP, Turkey plans to irrigate over 1.7 million hectares of land (1.1 million in the Euphrates basin and 0.6 million in the Tigris basin),[38] and to generate over 27 billion kilowatt hours of electricity by 2010.[39] With the full operation of GAP, the flow of the Euphrates to Syria could be reduced by up to 40 per cent and to Iraq by up to 80 per cent. This decrease in the water volume will also deteriorate the water quality due to upstream agricultural uses. However, the financial and technical constraints have delayed the working of the GAP project. GAP was funded almost entirely by Turkey's internal revenue till 1997.[40] World Bank and other international financial agencies have refused to support the project due to lack of agreement on this issue among the riparian states. GAP has become a huge economic burden for Turkey. In the early 1990s, it accounted for 6–9 per cent of the annual budget and its contribution to the annual rate of inflation in the country was to the tune of 70 per cent.[41]

Fear of future water scarcity has already brought Syria to a tense relationship with Turkey. At the regional level, the Euphrates-Tigris has become a central factor in the troubled relations between Turkey and Syria. According to a 1987 agreement with Turkey, Syria gets 15.75 cubic kilometres (500 cumecs) of water per year from the Euphrates, which is certainly going to be affected by the GAP, when it will be fully operational. This GAP project is also going to bring Iraq into the conflict in the near future. In the 1970s and 1980s, Iraq had developed a Master Plan to develop its water resources with the help of the Soviet Union. It led to its planned development and use of the Euphrates-Tigris water on a larger scale. In 1987, Iraq completed the Haditha Dam on the Euphrates with a storage capacity of 7 billion cubic metres. On the Tigris, a multi-purpose dam was built at Mosul (Saddam Dam). In December 1992, Iraq inaugurated its third waterway, the 565 kilometre long 'Saddam River'. This impressive canal starts near Baghdad and ends close to Basra and it is designed to remove excess drainage water from the area between two rivers and discharge it into Fao Peninsula to reclaim agricultural land.[42] The water projects, both completed and planned ones, are certainly going to be affected with the planned future water withdrawals in the upstream.

The decreased discharge from the Euphrates-Tigris might also bring environmental problems for the Gulf, which supports a rich and diverse marine life. Furthermore, the reduced flow of fresh water might increase water salinity in the Gulf, creating problems for the desalination plants of the Gulf countries. But Turkey is adamant over exploiting Euphrates and Tigris to its maximum advantage.[43] Turkey argues that the storage facilities are necessary for the proper management of Euphrates-Tigris water, as this river system suffers from high seasonal and annual flow fluctuations. The low-lying plains in Iraq and Syria do not provide ideal sites for the large dam building and associated reservoirs. Thus, Turkey claims that its reservoirs could provide water security to two downstream countries. To soothe the concerns of the Gulf countries, Turkey had even suggested in 1987 a twin 'Peace Pipeline' to divert waters from Turkish rivers to Sharjah and Jiddah. These pipeline projects are technically feasible but suffer from high economic cost and security risk.[44]

In spite of Turkey's claims and overtures, GAP has become a source of common concern for Syria and Iraq from the early 1990s. Turkey fears that they may forge an alliance against her on the use of Euphrates resources. Both Syria and Iraq are convinced that Turkey lacks willingness to supply them with sufficient water from the Euphrates-Tigris system to meet their future needs. In spite of their political conflicts, Syria and Iraq did sign the 1990 agreement following the impounding of the Ataturk Dam by Turkey.[45] The April 1990 Agreement between Syria and Iraq at Tunis, regulating allocation of water at the point where the Euphrates leaves Syria, allots 58 per cent to Iraq and 42 per cent to Syria.[46] With the decreasing runoff from the Turkish side, Syria may be forced to reduce the water supply to Iraq.[47] The signing of the Tunis Agreement between the two Arab antagonists, and the Syrian Agreement to drop its traditional demand for shares from over 50 per cent to 42 per cent was considered by the Turkish government as an unpleasant development. The 1991 Gulf War and the following UN sanctions on Iraq restricted the maturing of this front.

As Natasha Beschomer rightly points out: 'Water is only one of the factors souring relations between Turkey, Syria and Iraq, states traditionally competing for regional leadership.'[48] The relationship between Turkey and Syria has also not been smooth for a long time. Two major obstacles approach the Turkish–Syrian relationship: alleged Syrian help to the militant groups (Kurdish PKK, and left radical *Dev Sol*, etc.) within the Turkish state; and Syrian claim on the Turkish province of Hatay. Thus water issue has provided a good leverage to Turkey at the negotiation table to bargain with Syria. In the early 1990s, Turkey issued open threats to restrict the flow of the Euphrates River to pressure Syria to discontinue its support to PKK.[49] Turkey had bilateral agreements with Russia, Bulgaria and Greece over the sharing of the common water resources, but it refuses to do so with the Arab riparian countries of the Euphrates-Tigris system. Syria argues, 'The secret ideal of Turkey is to dominate the countries of the region economically and politically by making them dependent on water.'[50] Turkey continues its GAP development, and at the same time ensures the flow of the Euphrates meets the minimum levels per its agreements with Syria and Iraq. In future, Turkey may use water as a tool to manipulate Syrian and to some extent Iraqi policies.

The Baath regimes of Syria and Iraq were co-ordinating their actions on the Euphrates water issue till 2003, putting aside their political differences. In 1998, the two countries decided to boycott companies involved in the GAP. They were also openly critical of military agreement between the Turkish and Israeli armed forces. However, the overthrow of Saddam's regime in 2003 by the US-led coalition has brought some uncertainties about Iraq's future course of action. An American-backed regime may start collaborating with Turkey. On the other hand, the Turkey–Iraq collaboration may not affect the water situation in Syria. Rather, if Iraq manages to get a good bargain from Turkey on the

Euphrates-Tigris that may bring benefits to Syria as the water will have to pass through its territory. This may help to establish a basin-based institution to manage the Euphrates-Tigris. But if an Islamic Shia regime takes over the power in Iraq, the situation may get further conflictual. In the downstream alliance building, with Syria and Iraq, Iran may join. In that case, a stronger and tighter coalition against Turkey's upstream water withdrawal cannot be ruled out. Thus, the unfolding political changes in the region will determine whether the Euphrates-Tigris water will be used to further aggravate the riparian tension or be the source of cooperation and peace in this troubled region.

THE NILE RIVER

Ten years back, Homer-Dixon had concluded that the Nile River was one of the few international rivers that had the potential to bring its basin countries into an armed conflict situation.[51] His assessment was rationalized on the ground that the conflict over an international river was more likely when a downstream country was highly dependent on the shared water and was powerful in comparison to upstream riparians. The Nile River has also been considered, by many others, as having the high potential to induce inter-state armed conflict.[52] At least for the last 75 years, the Nile River has been the source of political tensions and low intensity conflict among three of its major riparians, Egypt, Ethiopia and Sudan.

The Nile River is the longest international river in the world. It flows through ten countries in the north-eastern part of Africa – Rwanda, Burundi, Zaire, Tanzania, Kenya, Uganda, Eritrea, Ethiopia, Sudan and Egypt – before emptying into the Mediterranean Sea. The White Nile and the Blue Nile are the two main tributaries of the Nile. From its major source, Lake Victoria in eastern-central Africa, the White Nile flows generally north through Uganda and into Sudan where it meets the Blue Nile at Khartoum, which rises in the Ethiopian highlands. From the confluence of the White and Blue Nile, the river moves northwards into Egypt and on to the Mediterranean Sea. From its remotest headstream, the Ruvyironza River in Burundi to the Mediterranean Sea, the river is 6,671 kilometres long. For almost half its length, the Nile runs through arid and desert lands. The basin extends over an area of 2.9 million square kilometres, which covers one-tenth of Africa's total land mass.

The White Nile contributes a relatively small but regular flow of water as it is supplied by permanent snows of the Ruwenzori Mountain and supported by several Equatorial Lakes. However, the Blue Nile, which is the primary water provider, proceeds from the Ethiopian

Map 2 The Nile River

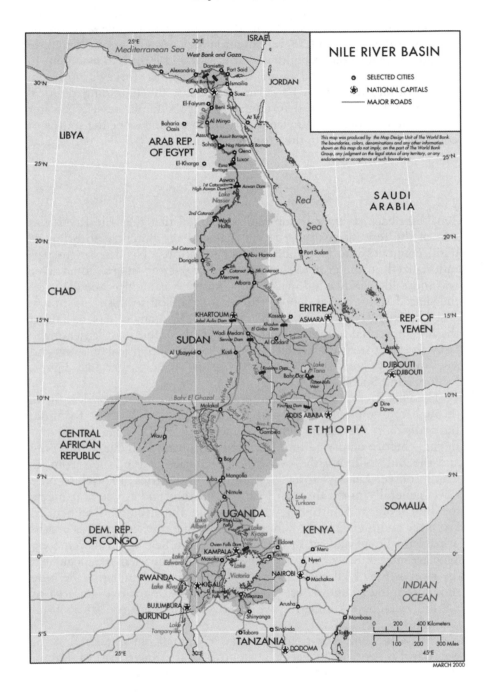

Table 3.1 Illustrative Data for Nile Basin Countries

Country	Population 1995	Population 2025	GNP per capita 1996	Population below poverty line (1 USD/day PPP) (%)	Per capita water availability 1990	Per capita water availability 2025
	(millions)	(millions)	(USD)		(cu. mts)	(cu. mts)
Burundi	6.4	13.5	170	–	655	269
Congo	43.9	104.6	160	–	359,803	139,309
Egypt	62.9	97.3	1,090	7.6	1,123	630
Eritrea	3.5	7.0	–	–	–	–
Ethiopia	55.1	126.9	100	33.8	2,207	842
Kenya	28.3	63.4	320	50.2	636	235
Rwanda	8.0	15.8	190	45.7	897	306
Sudan	28.1	58.4	–	–	4,792	1,993
Tanzania	29.7	62.9	170	16.4	2,924	1,025
Uganda	21.3	48.1	300	50.0	3,759	1,437

Sources: African Development Bank, *Policy for Integrated Water Resources Management: Draft*, February 2000; R. Engelman and P. LeRoy, *Sustaining Water: Population and the Future of Renewable Water Supplies* (Washington DC: Population and Environment Program, Population Action International, 1993). Population and water availability in the year 2025 are based on the medium projection of population growth.

highlands and suffers from strong seasonal fluctuations. The Ethiopian highlands provide 86 per cent of the Nile flow (Blue Nile 59 per cent, Baro-Akobo (Sobat) 14 per cent, Tekezze (Atbara) 13 per cent), while the contribution from the Equatorial Lakes Region is only 14 per cent.[53]

The total population of the Nile basin countries was 287 million people in 1995, and it is estimated that over half of this population is dependent on the Nile. By the year 2025, the total population of the basin is estimated to reach 597 million. As Table 3.1 shows, because of the increasing population, the per capita water availability is also decreasing rapidly in the basin. The Nilotic countries are among the poorest in the world. Though the Nile is a long river system and runs through ten countries and supports a large population, its average annual runoff is modest in comparison to the other major river systems in Africa (see Table 3.2).

Moreover, the flow variations of the Ethiopian tributaries are very sharp between the wet and dry seasons. During the rainy season, the water coming from Ethiopia can go up to 95 per cent of the Nile flow. The annual flow of the Nile water reaching Egypt also varies significantly as per the intensity of the rainy season – 104 billion cubic metres in a good rainfall year like 1946 to 45 billion cubic meters in a poor rainy season year as in 1913. Moreover, the average annual flow of the Nile has reduced over the years at Aswan in Egypt. In the late

Table 3.2 Comparing the Nile with other Major River Systems in Africa

Name of basin	Number of riparian countries	Catchment area '000 km²	Average annual discharge billion m³
Nile	10	2,850	84
Congo/Zaire	9	3,690	1,250
Niger	9	2,230	180
Zambezi	7	1,290	230
Volta	6	390	390

Source: R. Rangeley, B. M. Thiam, R. A. Andersen and C. A. Lyle, *International River Basin Organizations in Sub-Saharan Africa* (Washington DC: World Bank Technical Paper No. 250, 1994).

nineteenth century, annual average river flow at Aswan was 110 billion cubic metres while in the late twentieth century it has slipped to just above 80 billion cubic metres.[54]

Agriculture is the most predominant economic activity of all the Nile basin countries. It is not only that many countries in the Nile basin are having a lesser share of the water resource, but also their agro-based economy needs and consumes more water. The major riparian countries of the Nile River – Egypt, Sudan and Ethiopia withdraw most of their water for agricultural purposes. In the Great Lake region, with small-scale agriculture, rainwater contributes significantly. However, in the Lower Basin, the availability of rainwater is very small. In these areas, even small-scale farming has to a large extent depended on runoff in rivers, lakes and groundwater aquifers. The two downstreamers, Egypt and Sudan, are already very much dependent on irrigation for their agricultural production. To achieve food security in the face of increasing demand of the growing population, more Nilotic countries are becoming dependent on irrigated agriculture.

Riparian Agreements over the Nile

The famous Greek historian Herodotus had described Egypt as the gift of the Nile in the fifth century BC. The Nile River had brought ancient civilizations to its lower reaches in Egypt.[55] In pre-historic days, the Nile was being revered as God Hapi by the Egyptians.[56] The prosperity brought by the Nile River system in the vast arid desert attracted many invaders to the region throughout history. The dependence of Egypt on the Nile has not diminished in recent years. Since time immemorial, Egypt consumes most of the Nile water, and to a greater extent controls the basin.

After the fall of the Ottoman Empire in the eighteenth century, Egypt wished to control the water source of the Nile. That led Egypt to wage two major wars against Ethiopia in the 1870s. However, Yohnnes IV of Ethiopia was successful in defending his country's territory from the Egyptian attacks, first at Gundet in 1875, and then at Guta in 1876.[57] A few years later, in their Berlin Summit in 1884, the European colonial powers, Britain, France, Belgium and Italy, divided the region into their influence zones. Britain ruled Egypt from the late nineteenth century to 1937, and it controlled Sudan from 1899 to 1956.[58] Around that period, Italy had control over Eritrea and Ethiopia, and France and Belgium over the Equatorial Region. However, Britain was able to protect the Nile water flow to Egypt. Several treaties were signed among the colonial powers in giving priority to the Egyptian demands of the Nile's water.

Italy and Britain signed a Protocol for the division of their spheres of influence in Eastern Africa on 15 April 1891. This treaty prohibited the construction of any water development projects on the Atbara River, a tributary of the Nile originating from the Ethiopian highlands. On 15 May 1902, Menlik II of Ethiopia and Britain (for Sudan and Egypt) signed an agreement not to construct or allow any works to be constructed across the Blue Nile, Lake Tana or Sobat, which might obstruct the flow of the Nile. However, this was the only treaty between Ethiopia with the downstream riparian countries, which had addressed the management of the Nile. On 9 May 1906, Britain signed a similar agreement with the Independent State of the Congo in preventing any construction that would diminish the flow of the White Nile water reaching Sudan. The agreement among France, Italy and Britain on 13 December 1906 and the follow-up agreement between Italy and Britain in December 1925 also protected the Nile River from any upstream diversion.[59] Due to fluid political control of the colonial powers in the region and Britain's 'dual-flag' policy of establishing Anglo-Egyptian Condominium on Sudanese affairs, the legality of these agreements became complicated. However, all of these agreements were considered to have collapsed after the independence of the Nile basin countries from colonial rule.

The first Aswan Dam was built in 1889. Till then, the Nile was flowing freely through Sudan and Egypt. The dam was able to store some floodwater for agricultural use in Egypt. After achieving its independence in 1922, Egypt constructed the first Big Aswan Dam in 1928. Its increased storage capacity improved the flood situation and expanded the irrigation facilities. After the construction of this dam, the Egyptians became apprehensive about the possible exploitation of the upstream water resource.[60] Britain's projects to increase cotton production in Sudan brought anxiety to the Egyptians. The Nile water was being used by the British administration in Sudan as a carrot and stick *vis-à-vis* Egyptian nationalism.[61] On 7 May 1929, Egypt and the British government (on behalf of Sudan and the riparian countries of Lake Victoria) came to an agreement over sharing of the Nile water. The 1929 Nile Agreement came at a difficult time when there was a revolt of the Egyptian Army and Sudanese defence forces against the British domination in Sudan.

The 1929 Agreement differed from the earlier agreements as it specifically and exclusively dealt with the Nile River water-sharing issues. However, this arrangement excluded Ethiopia, which provides most of the water. According to the 1929 Agreement, Sudan got the rights over only 4 billion cubic metres of water per year while Egypt was allocated 48 billion cubic metres and the entire timely flow (from 20 January to 15 July). The Agreement stipulated that the East African countries were not to construct any water development schemes in the Equatorial Lakes without consulting Egypt and Sudan. Egypt thus enjoyed the overwhelming rights as against Sudan in the utilization of the Nile water. Egypt's claim to the entire timely flow limited Sudan to grow cotton only in winter months. The Agreement did not have any specific time period as Egypt was uncertain about the political future of Sudan. Egyptian nationalists were opposing the Anglo-Egyptian Condominium over Sudan, while demanding the unity of Sudan with Egypt.

Following revolution in Egypt in 1952, the new government started planning for the Aswan High Dam. This provoked the local administration in Sudan to demand renegotiations of the water agreement with Egypt. According to the Anglo-Egyptian Agreement of 1953, the Sudanese were given a chance to decide their future. They overwhelmingly rejected unity with Egypt and chose independence, and in 1956 the Republic of Sudan was born. Immediately after, Sudanese first Prime Minister Ismail al-Azhari demanded the revision of the 1929 Agreement. It came at a time when President Nasser of Egypt was planning to build a massive dam at Aswan. The period 1956–58 witnessed a bitter dispute between Sudan and Egypt over sharing of the Nile. Coinciding with Sudanese opposition to the Aswan High Dam, Egypt refused to provide assistance to Sudan in building the Roseires Dam on the Blue Nile, though it was agreed in the earlier agreement. The bilateral relations deteriorated further when Sudan unilaterally withdrew from the 1929 Agreement. In this tense period, the Egyptian Army started its consolidation in the border areas as a show of force.[62]

A new regime came to power in Sudan after a military coup in 1958. The military ruler, General Ibrahim Abbud, began to cooperate with Egypt and that led to the signing of a new agreement in 1959 between the two countries over the sharing of the Nile River water. From the newly calculated average annual discharge of 84 billion cubic metres of water at Aswan, Egypt received 55.5 billion cubic metres, 18.5 billion of which was allocated to Sudan. The remaining 10 billion cubic metres were reserved for mean annual evaporation and seepage losses from Lake Nasser behind the Aswan High Dam. The Agreement also included some provisions in regulating the filling of the storage created by the Aswan Dam. Since Sudan was unable to use the increased share of water at the time, the 1959 Treaty had a provision for Sudanese water loan to Egypt of up to 1,500 billion cubic metres every year to 1977. The Treaty removed the controversial restrictions imposed by the 1929 Agreement, prohibiting water withdrawal by Sudan from the Nile during the December to July period.

Egypt paid 15 million Egyptian pounds as compensation to Sudan for the resettlement of the displaced people. Lake Nasser was extended 150 kilometres into Sudanese territory and displaced 50,000 population. Sudan was permitted to build the Roseires Reservoir on the Blue Nile as well as other necessary projects to utilize its own water share. Both countries also expressed their desire to work for developing the water resources lost in the Sudanese swamps on a cost-sharing basis. Moreover, both countries committed that they would not negotiate with any third party over Nile water before they develop a common position. As per this agreement, the two countries signed a Protocol on 17 January 1960 to establish a Permanent Joint Technical Committee to facilitate technical cooperation on the projects.[63]

The High Aswan Dam and Lake Nasser

When Nasser came to power in Egypt after Nagib, he wanted to build the High Aswan Dam, which was originally envisaged by the Greek engineer Daninos in 1948. Nasser hoped that this huge project would provide him with an opportunity to strengthen his support base at home and bring legitimacy to his regime. However, Egypt did not have the economic strength to undertake the project on its own. Meanwhile, the West was becoming critical of Nasser's non-aligned foreign policy, which was considered close to the Soviet camp. Due to Western pressure, the World Bank withdrew from its commitment to finance the High Aswan Dam project. This infuriated Nasser and in retaliation, he nationalized the Suez Canal. Then, Egypt approached the Soviet Union for financial and technical support for the construction of the dam. Soviet leader Khruschev was eager to support the project in order to find an ally in the region. With Soviet assistance, the construction of the High Aswan Dam started in 1960, seven kilometres south of the old Aswan Dam, and it came into operation in 1971.

The High Aswan Dam created one of the largest man-made lake in the world, Lake Nasser, with the carrying capacity of 164 billion cubic metres of water. More than 55 million people are directly dependent upon the High Aswan Dam for their water supply. Without the Aswan, Egypt would undoubtedly have been in serious economic crisis. The water reservoir has brought significant increase in the welfare of the country owing to the supply of reliable and adequate water for irrigation, municipal and industrial use.[64] It is also the major supplier of the electricity in the country, with power generating capacity of 2,100 megawatts. The High Dam at Aswan has helped to prevent the flooding, and at the same time improved the drought situation in the region. Aswan not only saved Egypt from the drought of 1972–73, it also provided water for farming and drinking during a prolonged drought period in the 1980s. However, the dam has caused a series of environmental problems on its location and in the downstream of the river: water-logging, salinization, riverbed erosion, etc. Because of Lake Nasser, only about 2 per cent of the Nile's fresh water flow reaches the sea.[65]

It was not only the environmental concern, but also the Cold War political rivalry that invited a lot of criticism to the construction of the High Aswan Dam.[66] Soviet support to the dam building brought suspicion among the Western powers and also led to their involvement in the regional hydro-politics. Ethiopia criticized the 1959 Agreement, and asked for its legitimate rights to the water originating from its highlands. The United States was keen to gain from this dispute. With the help of the US Bureau of Reclamation, Ethiopia conducted a study to identify power and irrigation projects within its own Nile basin areas. This study was concluded in 1963 and it called for 6 billion cubic metres of water to irrigate lands in the Blue Nile catchment areas. The East African countries of the White Nile catchment areas, who were then under British Administration, also objected to their exclusion from the 1959 Agreement.

The 1959 Agreement between Egypt and Sudan further exacerbated the existing fissure in the Nile riparian relations. However, the relationship between Egypt and Sudan improved after their agreement to share the Nile water. It took a further upward turn in May 1969, when another military coup brought Jafar al-Numayri to power in Sudan. At the end of that year, three socialist republics of the region, Egypt, Sudan and Libya, committed themselves to the 'Tripoli Charter', for greater political, military and economic cooperation.[67] After the death of Nasser, Anwar Sadat of Egypt pursued the Nile policy vigorously with Sudan. His direct military support rescued Numayri's regime twice: in July 1971 and July 1976. In 1974, both Sadat and Numayri signed the 'integration agreement', which revived the agenda of United Nile Valley again. When Egypt drifted towards the West, Sadat saw Sudan as an important ally, because pro-Soviet regimes in Libya, Chad, Somalia and Ethiopia had encircled his country. Even after the Camp David Accord and the Arab Summit in Baghdad, Sudan did not withdraw its support to Egypt.

The Jonglei Canal Project

Since the 1959 Nile Agreement, Egypt had a friendly regime in Sudan until the departure of Sudanese President Numayri in 1985. In return for its support of the Numayri regime, Egypt received several concessions from Sudan. One of them was to execute the Jonglei Canal project in 1976. The Jonglei I Project was designed to reduce the loss of water from the White Nile while it passes through the Sudd swamps in the southern part of Sudan.[68] The 360 kilometres long canal was planned to re-direct part of the flow from the Bor tributary to the Sobat tributary's mouth in order to decrease the river flow to the Sudd and its evaporation. The second stage of the project, Jonglei II, needed the construction of a parallel bypass canal and a reservoir at Murchison Falls in Uganda. These projects, besides decreasing the evaporation from the swamps, could also reduce the flooding areas. The Jonglei I project had the potential to supplement an annual flow of 4.7 billion cubic metres of water, of which Lake Nasser's share was 3.8 billion.

The need for enhancing the supply arose owing to a noticeable decrease in the quantity of water flowing into Lake Nasser as a result of population growth and continuing drought in the upstream areas. With the help of the 1959 Agreement, Egypt wanted to develop the White Nile waters in Sudan and held a claim on the anticipated increased flow of the water.[69] However, the planning and implementation of the Jonglei I project, like the Aswan High Dam, received wide public scrutiny. The water diversion issue became highly politicized within and outside the basin. The seasonally flooded areas of the Bor River are a vital component of the Sudd region, which would have been adversely affected by the Jonglei Canal. The river water fed grasslands provide grazing ground for the animal population in the area.[70] This project would certainly have had a damaging impact on the 40,000 pastorialists living in Sudd swamplands. It was also appreciated that the Jonglei Canal, by reducing the evaporation to the atmosphere could affect the rainfall and climate of the region.[71] The canal was also bound to create communication problems in its area. It was widely believed in the south of Sudan that the Jonglei I scheme was implemented to bring benefits for the people of the northern Sudan and Egypt at their cost.

The construction of the Jonglei I Canal was started in 1978 by a French company. However, after having completed 250 kilometres of the proposed 360 kilometre long canal, the work was forcibly suspended in 1984. A series of attacks on the construction site and kidnapping of a number of project officials, by the southern Sudanese armed opposition – the Sudanese People's Liberation Army (SPLA) – brought this eventuality.[72] With this, the first serious effort to increase the yield of the Nile came to an end. The southern Christian Sudanese population opposed this water transfer project as they considered that 'it was carrying water from their "homes" to the Arab north'.[73] The unfinished Jonglei I Canal has now become a terrible trench for the human beings and wildlife of the region, which is already ravaged by a long civil war.

Not deterred by the internal opposition, President Numayri maintained friendly relationships with Egypt. After the assassination of Anwar Sadat, Egypt's new President, Hosni Mubarak, also followed the policy of his predecessor in keeping good relations with Sudan in general and with Numayri in particular. In spite of Numayri's late conversion to the Islamic path in 1983, Egypt maintained cordial relations with him, and offered asylum after he was removed from office in 1985. The post-Numayri administrations in Sudan have also failed to bring peace in the southern part of Sudan. In spite of recent peace talks, there is very little immediate hope for the operation of Jonglei Canal and the augmentation of the Nile's flow.

The relationship between Sudan and Egypt also deteriorated badly after the take-over of power in Khartoum by the military-Islamic-fundamentalist dictatorship in 1989.[74] Sudan has unilaterally abolished the integration agreement with Egypt, and at the same time is supporting anti-Egypt forces from its land. Sudanese support to Saddam Hussain's regime in the 1991 Gulf War, and its proximity with Islamic fundamentalist regime in Iran have been the source of headache for the Egyptian administration.

Egypt's improved relationship with Israel since the Camp David Accord has also brought further complications to the relations among the Nile riparian countries. In 1981, President Anwar Sadat of Egypt had reportedly offered Israeli Prime Minister Menachem Begin 365 million cubic metres of Nile water per year 'in exchange for the solution to the Palestinian problem and the liberation of Jerusalem'.[75] Ethiopia immediately brought objections to this proposal of water transfer to Israel. Sudan was also opposed to this idea. The Sudanese country paper, presented to the Nile 2002 Conference in 1996 at Kampala, Uganda, clearly states, 'The use of the waters of the Nile and other shared water resources should be exclusive right of the co-riparian countries alone and no transfer should be permitted to any non-riparian country.' Not only the upper riparian states, but the Egyptian nationalists and armed forces are also opposed to this water transfer idea; thus it has not been implemented since then.[76]

Growing Water Scarcity in Egypt and Sudan

John Waterbury predicts a critical water shortfall in Egypt in the near future.[77] With Egypt's population increasing by a million every nine months, the need for water in meeting the basic human needs and growing crops is rising alarmingly.[78] Egypt's water demands have further increased due to greater irrigation works resulting from land reclamation projects. Adding to the country's woe, the evaporation from the surface of the 600 kilometres long Nasser Lake apparently exceeds the earlier calculations. Egypt is heavily dependent on imported food; nearly 50 per cent of the food comes from abroad.[79] To achieve food security in the face of rapid population increase, Egypt needs an increasing supply of water from the Nile.

Egypt is almost completely dependent on the waters of the Nile. The river provides more than 95 per cent of the total water used in Egypt each year.[80] The rest Egypt supplements with small amounts of groundwater, agricultural drainage water and treated municipal water.[81] However, there is very little reliable data on Egypt's water availability. With World Bank's support, Egypt has conducted a comprehensive survey of the country's available water resources, but keeps the information secret. There has also been a lot of independent research, which clearly projects that intense water scarcity is going to trouble Egypt in the coming years.

Sudan is Africa's largest country. Its 26.5 million population is growing at an annual rate of 2.8 per cent. The northern part of the country receives very scanty rainfall, thus it depends almost completely on irrigation for agricultural activities. After the 1959 Agreement, some dams and storages have been built in Sudan to control the Nile water. The important ones are Roseires Dam and Sennar Dam on the Blue Nile, and Kashm el Girba Dam on the Atbara River. Moreover, Sudan is at present planning to build a number of new dams on the Nile system. Because of rapid population growth, Sudan is in need of more water to meet the demands of its food production. The increased desertification and land degradation have multiplied the country's water problem.[82] In the late 1980s, there was some speculation about Sudan's future plans to introduce a new irrigation system, which might raise demand by as much as 10 billion cubic metres yearly.[83] However, in the mid-1990s, Sudan expressed her future water requirements needs officially. Sudan claims that it has virtually consumed all of its share from the Nile water. The potential demand of the country from the Nile water is estimated at 32 billion cubic metres by the year 2025 for food security and other essential uses. Thus Sudan has planned to construct Upper Atbara Dam and has also started implementing the Merowe Dam and heightening of the Roseires Dam.

In the early 1990s, Sudan asked for the revision of the 1959 Agreement in order to increase the country's share, which was strongly opposed by Egypt. Sudan's alleged hand in the unsuccessful attempt on the life of the Egyptian President Mubarak at Addis Ababa in June 1995 brought further deterioration to the bilateral relationship. In this charged atmosphere, Sudan threatened to stop the water to Egypt by re-directing the Nile's flow. This caused alarm in Egypt and led to hectic official deliberations in Cairo. President Mubarak responded with an aggressive warning, 'Those who play with fire in Khartoum ... will push us to confrontation and to defend our rights and lives.'[84] Egypt has always used the threat of war to stop the water development plans of the Nile upstream countries.

Egypt regularly pronounces its historic right to exploit the waters of the Nile, which goes back 5,500 years. Egypt argues that the other Nile riparian countries have alternative sources of water supply while her survival completely depends upon the Nile water. Egypt is extremely sensitive about the water diversion upstream of the river. The Nile River has remained the focus of Egyptian regional foreign policy. But, the question increasingly being posed is whether Egypt can afford to continue using large quantities of water for agriculture when the need of other countries upstream are growing. Ethiopia now plans to harness the waters of the Blue Nile, and Kenya and Uganda wish to develop the water resources of Lake Victoria.

While Egypt is seriously averse to the idea of any agricultural water diversion in the upstream, it encourages the exploitation of the hydropower potentials in the Nile system. The dams, which came up in Sudan after the 1959 Agreement, have been advantageous for Egypt to a large extent. The Sudanese dams have acted as 'siltation basins', stopping most of the sediment load before reaching Lake Nasser. The reservoir of the Kashm el Girba Dam is already covered by its 40 per cent sediments, while the Roseires reservoir bed is filled by almost 60 per cent. Though the blockage of sediments in Sudan has resulted in the riverbed erosion in Egypt, it has reduced the threat to High Dam at Aswan. So, Egypt shows interest in hydropower development in the upstream, particularly in Sudan. Moreover, Egypt is keen on the opera-tion of the Jonglei Canal Project which will supplement the flow of the Nile. However, unless the peace process succeeds in southern Sudan, there is not much hope for the completion of the project in the near future. Moreover, the growing mutual suspicion between Khartoum and Cairo reduces the possibility of any other joint effort towards devel-oping water resources between the two neighbours.

The Ethiopian Factor

Ethiopia is often referred to as the 'great unknown' of the region. Ethiopia contributes nearly 86 per cent of the Nile flow, which rises to 95 per cent during the flood period. This massive upstream discharge undoubtedly confers a very important position to Ethiopia on the sharing of the Nile water. Moreover, the country is not bound by any agreement with Egypt and Sudan over the sharing of the river. Though Sudan refers to the existence of the 1902 Agreement between the Emperor of Ethiopia and the British government on behalf of Sudan with respect to Blue Nile, the Sobat and Lake Tana, Ethiopia refuses to accept its legitimacy, and has conducted several studies of its own to develop the water resources.

While most of the colonies of Black Africa were achieving independence, Ethiopia remained Africa's 'Hidden Empire' under Haile Selassie. The emperor's only concern was to maintain his power with the help of landed political aristocracy until his fall in 1974. The king did not have the will nor the financial strength to develop the water resources of the country. The Haile Selassie's regime collapsed, mainly due to the impact of the terrible Welo famine of 1972–74. After the fall and presumed execution of the Haile Selassie, Ethiopia became a socialist republic following the Soviet model under the leadership of Colonel Mengistu. During this Marxist regime, there was serious anxiety in Egypt about the possibility of politically motivated dam building. Under the guidance of the Soviet advisors, Ethiopians carried out feasibility studies in the Lake Tana area to develop the water resources. Ethiopia stressed at the 1977 UN Water Conference at Mar del Plata in Argentina that it was 'the sovereign right of any riparian state, in the absence of an international agreement, to proceed unilaterally with the development of water resources within its territory'.[85]

The water issue brought further tension between Egypt and Ethiopia, particularly after the Camp David Agreement.[86] Owing to objections from Ethiopia and its own nationalist forces, Egypt backed out from its 'water for peace' proposal with Israel. However, Ethiopia even objected to the Egyptian's transfer of water to the Sinai New Lands, arguing that water may get transferred to Israel. Since 1978, with the help of Nile water, Egypt is undertaking a massive project to achieve land reclamation of 1.26 million hectares. These New Lands are on the western corner of the Nile Delta, near the Suez Canal, and in the northern Sinai. Northern Sinai has to receive 3 billion cubic metres of Nile water per year via the al-Salam pipeline under the Suez Canal to irrigate 400,000 hectares of New Lands.[87] In 1979, Mengistu criticized the water transfer plan to Sinai and threatened to reduce Blue Nile flows in retaliation.[88] This did not stop Egypt; rather Egyptian President

Sadat responded by warning that: 'If Ethiopia takes any action to block our right to the Nile water, there will be no alternative for us but to use force.'[89]

In 1984, when Ethiopia was facing severe famine, the Mengistu regime drew up an action plan to resettle 1.5 million people in the western province of Welega, along the tributaries of the Nile. The plan had an aim to divert almost 40 per cent of the Blue Nile's water. Due to inadequate planning and lack of economic and organizational capacities, this resettlement plan became a failure.[90] Moreover, the internal civil war and separatist movements in Eritrea and Tigray kept the Mengistu regime occupied for venturing into any large-scale water resource development in the highlands. Like his predecessor Haile Selassie, the fall of Mengistu in 1991 was accelerated by the effects of the severe famine. Before his fall, Mengistu had unsuccessfully tried to obtain the support of Israel, whom he had earlier condemned as a reactionary Zionist state, in order to gain support from the US.[91] He even invited some Israeli engineers to help Ethiopia in developing its water potential.[92] On 7 July 1991, Egypt warned once again that it would consider any Ethiopian water diversions a *casus belli*.[93] The year before, in 1990, Egypt was instrumental in blocking an African Development Bank loan to the Mengistu regime of Ethiopia for a water development project, which could have reduced the flow to the Nile.[94] After the fall of the Mengistu's Marxist regime, Ethiopia is now going through a sort of semi-democratic experiment with a federal structure of administration.

Agriculture is the mainstay of Ethiopian economy. It contributes 40 per cent of the country's GNP, 90 per cent of the export income and provides employment to 85 per cent of the population. Ethiopia's large agricultural population is spread over high rainfall, highland areas. Nearly 88 per cent of the country's population lives in the highlands, which is only 44 per cent of the land area of the country. The highland areas also host 60 per cent of the livestock and account for 90 per cent of the rain-fed agricultural land of the country. In most parts of the highlands of Ethiopia, deforestation has been almost complete. The deforestation induced land and soil degradation have affected the agricultural production of the country. Ethiopia has witnessed two severe famines in the last 25 years, which have also led to the civil unrest and subsequent fall of the regimes. The present regime in Ethiopia is serious about achieving self-sufficiency in food production at any cost. For its own political future, it does not want the re-occurrence of the famines of the 1970s and 1980s.

At present, Ethiopia cultivates only 4 per cent of its potentially irrigable land. There is a growing domestic pressure towards developing water resources to increase the country's agricultural production. Moreover, Ethiopia's conversion to federalism has created new actors on the Nile sharing issue. The provincial administrations on the highlands are asking the centre to develop their water resources. It is projected that by 2025, Ethiopia will have more people to feed than Egypt.[95] With the rapid population growth and increasing food demands, Ethiopia now requires more water for her own use. There was speculation in the late 1980s about Ethiopia's unilateral plan to divert 4 billion cubic metres of the Blue Nile's water for its own irrigation project.[96] But the present government, learning from the past, did not undertake any surprise water diversion schemes. In the second half of the 1990s, after achieving some sort of political and economic stability, Ethiopia came up with concrete plans to expand its agricultural and irrigation capacities.

Ethiopia maintains its sovereign right to develop the water resources within its borders. The same philosophy also guides other basin countries. The major riparian countries of the Nile have been mostly pursuing state centric Nile water development programmes. However, this unilateral development of water-related infrastructure, particularly in Sudan and Egypt, in the absence of upstream-downstream cooperation, is untenable in the long run. The only alternative to meeting the growing water demand in the basin is cooperation. Yet the record of Nile basin cooperation is tentative at best.

Establishing Basin-wide Cooperation

Since the 1960s, there have been some attempts to achieve basin-wide cooperative arrangements among the Nile basin countries, but these were ultimately unsuccessful. In 1967, Egypt, Kenya, Sudan, Tanzania and Uganda launched the Hydromet Project with the assistance of the United Nations Development Program (UNDP) and the World Meteorological Organization (WMO). The purpose of the project was to evaluate the water balance of the Lake Victoria catchment area in order to assist in regulating the water level of the lake as well as the water flow of the Nile. Later, Rwanda and Burundi joined in the effort. This project lasted for 25 years, but did not include Ethiopia. In 1983 Egypt had also initiated a diplomatic initiative to activate a forum for discussion of problems affecting the Nile basin states. This forum was known as *undugu* group; *undugu* is the Swahili word for brotherhood.[97] All the Nile states were members of this organization, but Ethiopia and Kenya had refused to join this club. Through this forum, Egypt was advocating in favour of basin-based cooperation over hydropower generation. These initiatives, particularly due to their failure to include Ethiopia, did not develop as effective basin-wide arrangements.

In 1992, the Hydromet Project came to an end. In the same year, in the month of December, the water resource ministers from Egypt,

Sudan, Rwanda, Tanzania, Uganda and Congo gathered in Kampala and signed an agreement to establish a new outfit, the Technical Committee for the Promotion of the Development and Environmental Protection of the Nile Basin (TECCONILE). The other four riparian states, including Ethiopia, participated as observers. The TECCONILE came into operation on 1 January 1993 with its Secretariat located at Entebbe, Uganda.

A corresponding significant activity in the effort of bringing the basin-wide cooperation was the Nile 2002 Conference series, which was the byproduct of the TECCONILE.[98] In March 1998, the Council of Ministers of Water Affairs of the Nile Basin States reached a broad agreement at Arusha, Tanzania, over sharing and managing the Nile water, and endorsed a new programme of action. This led to the formal launching of the Nile Basin Initiative (NBI) in February 1999, of which all but Eritrea are members. In September 1999, NBI Secretariat, which supersedes the disbanded TECCONILE, was officially opened in Entebbe, Uganda. The NBI is based on a transitional arrangement until the member countries reach a permanent legal and institutional framework for sustainable development of the Nile basin.

The Nile Basin Initiative consists of a Council of Ministers of Water Affairs of the Nile Basin (Nile-COM), a Technical Advisory Committee (Nile-TAC) and the Secretariat (Nile-SEC). The NBI has formulated a shared vision 'to achieve sustainable socioeconomic development through the equitable utilization of, and benefit from, the common Nile Basin Water Resources', which includes seven co-ordinated projects.[99] In order to translate the shared vision into reality, two Subsidiary Action Programmes are being prepared: the Eastern Nile (EN-SAP) consisting of Egypt, Sudan and Ethiopia, and the Nile Equatorial Lakes Region (NEL-SAP) consisting of all the riparian countries except Ethiopia and Eritrea. Joint development of Nile waters needs huge financial resources. The World Bank is co-ordinating an International Consortium for Cooperation on the Nile (ICCON), which intends to aid transparent financing for cooperative water resources development and management in the basin. On 26 June 2001, ICCON was formally initiated at Geneva, where the donors pledged to contribute an initial amount of 140 million US dollars and expressed strong support to finance the first phase of the investment programme, which is expected to reach 3 billion US dollars.

The current President of the World Bank, James Wolfensohn, has taken personal interest in the Nile Basin Initiative. He contends that basin-wide cooperation will help reduce the poverty and conflicts in the region.[100] Owing to World Bank pressure, Egypt has brought some sort of a shift in its foreign policy over the Nile water issue. Egypt's economy is in a precarious state and the problem became more severe after the

World Bank reduced its lending to the country, from 550 million US dollars in 1990 to approximately 50 million US dollars in 2000. This strong economic pressure has practically forced Egypt into expressing its willingness to cooperate and relinquish its long-standing policy of defending its disproportionate consumption of Nile waters based on the principle of 'acquired rights'. For the first time in history, all the Nile riparian countries have expressed their willingness and commitment for a joint initiative. However, expressing concern over common fresh water resources and taking concrete steps are two different things. Though Egypt is committing itself to basin-wide cooperation within the NBI, at the same time it continues to develop massive new water projects unilaterally within its borders. Moreover, Egypt has not taken any particular measure to reduce its dependence on the Nile water. On the contrary, Egypt's demand for the Nile water is increasing considerably.

Starting from the Sub-Basin

Basin-wide development of irrigation, hydropower, water diversion or flood control projects can provide riparian countries greater net benefits than what they could have achieved through purely state-centric, unilateral development. The developing of the full economic potential of a river occurs most optimally at the basin-wide level in which the whole river basin is regarded as one economic, ecological and political unit, irrespective of state boundaries. Under an integrated programme of river development, water projects are located at optimum locations and the benefits of these projects are allocated taking into account the needs of riparian countries as well as the needs of those who have made sacrifices to implement the projects.[101]

However, a flexible approach should be taken when considering the extent to which all states within the entire hydrological catchment area of a river should be viewed as part of the same basin for the purposes of water development projects. The intention here is not to question the usefulness of a comprehensive basin-based approach; in some cases, however, a good starting point may be to look at the sub-basin level. Dagne, Mulugeta and Kaihara provide strong arguments in favour of introducing a sub-basin arrangement in the Nile basin. Such arrangements can lay a firm foundation for future basin-wide cooperation.[102] The ongoing institutional arrangement governing the management of the Mekong River is relevant for the Nile basin. The Lower Mekong Basin Initiative comprises only four out of the six riparian countries of the Mekong River – Thailand, Cambodia, Laos and Vietnam – and does not include two upper riparian countries – China and Burma. Although the Mekong headwaters originate in China, supplying most of the annual flow of the river, China has few incentives to seek regional cooperation. The lack of interest from the Chinese side in basin-wide cooperative management of the river is quite evident. China, being in the upstream, expects to exploit the Mekong water without any interference from the other riparian countries. Burma has also shown little interest in cooperating with its neighbours, mostly because of the limited catchment area within its borders and most of the catchment areas are under rebel control.[103] Nevertheless, the Lower Mekong basin countries reached an agreement in 1995 without these two upstream parties and have formed the Mekong River Commission, in which Burma and China participate only as observers. The lessons from the Mekong basin are quite indicative: unless they are interested in developing the hydrological potential of common water resources, countries have little incentive to participate in joint river basin initiatives.

The Nile basin would probably benefit from a similar initiative. Joint water management of the Nile should focus on the most important sub-basin, namely the lower basin comprising Egypt, Sudan and Ethiopia. The importance of the Nile water is not the same for all ten basin countries. Because their share of water resources is minimal, some riparian countries are less interested in cooperating on Nile water allocation and are therefore less committed towards basin-wide initiatives. In fact, only two states, Egypt and Sudan, currently account for most of the water abstraction from the Nile, and only the lower basin riparians – except, perhaps, for Eritrea – actively strive to retrieve yet larger shares of Nile waters. The remaining riparian states are dependent primarily on Lake Victoria as a source of fresh water. For them, the issue is how to manage the lake, which is threatened by depletion and pollution. As a result, these countries contribute a relatively small share to the Nile flow and their dependence on the river for fresh water is not as significant. Thus, any basin-wide initiative faces the problem of co-opting a large number of uninterested parties. Moreover, as long as the civil war continues in Sudan, any collaboration between the riparian countries in the Great Lakes region and those in the lower basin will be extremely difficult. Even if the countries in the Great Lakes region agree to cooperate, the situation in Sudan may impede any efforts to increase the water supply flowing downstream to Egypt. Moreover, the potential for additional flow from the Great Lakes area is not that significant.

Just and Netanyahu have found out that, 'the grand coalitions often envisioned by international agencies and championed by environmental interests may not be optimal arrangements'.[104] In the Nile basin, pragmatic consideration favours sub-basin cooperative management rather than the ambitious basin-based institutional arrangement. Moreover, any move to achieve basin-wide cooperation in the Nile basin will not be successful without finding a formula for the active and successful cooperation among Egypt, Sudan and Ethiopia. International support and assistance should therefore be directed towards water management issues in this core area. A comprehensive approach to manage the Nile water at the basin level can be taken as the next step, only after achieving effective and institutionalized riparian cooperation at the lower basin level.

The conflict of interest in the lower basin, particularly between Ethiopia and Egypt, if not addressed properly and urgently, will remain a major obstacle for achieving a negotiated settlement at the basin-wide level. Besides Nile water, there are other areas of conflicting national interest between Egypt and Ethiopia. These conflicts include Egypt's desire of converting the Red Sea into an Arab Lake; the status of the Copts in Egypt, which has always been of utmost concern to Ethiopia; and the conflict of entitlement to the Covenant of Dayr-es-Sultan in Jerusalem.[105] However, since the Blue Nile is the major source of fresh water for Egypt and equally crucial to Ethiopia's development, the emphasis of the international agencies in general and the World Bank in particular should focus on addressing the areas of conflict in the lower basin to build up cooperation from the sub-basin level.

The dispute between Egypt and Ethiopia is primarily based on conflicting visions and interpretations. Egypt emphasizes its historic rights on most of the Nile water, while Ethiopia asks for a more equitable water allocation between both countries. Given the increasing concern about water scarcity, efforts should be directed at increasing supply and decreasing demand. Since the conflict in Sudan prohibits any augmentation of water supply to reach the mainstream from the White Nile, the only option is to develop a water management scheme for the Blue Nile. Ethiopian highlands and Lake Tana can provide better water storage facilities than the present one at Lake Nasser, by decreasing the rate of seepage and evaporation.[106] As J. A. Allan estimates, after taking into account the evaporation and seepage at Lake Nasser, the Ethiopian storage facilities could increase water availability for Egypt by as much as 15 billion cubic metres per year.[107] Moreover, by building a series of dams in Ethiopia and Sudan, significant hydropower potential can be tapped, enabling these two countries to efficiently use the underground water as an alternative source of supply. The upstream dams in the Ethiopian highlands could also help prevent silts from entering Lake Nasser. International support should be targeted to promote and leverage these advantages and help build trust among Ethiopia, Sudan and Egypt, encouraging them to enter into a mutually dependent cooperative framework.

In a recently written paper, two World Bank officials have elaborated a series of possible benefits, which the Nile Basin Initiative is explicitly aiming at. These are: protecting the vast Nile ecosystem, bringing economic gains through proper flood and drought management, increasing hydropower generation and agricultural production, and finally, reducing conflicts and promoting regional cooperation.[108] There is nothing wrong with these exalted expectations from the NBI, but the way NBI is progressing, there are some serious questions about its future success. The NBI's present strategy of consensus building has only brought agreement among all the riparian countries on less controversial issues. A number of difficult but important issues have been kept aside. Failure to address core issues raises grave doubt over the success of the NBI in the long run. As an Ethiopian official warns, 'In fact, the failure of NBI would mean more mis-trust and suspicion among the riparian states, frustration on the part of the facilitators, and a full-fledged unilateralism, which would be a recipe for a conflict over the utilization of the Nile waters.'[109]

NOTES

1. This chapter has borrowed liberally from the author's earlier works: A. Swain, 'The Nile River Dispute: Ethiopia, the Sudan, and Egypt', *The Journal of Modern African Studies*, 35, 4 (1997), pp. 675–94; A. Swain, 'A New Challenge: Water Scarcity in the Arab World', *Arab Studies Quarterly*, 20, 1 (1998), pp. 1–11; A. Swain, 'The Nile Basin Initiative: Too Many Cooks, Too Little Broth', *SAIS Review*, 22, 2 (2002), pp. 293–308; A. Swain, 'Managing the Nile River: The Role of Sub-Basin Cooperation', in M. Chatterji, S. Arlosoroff and G. Guha (eds), *Conflict Management of Water Resources* (Aldershot: Ashgate Publisher, 2002), pp. 145–60.
2. See World Bank, *From Scarcity to Security: Averting a Water Crisis in the Middle East and North Africa* (Washington DC: World Bank, 1998).
3. See J. R. Starr, 'Water Wars', *Foreign Policy*, 82 (1991).
4. Egypt heads the list among the externally water dependent countries in this region, whose 97 per cent of total water flow originates outside of its border. It is followed by Syria (79%), Sudan (77%), Iraq (66%), Jordan (36%), Israel (21%). A large part of Israel's water supply comes from the disputed territories. World Resource Institute, *World Resources, 1991–92* (New York: Oxford University Press, 1991).
5. T. Homer-Dixon and V. Percival, *Environmental Scarcity and Violent Conflict: Briefing Book* (The Project on Environment, Population and Security, Association for the Advancement of Science of University College, University of Toronto, 1996).
6. S. Arlosoroff, 'The Water Sector in the Middle-East: Potential Conflict Resolutions', in M. Chatterji, S. Arlosoroff and G. Guha (eds), *Conflict Management of Water Resources* (Aldershot: Ashgate Publishers, 2002), pp. 47–68.
7. M. R. Lowi, 'Bridging the Divide: Transboundary Resource Disputes and the Case of West Bank Water', *International Security*, 18, 1 (1993), pp. 113–38.
8. S. Libiszewski, *Water Disputes in the Jordan Basin Region and their Role in the Resolution of the Arab-Israeli conflict* (Zurich: Centre for Security Studies and Conflict Research Occasional Paper No. 13, 1995).
9. M. Sherman, 'The Hydro-Political Implications of the Oslo Agreements: An Israeli Perspective', in M. Chatterji, S. Arlosoroff and G. Guha (eds), *Conflict Management of Water Resources* (Aldershot: Ashgate Publishers, 2002), pp. 69–85.
10. *Ha'aretz*, 21 December 1995.

11. K. Kelly and T. Homer-Dixon, *Environmental Scarcity and Violent Conflict: The Case of Gaza* (Toronto: AAAS and University of Toronto, the Project on Environment, Population and Security, 1995).

12. Saudi Arabia has the world's largest number of desalination plants. J. Bulloch and A. Darwish, *Water Wars: Coming Conflicts in the Middle East* (London: Victor Gollancz, 1993), p. 143.

13. M. J. Haddadin, 'Water Issues in the Middle East Challenges and Opportunities', *Water Policy*, 4 (2002), pp. 205–22.

14. A. T. Wolf, *Hydropolitics Along the Jordan River: Scarce Water and its Impact on the Arab-Israeli Conflict* (Tokyo: UNU Press, 1995).

15. N. S. Copaken, 'The Perception of Water as part of Territory in Israeli and Arab Ideologies between 1964 and 1993: Toward a Further Understanding of the Arab-Jewish Conflict' (University of Haifa, Working Paper No. 8, May 1996).

16. Wolf, *Hydropolitics along the Jordan River*, p. 43.

17. E. Feitelson, 'The Ebb and Flow of Arab-Israeli Water Conflicts: Are Past Confrontations likely to Resurface?', *Water Policy*, 2 (2000), pp. 343–63.

18. Israel and Syria reached a compromise, which allowed Israel to continue draining the Huleh only on the western bank of the Jordan River.

19. Israel was forced to shift the diversion point to an alternative site. From this new site at the Kinneret, Israel had to pump up the water from 212 metres below sea level.

20. M. Lowi, 'Rivers of Conflict, Rivers of Peace', *Journal of International Affairs*, 49 (1995), pp. 123–44.

21. S. S. Elmusa, *Negotiating Water: Israel and the Palestinians* (Washington DC: Institute for Palestine Studies, 1996).

22. M. Klein, 'Water Balance of the Upper Jordan River Basin', *Water International*, 23 (1998), pp. 244–48.

23. D. F. Shmueli and U. Shamir, 'Application of International Law of Water Quality to Recent Middle East Water Agreements', *Water Policy*, 3 (2001), pp. 405–23.

24. A good rainfall in 1992 also facilitated the change of this environmentally unsustainable policy.

25. J. A. Allan, 'Hydro-Peace in the Middle East: Why no Water Wars? A Case Study of the Jordan River Basin', *SAIS Review*, 22, 2 (2002), p. 264.

26. Tigris also receives 10 per cent of its flow from the tributaries, which originate in Iran.

27. See S. Kirmani and R. Rangeley, *International Inland Waters: Concept for a More Active World Bank Role* (Washington DC: World Bank Technical Paper No. 239, 1994).

28. J. S. Starr, *Covenant over Middle Eastern Waters: Key to World Survival* (New York: Henry Holt, 1995), p. 128.

29. M. E. Moris, 'Water and Conflict in the Middle East: Threat and Opportunities', *Studies in Conflict and Terrorism*, 20, 1 (1997).

30. S. N. Saliba, *The Jordan River Dispute* (The Hague: Martin Nijhoff, 1968), p. 59.

31. Moris, 'Water and Conflict in the Middle East: Threat and Opportunities'.

32. P. H. Gleick, 'Water, War, and Peace in the Middle East', *Environment*, 36, 3 (1994), pp. 6–42.

33. S. Guner, 'The Turkish-Syrian War of Attrition', *Studies in Conflict & Terrorism*, 20, 1 (1997).

34. P. Schweizer, 'The Spigot Strategy', *New York Times*, 11 November 1990.

35. *Boston Globe*, 26 July 1992.

36. J. Kolars, 'Problems of International River Management: The Case of the Euphrates', in A. K. Biswas, (ed.) *International Waters of the Middle East: From Euphrates-Tigris to Nile* (Bombay: Oxford University Press, 1994), pp. 44–94.

37. J. Kolars and W. A. Mitchell, *The Euphrates River and the Southeast Anatolia Development Project* (Carbondale: Southern Illinois University Press, 1991).
38. One of the major irrigation infrastructure of the GAP is the Sanliurfa Tunnel. This longest tunnel in the world is carrying irrigation water from the Ataturk Dam Reservoir to the Sanliurfa-Harran Plain.
39. GAP is already providing more than half of Turkey's total hydropower. The hydropower generated by the Karakaya and Ataturk Dams had reached 145.6 billion kilowatts per hour by the end of 1998.
40. In the second half of the 1990s, Turkey transformed the GAP into an integrated development project along the lines of United Nations Development Programme. This strategy has achieved limited success in securing some international funding. M. Yetim, 'Governing International Common Pool Resources: The International Water Courses of the Middle East', *Water Policy*, 4 (2002), pp. 305–21.
41. N. Beschorner, 'Water and Instability in the Middle East', *Adelphi Papers*, 273 (1992/93).
42. Kolars, 'Problems of International River Management: The Case of the Euphrates', p. 84.
43. Starr, *Covenant over Middle Eastern Waters: Key to World Survival*, p. 127.
44. Ö. Bilen, 'Prospects for Technical Cooperation in the Euphrates-Tigris Basin', in A. K. Biswas (ed.), *International Waters of the Middle East: From Euphrates-Tigris to Nile* (Bombay: Oxford University Press, 1994), pp. 95–116.
45. S. Guner, 'Water Alliances in the Euphrates-Tigris Basin' (Paper presented at the NATO Advanced Research Workshop, 9–12 October, 1997, Budapest, Hungary).
46. S. Bölükbasi, 'Turkey Challenges Iraq and Syria: The Euphrates Dispute', *Journal of South Asian and Middle Eastern Studies*, 16, 4 (1993), pp. 9–32.
47. Iraq asks for 700 cumecs of water from the Euphrates River on the basis of its historical claim. S. C. McCaffrey, 'Water, Politics, and International Law', in P. H. Gleick (ed.), *Water in Crisis: A Guide to World's Fresh Water Resources* (New York: Oxford University Press, 1993), pp. 92–104.
48. Beschorner, 'Water and Instability in the Middle East', p. 27.
49. P. J. Vesilind, 'Middle East Water: Critical Resource', *National Geographic*, 183, 5 (1993), pp. 38–60.
50. A. Nachmani, 'Water Jitters in the Middle East', *Studies in Conflict & Terrorism*, 20, 1 (1997), pp. 67–93.
51. T. F. Homer-Dixon, 'Environmental Scarcities and Violent Conflict: Evidence from Cases', *International Security*, 19, 1 (1994), pp. 5–40.
52. R. Clarke, *Water: The International Crisis* (London: Earthscan, 1991); P. H. Gleick, 'Water and Conflict', *International Security*, 18, 1 (1993), pp. 79–112; A. Swain, 'Water Scarcity: A Threat to Global Security', *Environment & Security*, 1, 1 (1996), pp. 156–72.
53. Swain, 'The Nile River Dispute: Ethiopia, the Sudan, and Egypt'.
54. M. N. Ezzat, M. A. Mohamadien and B. B. Attia, Arab Republic of Egypt's Country Paper, 'Integrated Approach to Water Resources Development', *The Nile 2002 Conference*, Kampala, Uganda, February 1996.
55. The Nile also brought Meroe and Auxum civilizations in its upper and middle reaches.
56. Y. L. Mageed, 'The Nile Basin: Lessons from the Past', in A. K. Biswas (ed.), *International Waters of the Middle East: From Euphrates-Tigris to Nile* (Bombay: Oxford University Press, 1994), p. 156.
57. H. Adhana, 'The Roots of Organised Internal Armed Conflicts in Ethiopia, 1960–1991', in T. Trevdt (ed.), *Conflict in the Horn of Africa: Human and Ecological Consequence of Warfare* (Uppsala: EPOS, 1993), pp. 27–45.

58. McCaffrey, 'Water, Politics, and International Law'.
59. C. O. Okidi, 'History of the Nile and Lake Victoria Basins through Treaties', in P. P. Howell and J. A. Allan (eds), *The Nile: Resources Evaluation, Resource Management and Hydropolicies and Legal Issues* (London: School of Oriental and African Studies, University of London and the Royal Geographical Society, 1990), pp. 193–224.
60. S. Christiansen, 'Shared Benefits, Shared Problems', in S. Lodgaard and A. H. af Ornäs (eds), *The Environment and International Security* (Oslo: PRIO Report No. 3, 1992).
61. N. A. L. Mohammed, 'Environmental Conflicts in Africa', Paper presented at the NATO Advanced Research Workshop on Conflict and the Environment, at Bolkesjø, Norway, 12–16 June 1996.
62. G. R. Warburg, 'The Nile in Egyptian-Sudanese Relations', *Orient*, 32, 4 (1991).
63. C. O. Okidi, 'Legal and Policy Considerations for Regional Cooperation on Lake Victoria and Nile River', *The Nile 2002 Conference*, Kampala, Uganda, February 1996.
64. S. E. Smith, 'General Impact of Aswan High Dam', *Journal of Water Resources Planning and Management*, 112, 4 (1986), pp. 551–62.
65. S. Postel, 'Dividing the Waters: Food Security, Ecosystem Health, and the New Politics of Scarcity', *Worldwatch Paper*, 132 (1996).
66. A. K. Biswas, 'Sustainable Water Development from the Perspective of the South: Issues and Constraints', in M. A. Abu-Zeid and A. K. Biswas (eds), *River Basin Planning and Management* (Calcutta: Oxford University Press, 1996), pp. 87–100.
67. G. R. Warburg, *Egypt and the Sudan: Studies in History and Politics* (London: Frank Cass, 1985).
68. R. O. Collins, *The Waters of the Nile: Hydropolitics of the Jonglei Canal, 1900–1988* (Oxford: Clarendon Press, 1990).
69. A. Dinar and A. Wolf, 'International Markets for Water and the Potential for Regional Cooperation: Economic and Political Perspectives in the Western Middle East', *Economic Development and Cultural Change*, 43, 1 (1994), p. 58.
70. P. P. Howell, J. M. Lock and S. M. Cobb, (eds), *The Jonglei Canal: Impact and Opportunity* (Cambridge: Cambridge University Press, 1988).
71. J. V. Sutcliffe and Y. P. Parks, 'Environmental Aspects of the Jonglei Canal', in M. A. Abu-Zeid and A. K. Biswas (eds), *River Basin Planning and Management* (Calcutta: Oxford University Press, 1996), pp. 126–50.
72. M. Suliman, *Civil War in Sudan: The Impact of Ecological Degradation* (Zürich & Bern: Environment and Conflict Project Occasional Paper No. 4, 1992), p. 21.
73. C. L. Kukk and D. A. Deese, 'At the Water's Edge: Regional Conflict and Cooperation over Fresh Water', *UCLA Journal of International Law & Foreign Affairs*, 21 (1996), p. 45.
74. Warburg, 'The Nile in Egyptian-Sudanese Relations', p. 572.
75. R. Krishna, 'The Legal Regime of the Nile River Basin', in J. Starr and D. C. Stoll (eds), *The Politics of Scarcity: Water in the Middle East* (Boulder, CO: Westview Press, 1988), pp. 23–41.
76. Bulloch and Darwish, *Water Wars: Coming Conflicts in the Middle East*, pp. 80–5.
77. J. Waterbury, *Hydropolitics of the Nile Valley* (Syracuse: Syracuse University Press, 1979); and J. Waterbury, *Riverains and Lacustrines: Toward International Cooperation in the Nile Basin* (Princeton University Research Programme in Development Studies, Discussion Paper No. 107, September 1982).
78. S. Postel, 'Where Have All the Rivers Gone?', *World Watch*, 8, 3 (1995), p. 12.
79. N. Sehmi, 'The Enigmatic Nile', *World Meteorological Organization Bulletin*, 45, 3 (1996).

80. M. A. Abu Zeid, 'The River Nile and Its Contribution to the Mediterranean Environment', Paper presented at the Stockholm Water Symposium, 10–14 August 1992, Stockholm, Sweden.

81. S. Postel, *Last Oasis: Facing Water Scarcity* (New York: W.W. Norton & Co., 1992), p. 78.

82. S. Lonergan, *Climate Warning, Water Resources and Geopolitical Conflict: A Study of Nations Dependent on the Nile, Litani and Jordan River System* (Ottawa: Operational Research and Analysis Establishment (ORAE) Extra-Mural Paper No. 55, 1991).

83. P. Beaumont, *Environmental Management and Development in Drylands* (London: Routledge, 1989).

84. Quoted in *Sudan Update,* 15 July 1995.

85. L. Timberlake and J. Tinker, *Environment and Conflict: Links Between Ecological Decay, Environmental Bankruptcy and Political and Military Instability* (London: Earthscan Briefing Document 40, November 1984), p. 65.

86. S. E. Smith and H. M. Al-Rawahy, 'The Blue Nile: Potential for Conflict and Alternatives for Meeting Future Demands', *Water International*, 15, 4 (1990), pp. 217–22.

87. In 1997, Egyptian President Hosni Mubarak inaugurated four large tunnels under the Suez Canal to transfer Nile water into the Sinia Peninsula. The same year, Egypt also started the construction of a pumping station to carry Lake Nasser water into its 'National Project' in the Western Desert. D. R. Ward, *Water Wars: Drought, Flood, Folly, and the Politics of Thirst* (New York: Riverhead Books, 2002), p. 183.

88. Beschorner, 'Water and Instability in the Middle East'.

89. Krishna, 'The Legal Regime of the Nile River Basin'.

90. A. Pankhurst, *Resettlement and Famine in Ethiopia: The Villagers' Experience* (Manchester: Manchester University Press, 1992).

91. K. Abraham, *Ethiopia from Bullets to the Ballot Box: The Bumpy Road to Democracy and the Political Economy of Transition* (Lawrenceville, NJ: The Read Sea Press, Inc., 1994).

92. F. Pearce, 'Africa at a Watershed', *New Scientist*, 23 (1991), pp. 34–41.

93. A. Soffer, *Rivers of Fire: The Conflict over Water in the Middle East* (Lanham: Rowman and Littlefield Publishers, 1999), p. 61.

94. A. Cowell, 'Now, a Little Steam. Later, Maybe a Water War', *New York Times*, 7 February 1990.

95. UNDP, *Human Development Report 1994* (UNDP & Oxford University Press, 1994).

96. Clarke, *Water: The International Crisis.*

97. S. Ahmed, 'Principles and Precedents in International Law Governing the Sharing of Nile Water', in P. P. Howell and J. A. Allan (eds), *The Nile: Sharing a Scarce Resource* (Cambridge: Cambridge University Press, 1994), p. 360.

98. Nile 2002 is the last in a series of ten annual conferences.

99. Information regarding the Nile Basin Initiative can be found in its website address: http://www.nilebasin.org/

100. J. Wolfensohn, 'Rich Nations Can Remove World Poverty as a Source of Conflict', *International Herald Tribune*, 6 October 2001.

101. A. Swain, 'Constructing Water Institutions: Appropriate Management of International River Water', *Cambridge Review of International Affairs* 12, 2 (1999), pp. 214–25.

102. N. Dagne, D. B. Mulugeta and K. Kaihara, 'Towards a Cooperative Use of the Nile: A Legal Perspective', *Cambridge Review of International Affairs* 12, 2 (1999), p. 236.

103. J. Öjendal, *Sharing the Good: Models of Managing Water Resources in the Lower Mekong River Basin* (Gothenburg: Department of Peace and Development Research PhD dissertation, 2000).
104. R. E. Just and S. Netanyahu, 'International Water Resource Conflicts: Experience and Potential', in their (eds), *Conflict and Cooperation on Trans-Boundary Water Resources* (Boston, MA: Kluwer Academic Publishers, 1998), p. 24.
105. D. Kendie, 'Egypt and the Hydro-Politics of the Blue Nile River', *Northeast African Studies* 6, 1 (1999), pp. 141–69.
106. Soffer, *Rivers of Fire: The Conflict over Water in the Middle East*, p. 62.
107. J. A. Allan, 'Nile Basin Water Management Strategies', in P. P. Howell and J. A. Allan (eds), *The Nile: Sharing Scarce Resource* (Cambridge: Cambridge University Press, 1994).
108. C. W. Sadoff and D. Grey, 'Beyond the River: The Benefits of Cooperation on International Rivers', *Water Policy*, 4, 5 (2002), p. 400.
109. S. Lemma, 'Cooperating on the Nile: Not a Zero-sum Game', *United Nations Chronicle*, 3 (2001).

4

Southeast Asia and the Mekong River[1]

The Mekong River is the most important and largest international river of mainland Southeast Asia. Six riparian states – China, Burma,[2] Thailand, Laos, Cambodia and Vietnam – share the resources of this river. The Mekong begins its flow from the mountainous region in Tibet, the Himalayas, then stretches down through Yunnan, southwestern Chinese province. The Mekong River, for a short length, forms the border between Laos and Burma before entering Laos and Thailand. Here, the Mekong itself creates a 900 kilometre long river border separating Laos from Thailand. The river continues its flow into Cambodia. Before draining into the South China Sea, the Mekong splits into a nine-tailed dragon, creating the Mekong delta in Southern Vietnam. The total population of the basin area around the Mekong River is an estimated 66 million people. It has a total length of 4,400 kilometres, which makes it the twelfth longest river and the eighth largest river in the world.[3] It includes an area of 795,000 square kilometres, and annually contributes 475 billion cubic metres of water to the South China Sea.

The part of the river system upstream of the Golden Triangle, where Thailand, Burma and Laos meet, comprises to a large extent mountain ranges and highlands. About 70 per cent of Laos consists of mountains, including its Thai border region where the river runs. The upstream 120 kilometres of the river in Cambodia has numerous rapids. The more even parts of the river are where it runs through the Korat Plateau in Thailand and Laos and the delta area in Vietnam. The Mekong basin has a tropical monsoon climate. In the flooding season, the Mekong experiences a reverse flow, which almost doubles the size of Cambodia's Tonle Saep, the largest fresh water lake of Southeast Asia.

People living in the basin depend on the Mekong and its tributaries for food, water and transport. Its annual flood–drought cycles are essential for the sustainable production of rice and vegetables. The river also supports one of the world's most diverse fisheries. The Upper

Map 3 The Mekong River

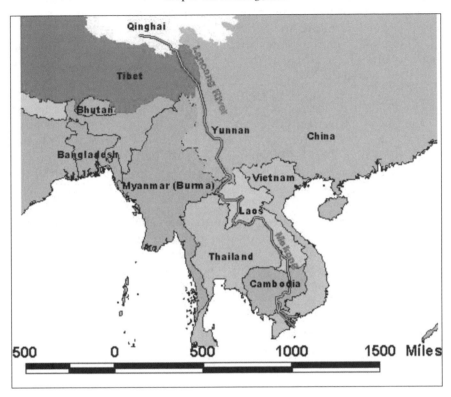

Table 4.1 The Mekong River Basin and the Riparian States

Country	Share of the basin	Share of the basin	Basin's relative size within country's total land mass
	(sq km)	(%)	(%)
China	165,000	21	1.7
Myanmar (Burma)	2,400	3	3.5
Laos	202,400	25	85.3
Thailand	184,000	23	35.9
Cambodia	154,700	20	85.6
Vietnam	65,200	8	20

Source: H. Hori, The Mekong: Environment and Development (Tokyo: The UNU Press, 2000).

117

Mekong basin is fairly unexploited but is gradually gaining importance as a generator of hydropower. In its lower part, the Mekong system is essential for agriculture and fishery.

Though six riparian states share the Mekong, the Lower Mekong basin is often referred to, as the four lower basin countries have long together created the Mekong Committee. This cooperation in the lower basin excludes two upper riparian countries, China and Burma. Only 3 per cent of the basin area is in Burma. However, nearly half the length of the Mekong River runs through China. The basin covers only a small part of China, but represents 21 per cent of the total area of the basin. It is from China that the Mekong receives 18 per cent of its flow. The basin covers 38 per cent of China's Yunnan province. The stretch of the river in Yunnan province is extremely favourable for hydropower development.

Among the six basin states, Laos contributes about 35 per cent of the total flow. More than 85 per cent of the land area of Laos is in the Mekong basin. In Laos, most of the wet-rice cultivation is taking place in the vicinity of the Mekong, which is the most populated part of the country. Similarly, for Cambodia the river is the life-line. Nearly 86 per cent of Cambodia's land area lies within the Mekong basin. The capital of Cambodia is well integrated with the river and the river system provides water for domestic use, irrigation, fisheries and navigation. For Vietnam the river is the main water supplier for rice cultivation. The Mekong delta provides half of the total rice produced in Vietnam and 40 per cent of total agricultural production. More than a third of Thailand, which is a local economic force in the region, falls within the Mekong basin. Thus, in the Lower Mekong basin, the river is essential for the economic development and food security of the countries.

The efforts to harness the Mekong River started in the late 1940s and the 1950s. This period was the time when Southeast Asia politics, like the rest of the world, was influenced by Cold War superpower rivalry. Since 1954, the US has replaced the French influence in the region and become directly involved in Southeast Asian politics. Mekong was seen then as a potential resource to develop the region's economy in both agricultural and industrial spheres.

USES OF THE MEKONG WATER

The countries of the Lower Mekong River are not highly urbanized or developed, particularly the areas around the river. The largest city on the bank of the river is Phnom Penh, with an estimated population of 1 million. Among the countries in the Lower Mekong basin, Thailand is the most developed country, with a GDP (gross domestic product) that is ten times greater than the combined GDP of the other three countries. Laos and Vietnam are gradually liberalizing their centralized economies, and Cambodia is in the midst of a process of democratization. Agriculture is the source and strength of economy of these countries, with an estimated 75 per cent of the population dependent on it in some form for their income and survival. Water intensive rice is by far the most important crop in the region.[4] Over 90 per cent of the agricultural land of the delta is utilized for rice. Mekong delta rice significantly contributes to the national economy and also forms the bulk of the rice export.[5] The competition for productive land, combined with an increase in population growth in the basin leads to unsustainable land use, such as an increase in the use of pesticides and fertilizer. During the 1970s and 1980s, intensive rice cultivation spread rapidly throughout the delta. The total area of irrigated rice within the delta has nearly quadrupled between 1975 and 1995 to 1.1 million hectares.[6] The agricultural pollution is adversely affecting the fishery sector, which is extremely important in economic terms, especially in the Tonle Saep Lake and the delta area.[7]

Building Big Dams

Mekong as a source of hydropower has received a tremendous amount of attention from its riparian countries. However, very low amounts of this hydropower potential have so far been tapped. The Mekong River and its tributaries have a potential hydropower generating capacity of 30,000–58,000 megawatts, out of which the potential of the Lower Mekong basin outside the main river is estimated at about 17,000 megawatts. Eleven hydropower dam projects have been constructed in the lower basin totalling some 1,600 megawatts, which is only 9 per cent of the potential.[8] The projected demand for electricity within the Lower Mekong basin is much less compared to the potential. Thailand, and to some extent Vietnam, together account for 98 per cent of the demand in the region. This can be attributed to the low level of industrialization in Laos and Cambodia, a situation that is expected to change as these countries continue to liberalize their economies and increasingly industrialize. The demand for energy is also likely to increase much more in Vietnam, as its economy continues to develop.

In terms of supplying hydropower, Laos has the most potential, with an estimated country-wide capacity to generate around 18,000 megawatts of hydropower. There is at present only one hydropower facility in Laos, on the Nam Ngum, generating 150 megawatts. Laos currently exports around 80 per cent of its 220 megawatts of hydropower to Thailand. It has also signed agreements with Thailand to export another 3,000 megawatts, and with Vietnam to export 1,500 megawatts, of electricity by 2009.[9] Laos and Cambodia have large hydropower potential and its development is in the interests of both Thailand and Vietnam as a source of cheap energy. However, what complicates the matter is the complex ecological balance in the Mekong, and the uncertainty over the effects that the building of dams and other projects will have on the nature of the Mekong system.

The notion of building big dams in the basin is not a recent development. In the 1950s building big dams was very much in fashion in the developed world. A team of American engineers, headed by Raymond Wheeler, a retired general of the US Army Corps of Engineers, was assigned with the task of measuring the Mekong River potential. The Wheeler Mission, taking large dams as the model, recommended the construction of ten multi-purpose dams to generate hydroelectricity, flood control, irrigation, improved navigation and also to promote tourism. These recommendations were adopted as key to cooperation and development in the region and led to the formation of the Mekong Committee.

The history of the Mekong Committee was the history of planning for the large-scale projects. In 1957, the four countries in the Lower Mekong, Thailand, Laos, Cambodia and Vietnam (South) formed the Committee for the Coordination of Investigations of the Lower Mekong basin, better known as the Mekong Committee, in an aim to collaborate in the development of hydro-projects. A Secretariat was founded in Bangkok under the auspices of the UN. In the Mekong Committee, each member country had the right to veto others' plans. Besides the Economic Commission for Asia and the Far East (ECAFE), the US government was the other initiator of this cooperation as it viewed the cooperation among the then non-communist countries as a way of preserving its interest in the region. The four Lower Mekong riparian countries were positive about this cooperative effort as three of them were newly independent states,[10] and Thailand was an underdeveloped country in need of assistance. The member countries of the Committee hoped to address their economic and political problems through better water management in terms of irrigation, hydropower generation and flood control.[11]

However, the Indochina War in the late 1960s and early 1970s made implementation of the proposed hydro-projects impossible. Only a few small hydro-projects could be put in place. In 1970, the Mekong Committee came up with a long-term programme known as the Indicative Basin Plan. This plan contained provisions for the creation of a number of dams in the basin, with the goal of providing energy as well as irrigation in the region. The Plan, within both its short-term as well as long-term goals, contained potential for 17 mainstream and 87 tributary hydro-projects. The Indicative Basin Plan viewed the basin as a single integrated unit, with the idea that a comprehensive approach for the use of the Mekong would increase the benefits among all the riparian states. The focus was therefore on utilizing and managing the basin in a way that would maximize the benefits for all the riparian countries. The political crisis and instability in the 1970s brought a halt to the activities of the Mekong Committee. Following the unification of Vietnam and the victory of Khmer Rouge in Cambodia, an 'Interim Mekong Committee' was formed in 1978 by Thailand, Laos and Vietnam. However, the Khmer Rouge regime of Cambodia refused to participate in this arrangement.[12] The non-participation of Cambodia reduced the possibility for the Interim Mekong Committee to take up large hydro-projects in a cooperative way. Thus, the Interim Mekong Committee only aimed at protecting the rights of all the lower riparian countries to use the Mekong water.[13]

In 1988, the Indicative Basin Plan was revised, as subsequent events in the region had made its recommendations and planned projects untenable, and a follow-up study was presented. The new document, entitled 'Perspectives for Mekong Development', in short, stated that the Pa Mong Dam would be completed by the year 2000, as would the Nam Theun 2 Dam, named after the Nam Theun tributary in Laos. The new Pa Mong Dam estimation, apart from providing a new date for completion, also proposed some changes to the size of the dam, making it smaller. The Nam Theun 2 Dam was estimated to be able to generate 600 megawatts of energy, as well as to provide water during the dry season. The third proposed project in the 1988 report was the Nam Ngum 2 Dam project, which would be able to provide an estimated 400 megawatts of energy. The Nam Ngum 2 Dam project, it was stated, would be constructed after the first two projects had been completed.[14]

The reaction over these planned dam-projects has been mixed around the Mekong basin. One problem has been the general lack of information regarding the short- and long-term effects that these projects will have on the nature and aquatic life of the Mekong. Protests stem from the different uses of the river, as well as who actually benefits from the planned projects. Often, there is also confusion over the scope and intentions of the proposed projects. Construction of dams, in particular, has tremendous direct effects on the communities living around the dam areas, in addition to the long-term effects. The direct effect is that people are forced to move from their communities, as large areas surrounding the dams are flooded. The problem is that the benefits of these projects are often not distributed to those who are forced to sacrifice for their construction.

The proposed Nam Theun 2 Dam is an example of this situation. This project is expected to provide 100 million US dollars annually for the Lao government, representing around 10 per cent of the current

GDP.[15] However, it will also flood around 20 villages in the surrounding area, causing the relocation of around 5,000 villagers, mostly minorities living in the highlands. Along with these communities, an estimated additional 50,000 people will be affected owing to the increased flow of the river, and the project will have negative consequences for wildlife and the eco-system in the area. There is some understanding among the countries of the Mekong basin to address the negative effects of the construction of these dams. Individual countries have provisions, such as STEA (Science, Technology and Environment Agency) in Laos, which have guidelines over how projects are implemented. However, the lack of transparency and democracy in many of these countries means that often decisions are made without consultation of the affected local communities.

The dearth of social movement tradition in the region further hampers the ability of local communities to make their voices and interests heard in relation to these projects. In all these countries, the decision-making is very much centralized. Even the decisions as to whom and which regions should benefit from the projects are decided in the capitals. In this region, the only effective and organized protests have come from local villagers and organizations in Thailand, as a result of the open society that currently exists there compared to the other countries in the Mekong basin. One such protest relates to the issue of the construction of the Pak Moon Dam.[16] This dam is built on the Pak Moon River in Thailand, a tributary of the Mekong. The construction of the dam was completed in 1994. It was built on the mouth of the river in order to generate electricity and to prevent flooding.[17] The building of the dam and its subsequent effects have caused damage to the local communities, as fish habitats and aquatic life have been disrupted, and fish were prevented from travelling down the river.

In the summer of 2001, after concerted protests, the floodgates were opened for a one-year duration in order for the government to study the impact that the dam had had on the surrounding environment.[18] So far, the results of the study have shown that fish species have returned, as well as farmland, previously submerged by the reservoir.[19] Members of one of the local organizations that had campaigned against the dam project, 'the Assembly of the Poor', are pressing for the dam gates to stay permanently open. They claim that the benefits to be obtained from the operating of the Pak Moon Dam is minimal, whereas the effect on the local environment and the local communities living around the river was substantial, in terms of loss of income and way of life.[20] The strong lobbying by the environmental groups, as well as growing popular protests in Thailand have led to a declaration in June 2002 by the Director General of the Thai Irrigation Department that the country would not construct large-scale dams that were opposed by local communities, taking into account the concerns of those directly affected.[21]

Dredging the River for Navigation

Throughout its course, the Mekong changes character in a number of places. At some places it is shallow, and at other places it is deep, and the flow is sometimes powerful, sometimes sedate; it also changes intermittently between being a wide and a narrow river. In addition to this, there are a number of natural obstacles that impede journey on its waters. At best, in its present state it is possible to travel in regional patches, but not the entire length. Moreover, parts of the river are only fit for cargo ships during the rainy season, resulting in fleets being out of use during the rest of the year.

A number of projects have been attempted at providing regular transportation, both of people and of cargo, between long stretches of the river. As early as 1866, a French naval expedition was launched in order to determine the feasibility of commercial shipping between the lower parts of the Mekong basin and China.[22] The goal of the expedition was to establish a commercial shipping route through Khone Falls. A number of attempts were made to try to go around this obstacle. One strategy, attempted by the French in 1897, was to construct railway tracks, on which goods could be loaded and transported through the stretch of the Khone Falls, and then resume the trip on the river. Eventually, when the difficulties of using the total length of the Mekong for transportation were recognized, these large-scale attempts were abandoned. Attempts to facilitate navigation have in recent times resumed, one of the most notable including a Chinese initiative in 1990, of providing regular services of cargo ships between Simao Port in Yunnan province and Vientiane. The low amount of cargo that was obtainable for shipping, as well as the availability of this mode of transportation only during a limited part of the year, caused the termination of this venture. Similarly, a venture between Thailand and China to provide transportation between these two countries across the river failed, due to lack of tourists and the high costs of making the river navigable.[23]

The Khone Falls is the primary obstacle to navigation in the Mekong River. The Falls basically divides the Mekong into two parts: the area between the Khone Falls and the South China Sea, and the area between the Khone Falls and the northern regions. However, many other areas of the river are affected by rapids, shoals and boulders, which impede the flow of the river and prevent large cargo ships from travelling longer stretches down the Mekong, except during the wet season. There are ongoing attempts by the countries in the Mekong basin to improve navigation, by using modern techniques for dredging the river, as well as removing reefs and shoals by using explosives. These actions have significant impact on the ecological balance of the Mekong basin. Moreover, the destruction of nature directly affects the livelihoods of local communities, particularly those who are dependent on the fishing industry.

There are a number of incentives for the regimes in the Mekong basin to develop the shipping routes of the river. Incentives involve opening up of the markets in the Lower Mekong basin to Chinese goods, as well as providing an outlet at the South China Sea. There will also be upstream traffic. Goods from the countries in the Lower Mekong basin would be able to reach Yunnan, and from there to other major commercial centres of China, such as Sichuan, Qinghai and Gansu.[24] It will also give a boost to the tourism industry in the Mekong basin. Moreover, the river can provide a safer way of transportation between some areas, such as between Thailand and China, than the road route, which in this case goes through unstable parts of Burma. In particular China is now the biggest supporter of improving transportation activities in the Mekong, as it is seen as a step in developing its inland provinces which have not benefited as much as the coastal provinces from the infusion of foreign investment. The goal is to be able to reach Thai ports such as Laem Chabong in Chon Buri, which would enable Chinese goods to be exported worldwide, as well as provide a link with the inland provinces and the international markets.

A major large-scale initiative to improve navigation is currently underway in the Upper Mekong basin. With the help of Commercial Navigation Agreement signed in April 2002 between China, Burma, Laos and Thailand, obstacles are now being removed in the river. The intention is to enable vessels to travel freely between the Port of Simao in Yunnan and the city of Luang Prabang in Laos, a distance of 886 kilometres.[25] The Agreement as such contains six common navigation rules, entitled 'Guidelines on the Maintenance and Improvement of Navigability of the Lancang-Mekong River', and it is expected to be completed during two dry seasons at a cost of 5.3 million US dollars, to be provided by China. In order to complete this project, 11 major rapids, shoals, as well as 10 reefs will be removed using explosives, along with several minor obstacles.[26] The goal is for vessels of 500 tonnes to be able to navigate the outlined stretch of the river during 95 per cent of the year. Another part of this project is the construction of piers around Chiang Rai, which has been approved by Thai and Lao authorities.[27] However, there is a concern that the construction of the piers would change the course of the river and erode the riverbanks on the Laotian side.[28] The building of the piers will allow Chinese ships to dock in the area. The busiest traffic will take place in the route between the Port of Simao and the Thai city of Chiang Rai. As per the 2002 Agreement, the four countries have already opened their waterways for commercial shipping. In just three months, there was a 40 per cent increase in trade in terms of the amount of Chinese cargo ships reaching Chiang Rai in Thailand.[29]

According to the signatories, this project will improve trade between the countries by making it easier and faster to navigate the river, and safer by preventing accidents as a result of the obstacles. However, the removal of the reefs and shoals in this area means that the spawning and breeding grounds of a number of species of fish are also being removed. The local population is getting concerned as fish is the source of livelihood for many of them. There is also apprehension that tourism will suffer, as many of the boulders act as tourist attractions. However, supporters of the plan claim the opposite, that tourism will grow as a result of the wider accessibility to the region.[30] Certainly there is lack of a proper study on the possible adverse effects of the removal of boulders and other physical characteristics of the river on the ecological balance of the area. According to the Southeast Asia Rivers Network (SEARIN), there are many species of fish, as well as plants, that depend on the various reefs and shoals for their eco-system.[31] Rapids also function as cleaning mechanisms for the water that passes through them and, if removed, the water downstream will be more polluted. However, the official Environmental Impact Assessment (EIA) conducted by the Agreement in order to study the feasibility of this project did not produce any evidence of substantial damage to the ecology of the river. This EIA study was criticized by SEARIN for failing to take into account the social as well as environmental consequences of the project. In addition, the clearing of the river would have effects on the flow, which means that the downstream countries would be adversely affected. There are also fears that the depletion of fish as a result of the explosions will lead to more competition over fish-stocks, and lead to the further increased use of explosives by local fishermen. The protests by the people living in the affected areas, and the subsequent negative publicity, have led to increased opposition to these plans.

Another ongoing project to improve navigation is a Chinese-sponsored initiative to clear the Sambor Rapids, situated on the Cambodian side of the Mekong.[32] Besides improving navigation in the Upper Mekong basin, this initiative aims to facilitate commercial shipping as well as other forms of travel, such as tourism, and link the countries in the Mekong basin closer together. However, unlike the project on the Upper Mekong basin, much less is known about this project. The Sambor Rapids are an important habitat for fish species, as well as the Irawaddy dolphins, a species threatened with extinction.[33] The rapids also perform the same function at Sambor as they do upstream. They are instrumental in creating conditions for fish species to reproduce and survive.

The River and Its Fish Resources

In the Mekong basin, there are an estimated 1,700 species of fresh water fish in existence.[34] Of these, around 20 species account for the majority of the fish that is traded. It is difficult to provide exact figures on the amount of fish that is caught, consumed and traded, but some figures point to around 150,000 to 200,000 tonnes of fish being sold annually, with another 100,000 tonnes being consumed locally.[35] The value of fish being caught in the Lower Mekong basin every year has been placed at around 1.4 million US dollars.[36]

Fish, along with rice, is the staple diet of the population in the Lower Mekong basin. It provides them with their nutritional requirements, with fish representing the single most important source of animal protein.[37] A number of products are also produced from fish, such as fish paste. It is estimated that, per capita, 20 kilograms of fish are consumed each year in the basin area, with this figure rising to around 79 kilograms in the area around the Tonle Saep Lake in Cambodia.[38] In Cambodia, fish comprise around 80 per cent of the protein needs of the rural population.[39] Activities such as clearing reefs and similar natural habitats, and spawning grounds of fish have tremendous effect on the fisheries sector. Not only do they instantly kill a large number of fish, as well as remove their habitats, but these practices also change the flow and nature of the river, affecting downstream countries.

The fish in the Lower Mekong basin migrate during the wet and the dry season across various parts of the river, spawning and breeding in certain places where the conditions are suitable. Certain species of fish migrate for long distances of the river. Fish migrations are an important feature of tropical river ecology. In the Mekong basin, many important fish-stocks are shared between the riparian countries, thus fish migrations have great implication for regional development and planning. In the Mekong River system, the most significant fish migrations are along the main river and on to the flood plain. The most obvious impact on fish movements are being caused by the recently constructed large dams on the river system.[40]

Controlling Floods

The issue of flooding is intimately linked with deforestation in the Mekong basin, since trees act to prevent rainwater, as well as material brought by rainwater, from entering the Mekong or its tributaries. In this way, forests act as a kind of barrier, protecting the river from siltation, which makes the riverbed increasingly shallow. Deforestation has the effect of changing the nature of the river, causing increasingly severe flooding that mostly affects the downstream countries. Many areas of the downstream, in particular the Mekong delta, have very low elevation, which means that slight changes in the amount of water can have significant impact on the agriculture and fishery sector of those areas. In recent years, floods have caused serious damage to the region, in particular to the Lower Mekong basin.[41]

In the Mekong delta, flooding also brings some benefits. Annually, an estimated 9 to 13 million tonnes of sediments are deposited by floods in the Mekong delta. This land is extremely productive for rice and other crops. The flood flushes away the acidic soil elements, and also reduces the rat population. Flooding also provides suitable conditions for fresh water fish development. Annually, approximately 35 million fish hatching are taken from floodwater. Moreover, the floodwater is very important for irrigation.

After the devastating flood in the year 2000, countries in the Lower Mekong basin have taken up a number of proposals in order to control flooding. The lower basin countries have also come into an agreement in 2002 with China to receive daily flood data.[42] The aim in the lower basin is complete flood control by constructing embankments and flood-ways in the border areas, and a dyke system. However, in view of the flood benefits, flood control in the Mekong delta should be carried out in a comprehensive manner to take advantage of the flood benefits, and minimize environmental impacts.

MANAGING THE MEKONG RIVER IN RECENT YEARS

After the 1991 Paris Peace Agreement on Cambodia, the question of readmission of Cambodia into the Mekong Committee came up. Thailand's reluctance blocked any advances in this regard for some years. Thailand devised another way of cooperation beyond the framework of the Mekong Committee. In early 1993, Thailand together with China, proposed the quadripartite economic cooperation among the four upstream riparian states – China, Burma, Thailand and Laos. The focus of this proposed initiative was to improve trade, transportation and tourism in that part of the basin. In October 1994 the four countries agreed on the draft of a 'Commercial Navigation on the Lancang-Mekong River' to ensure free navigation along the portion running from Simao of China to Luang Prabang of Laos. However, the lack of interest from the Burmese side was the hindrance to the speedy implementation of the Agreement. The major task of the Quadrangle Economic Cooperation was to create a transportation network linking four member countries together for further economic cooperation especially in trade and tourism. The activities of the Quadrangle Cooperation highlighted Thailand's dream to become the centre of the sub-regional transportation network.[43]

In February 1995, another framework for cooperation was promoted by Japan in co-ordination with other donors, France and UNDP. The forum was named as Comprehensive Development in Indochina and it aimed to assist the integration of the three Indochina countries into the greater ASEAN association. Later, Japan pushed forward the co-ordination between ASEAN economic ministers and Ministry of Trade and Industry to promote economic development in the Indochina countries and Burma. The forum concentrated mainly on assisting the transformation of centrally commanded economies into a market one in these states.[44]

Finally, in April 1995, at Chiang Rai, Thailand, four Lower Mekong riparian countries – Thailand, Laos, Cambodia and Vietnam – came together and signed an agreement on Cooperation for Sustainable Development of the Mekong River basin giving birth to the Mekong River Commission. In fact, the new Commission is in reality a replacement of the former Mekong Committee in existence since 1957. What is new of this newly born Commission is much to do with its capacity to regulate the efforts to develop the water resource of the Mekong River. The Mekong River Commission (MRC) was created amidst an atmosphere of cooperation around the Mekong. This initiative had the support of the World Bank, the Asian Development Bank, various donor agencies and international organizations.[45]

The Mekong River Commission

The 1995 Agreement encompasses two main principles: firstly, to 'reflect and protect the sovereign interest of each co-riparian', and secondly, 'to ensure the integrity of the final Agreement'. The Agreement calls for the creation of three permanent bodies: the Council (policy and decision-making), Joint Committee (co-ordination and technical expertise) and the Secretariat (executing branch). The Council is the highest political level, with the authority to look at issues such as disputes on political grounds. It is composed of one senior member (at least of ministerial or cabinet level) of each of the participating riparian countries, with the chairmanship rotating among the riparians for one-year periods, and it meets annually; the Council is supported by a Joint Committee, which has regular meetings by senior representatives of a more technical nature.

The Joint Committee is composed of one representative of each riparian country at no less than the Head of Department level, with the chairmanship rotating on an annual basis. The Joint Committee meets twice every year. The executive body is the Mekong Secretariat, which executes the decisions of the Joint Committee, after having been approved by the Council. It provides technical and administrative services, under the supervision of the Joint Committee. The MRC Secretariat, the executing branch, provides technical and administrative support to the Joint Committee, and is in charge of implementation of the MRC programmes. The Secretariat is headed by a Chief Executive Officer, selected by the Joint Committee, and composed of technical staff from the riparian countries.

Apart from the Council, the Joint Committee and the MRC Secretariat, the MRC structure also includes the National Mekong Committees. These National Mekong Committees, or NMCs, are tasked to serve the needs of the Joint Committee members of each country by providing a link between the MRC and national govern-ments and by co-ordinating MRC related activities at the national level. The structure of the National Mekong Committees varies from one country to another. The NMCs, therefore, are intended to serve as a facilitating mechanism between the governments of the MRC process and the MRC Secretariat. The National Mekong Committees are differ-ently organized in the four member countries, each reporting to their 'line ministries'. The last structure attached to the MRC process is the Donor Consultative Group, which is composed of donor countries and cooperating institutions, and acts to provide a link between the donor countries and the MRC process, and address concerns from both parties.

The Agreement stipulates that the member-riparian countries cooperate in all fields of sustainable development, utilization, manage-ment and conservation of the water and related resources of the Mekong River basin in a manner to optimize the multiple-use and mutual benefits of all riparians. The Agreement contains provisions that it works within the framework of international laws and the Charter of the United Nations, including the principles of equitable usage and to do no significant harm to the previous users. The Agreement replaces the 1957, 1975 and 1978 declarations. In terms of membership of the Commission, the Agreement leaves the door open for any other ripar-ian country to join, i.e. China and Burma, provided that they accept all the articles of the Agreement, and are accepted by the existing members. When the 1995 Agreement was signed, it immediately came under criti-cism for its failure to include the unanimous principle of the Mekong Committee, e.g. other countries can veto diversion, dam or any project on both Mekong mainstream and tributaries that are considered to cause detrimental effects on them. The exclusion of this principle in fact gives individual riparian nations free hands to go ahead with their own individual plans. The 1995 Agreement is being criticized for excluding the 1975 spirit of cooperation and of promoting an essentially 'dam-building' agenda.[46]

In terms of the mechanisms within the MRC process for resolving disputes and differences among the riparian countries, should they arise, the tactic of 'gentle pressure' is relied upon. The Agreement states that, in cases of disputes between two or more parties, 'the Commission shall first make every effort to resolve the issue' through the mechanisms outlined in the Agreement, firstly by the Joint Committee, and secondly by the Council. If the dispute is unable to be resolved by these two instances, the matter is passed to the governments of the riparian countries for resolution, who may in turn ask for a third party or mediator to assist in the dispute, in conjunction with the principles of international law.

Therefore, any disagreements over the actions of one of the countries involved in the process is first dealt with in the Secretariat, and is subsequently moved up to higher levels if there is no resolution, culminating in the Joint Committee and, ultimately, to the Council itself. This is partly out of necessity, as a result of the culture of consensus that exists in this part of the world, which is also apparent in other international organizations that operate in this region, such as ASEAN.[47] The concept of the 'Mekong Spirit' can also be seen as being a reflection of this culture.[48]

The MRC has installed a network of 21 monitoring stations along the Mekong, which track the level of the river, and is used primarily in terms of flood control. As of yet, these stations do not monitor the quality of the water. Added to the problems associated with the gathering and sharing of information between the MRC countries is the issue of information exchanges with upstream countries, in particular with China. China is the most upstream riparian, the country where the Mekong originates. It is important for the purposes of planning and preparedness that the information is shared between China and the MRC countries, especially given the number of planned water development schemes on the river by China, such as the construction of large dams. Although little and select information has been shared up till now between China and the MRC countries, the situation is gradually improving. Under an agreement between the two parties, China has agreed in 2002 to share information daily regarding the water level during the flooding season, between 15 June and 15 October, from two stations in Yunnan province in China.[49]

The MRC can be seen as an organization that focuses on fostering cooperation between the governments of the four riparian countries in the region. The MRC is not an independent or supra-national institution, and is dependent on the member governments in the planning of its activities. This means that local groups and stakeholders are dependent on their government representatives to promote their concerns. This can be a problematic situation as only two countries in this region are democracies (Thailand and Cambodia), and only one has a tradition of public participation (Thailand). However, NGOs, both national and international, are active in the basin area.

Overall, the 1995 Agreement is considered one of the most encompassing and holistic international water management agreements in the world, as it takes into account sustainable development, full utilization of the river resources and the protection of the environment in the first three articles. The mixture of political and technical aspects is a common and perhaps a necessary factor in international agreements on natural resources. However, it also means that in practice the comprehensive development of the Mekong River has not always been pursued due to political reasons, and for the sake of unanimity. Difficulties arise when there is a discrepancy between the governments and the implementing institution. The activities and programmes of the MRC Secretariat are hindered if there is a lack of political will to implement the programmes. The National Mekong Committees are also an unstable component of the process, since they differ in their capacity in the four countries. There are concerns that these institutions serve to halt the momentum of the MRC process.

One issue that perhaps reflects the difficulties of dealing with an international body concerns the location of the headquarters, the MRC Secretariat. Originally, the headquarters was located in Bangkok, but it was felt that the Secretariat should be placed in the headquarters of one of the smaller countries, located in the Mekong basin area. The choice was between Vientiane in Laos and Phnom Penh in Cambodia, as both of these capitals were located in the basin region, along the Mekong River. During the negotiations, it was agreed that the headquarters would rotate between these two capitals on a five-year basis, with Phnom Penh having it between 1998 and 2003, and Vientiane receiving it after that. However, this issue became controversial, since officials in the MRC Secretariat in Phnom Penh unsuccessfully complained that it is impractical to move the headquarters, pointing to the cost, as well as to the loss of momentum in that several support staff in Laos will have to be trained. In addition, it is feared that the general lack of an open political environment in Laos might hamper the activities of the MRC Secretariat.

The other drawback with the MRC is that it is not easy to pin-point where the responsibility lies when actions are taken that are detrimental to the Mekong River. The state-centric nature of the MRC process makes it difficult for local communities and stakeholders, those who are not adequately represented by their governments, to make their voices heard in terms of the planning and implementation of the programmes. The Commission does not consider itself as responsible for soliciting public participation, nor does it see itself as answerable to the public. The MRC does little to influence the governments of member countries, and acts more like an advocacy organization for development in the form of hydropower. On the whole, the MRC process is interesting for many reasons, not least since it has brought countries that have had difficult relationships together in cooperation over natural resources.[50]

DEMAND FOR IRRIGATION AND HYDROPOWER: PROBLEMS AHEAD

The 1995 Agreement outlines a wide scope of cooperation among four lower basin riparian countries that includes 'irrigation, hydropower, navigation, flood control, fisheries, timber floating, recreation and tourism' and other areas beyond those spheres. The wide scope of cooperation is added by the emphasis on the joint and basin-wide perspective stipulated in Article 2 by developing a basin development plan. Besides, priority is given to sustainable development in which the protection of the environment and ecology of the basin area is emphasized. However, this cooperation spirit in the Agreement is only on paper; what member states actually do is another matter. To ensure the cooperative development of the basin water resources, further work needs to be done to prepare a comprehensive implementation strategy.

The Mekong basin countries are situated in a tropical region with plenty of rainfall in the rainy season, usually from June to September or October, and then the dry season for the rest of the year. Looking at the general water availability per capita around the year, Mekong basin nations can be judged as abundant in water supply. However, these countries are subjected to regional and seasonal water scarcity. Among the four lower basin countries, Thailand is the most economically developed and the demand for water in Thailand is increasing. Though not ranked as a water shortage country yet, water in Thailand is not evenly spread and rainfall is unpredictable. The north-eastern Thailand of the Korat Plateau faces uneven and unreliable rainfall that causes both floods and droughts. The plateau covers a large area, 6.6 million hectares of land. This area is densely populated and industrially backward compared to other parts of the country. Though agriculture is the main economic activity of the region, land here suffers from water scarcity because of unreliable rainfall. Being a large constituency, the support of the region's population is important in Thai politics. Thus, the Thai government has long planned to improve the economic situation of this area.

In order to improve agriculture in the north-eastern part of Thailand

and to supply water for the Central Plain, Thailand is seriously considering diverting waters from Chieng Khan, a Mekong tributary in the North to the Chao Praya River. This plan has been opposed by the downstream countries, and also by the environmental groups within the country. Similarly, Thailand's plan to build other dams on the Mekong tributaries has also been halted owing to lack of agreement with Laos and growing internal opposition. The construction of the dams is increasingly being subjected to a lot of criticism and opposition from the domestic community whose life used to inter-link to the river system.

In Laos, the internal opposition to dam building is negligible compared to Thailand. Among the socialist states, Laos was one of the earlier states in taking a decision to transform its former centrally planned economy to a market oriented one. Laos is famous for its hydropower potential, which is mainly found in the Mekong and its tributaries. Laos is undoubtedly considered as a potential hydropower house of the region. Seen as Laos' most promising export good, at least 23 dams are planned by the Laos government to be built in the country up to the year 2020.[51] Two dams, Theun Hinboun and the Nam Theun II have been already built and they have attracted criticism for their cost and effect calculation of the BOT (build-operation-transfer) investment mechanism. Moreover, with the strategy of building dams for sale of hydroelectricity, Laos is facing another problem: finding the market. In 1996, Laos reached an agreement to sell hydropower to Vietnam; however, Thailand is still the only main purchaser of Laos' hydropower. But, this has not dampened the plan of Laos to build a series of other dams for power selling.

Among the lower riparian countries of the Mekong River, Cambodia is second to Laos in water contribution to the river. In Cambodia, hydropower potential from the Mekong is also very high. Cambodia, however, owing to its delicate internal political situation, is somewhat behind in implementing its dam construction plan. Plans for dams in Cambodia, like other Mekong lower basin countries, have been under proposal since the 1950s and at present they are being resurrected. There are about eight projects mainly on the Mekong tributaries that are considered priority by either the Mekong Commission or the Cambodian National Mekong Committee. Of these proposed dams, Sambor Dam is to be built on the mainstream and was included in the Mekong work programme of 1998. The electricity generated from this dam, about 3,300 megawatts, is planned for export to Thailand or Vietnam.

The Mekong delta is Vietnam's hope to remain self-sufficient in food supply. Owing to war, the delta area was not developed, and a lot of potential in the region remains unexploited. Furthermore, the climate in the delta is more favourable for agricultural cultivation than in the North. For the success of the agricultural development plan of Vietnamese government, the water supply of the Mekong River is the core, especially in the dry season. The Mekong delta is productive land for agricultural development, which is known as the 'rice bowl' in Vietnam. Covering only 12 per cent of the total surface area of Vietnam, it produces 45–50 per cent of the national rice output. Besides the need of water for irrigational use, Vietnam is also in search of hydropower. Thanks to current economic growth, the country's demand for electricity has been increasing at over 10 per cent annually since 1986. The northern part of the country is providing hydropower to the rapidly industrializing south. In the future, Vietnam plans to exploit the potential hydroelectricity of the Mekong tributaries.

Due to the increasing demand of irrigation and hydropower, the countries in the Lower Mekong basin will be tempted to withdraw a larger share of water from the Mekong. It has the potential to bring in the quantity issue as a source of conflict. Both Cambodia and Laos are dependent on agriculture and plan to expand the sector. However, taking into consideration the size of their economy and the water availability, the need to withdraw massive amounts of water from the Mekong River is not an important priority for them. Vietnam and Thailand are the main potential rivals in this matter. Its geographical location gives Thailand an advantageous position compared to Vietnam. Thailand has also consistently shown its intention and determination to carry out large-scale water diversion projects.

Thailand's water diversion projects, besides being opposed internally by the affected people, are also being opposed by Vietnam who would bear some serious impact if the projects were carried out. Thailand's position is that it is entitled to the amount of water equal to that contributed to the flow of Mekong from its tributaries. In Vietnam, there is a fear that if Thailand carries out its proposed water diversion projects, there will be a significant reduction in the dry-season flow of the Mekong River, resulting in eventual saltwater intrusion into the Mekong delta of South Vietnam. If there is a large-scale withdrawal in Thailand, it might also cause water scarcity for the Mekong delta in the dry season, which would negatively affect the cultivation productivity of the area. These opposing interests in the use of the Mekong water between upstream and downstream countries in the Lower Mekong basin, e.g. Thailand and Vietnam, is a potential contradiction that may lead to future conflict. However, as has been discussed before, the continuing opposition and demonstration against dam building in Thailand, together with strong opposition from Thai NGOs in protection of the Mekong environment, has decisively contributed to the cessation of dam construction and large-scale water diversion in

Thailand. However, the serious threat now emanates from further upstream.

Unrestrained economic development and rapid societal change have placed China's already dwindling water supply under severe stress. Of the 640 major urban centres in China, more than 300 face water shortages, with 100 facing severe scarcities. To meet the shortfall, the state is actively diverting water from the agriculture sector. Since the beginning of economic reform in 1978, water scarcity in the northern part of China has been further complicated. Northern China is very water-poor, with only 750 cubic metres per capita availability. This region has one-fifth of the per capita water resources of southern China. Besides exploiting the southern rivers for hydropower generation, China is also planning to divert the water from these rivers (including the Mekong) to the urban and industrial centres in the North.

The Mekong Committee of 1957 was a product of the Cold War politics, and that had resulted in the exclusion of China and Burma. The 1995 Agreements also came about without the participation of these two upstream countries. The absence of China is a serious limit to the capacity of the Commission to manage the conflicts and to promote riparian cooperation. Burma's importance is limited as the portion of the Mekong that runs through the country is very short and the area is sparsely populated. Furthermore, Burma is not keen in developing the Mekong River because of its volatile political situation. On the contrary, China's role is of great importance not only because the country hosts a long stretch of the river but also because of its furthermost upstream position. Moreover, China is a big and powerful country which is on the way to rapid modernization and industrialization. Its industrialization and urbanization require vast energy, and that prompts the desire for the exploitation of the Mekong River. Compared to the other Mekong riparian states, China is in the advantageous position not only geographically but also politically and to a large extent economically as well.

In the Yunnan province, China has a plan to build a total of 14 dams on the Upper Mekong, known locally as the Lancang River. China has already built two large hydropower dams (Manwan and Dachaoshan), and is currently constructing the third, the 292 metres high Xiaowan hydroelectric dam, which is due to be completed in 2012.[52] The Xiaowan Dam is second in size only to the Three Gorges Dam on the Yangtze and will have about 20 times more storage of Manwan and Dachaoshan combined. The construction of Jinghong Dam is also going to begin soon. This cascade of dams would have a total installed capacity of 7,700 megawatts, nearly 20 per cent of China's current energy consumption. The remote Yunnan province plans to export part of this hydropower to Thailand to earn export dollars.

All these dams on the Mekong mainstream will certainly alter the flow of the river by reducing the amount of water during the flood period and increase the water supply for downstream countries in the dry season. This may allow Thailand to withdraw more water for the irrigation project in its north-eastern part. However, there is lack of authoritative studies to assess the combined impact of these huge dams on the downstream environment and fisheries and flooding mechanism. This concern has already been expressed by the downstream riparian countries. Moreover, China has another ambitious proposal to divert water from the Mekong into the Yellow River to address north-east China's growing water problem. This situation demonstrates the fact that, for the sustainable development of the river as a whole, cooperation on the side of China is significantly needed.

Though China and Burma are not yet members of the Mekong Commission, since 1995 they have observer status within the organization. In order to treat the Mekong basin as one single ecological system, there is an absolute need to include China and Burma in the cooperation mechanism of the basin. The 1995 Agreement invites both countries to join. Burma is reluctant to join the Commission as it does not see any benefit out of it, because of its token involvement in the basin. China's motivations for non-participation are more complex. China is in an advantageous position and it has been under no pressure to cooperate with other downstream countries in order to utilize Mekong resources. Rather, membership of the Mekong River Commission may interfere in the country's Upper Mekong development plans. The 1995 Agreement implies that dam construction or water diversion would be done only after reaching a consensus among the riparian countries, which China is worried about.

However, China has a need to expand economic relations with Southeast Asia and so far it has shown an interest in connecting the land-locked Yunnan province to the East Sea through the Mekong River. Beijing has already prodded Burma, Laos and Thailand to collaborate on a scheme to clear the rapids and shoals that have long hindered navigation of the river. This cooperation with some Lower Mekong riparian countries may possibly bring China within the fold of the Commission.

FUTURE CHALLENGES

The Mekong basin area is undoubtedly a contentious area. The six riparian countries share a difficult history of tension with one another, having frequently conducted armed conflicts, and conducting illicit activities in each other's territories. Cultural differences and border disputes also exist between the riparian states. Moreover, there is also a clear disparity in the relative strengths of the riparian states, with China being, at the very least, a regional superpower, if not a global one. Thailand is the dominant regional country in the Lower Mekong basin, with cultural ties with Laos. Vietnam is behind Thailand in terms of development in the Lower Mekong basin, but has strong influence in Cambodia and in Laos. Cambodia and Laos are the weakest countries in the whole basin area, in terms of population, development, as well as military. Burma, in the Upper Mekong basin, has a large population, but is affected by and is dependent on the Mekong in a limited way, as the river only passes through a very small portion of its territory. The upstream country, China, is the most powerful in the basin, and also the least dependent on the resources of the river. Issues relating to the principle of sovereignty in the basin are very important, and actions that impinge on this principle are treated with scepticism. All of these conditions make it difficult to create a successful basin-based water management regime.

Taking into account the pre-conditions that exist, in many ways the present management of the river can be viewed as somewhat satisfactory. Four of the riparian countries are continuing a partnership and collaboration that has its roots in the Cold War of the 1950s. From that period until now, these countries have witnessed a tremendous amount of change and events, such as the Vietnam War, the Khmer Rouge regime, the rapid development of Thailand, and the gradual liberalization of the regimes in the former Indochina. Despite these, the four lower riparian countries are continuing to collaborate and share the resources of the river. Given the history of the region, and the diverse and problematic nature of the relations between the riparian countries, the ongoing collaboration is a significant achievement. These developments reflect the high hopes that many actors, both within and outside the basin region, have on the potential of the Mekong to become a significant factor in the continued development of the region. However, the exclusion of two of the upper riparian states, and particularly the absence of China in the Mekong water management mechanism, is a major future problem.

NOTES

1. This chapter was written with substantial research assistance from Peter Holtsberg.
2. This chapter does not use the name 'Myanmar' given to Burma by the military regime in 1998. Besides many countries and leading publications, the Burmese National League for Democracy also uses the old name.
3. V. R. Pantalu, 'The Mekong River System', in B. R. Davies and K. F. Walker (eds), *The Ecology of River Systems, Monographiae Biologicae*, 60 (Dordrecht: Dr W. Junk Publishers), pp. 695–719.
4. J. Öjendal, *Sharing the Good: Models of Managing Water Resources in the Lower Mekong River Basin* (Gothenburg: Department of Peace and Development Research, 2000).
5. NEDECO, *Mekong Delta Master Plan, Working Paper No. 4: Agriculture* (Mekong Secretariat, 1991).
6. D. K. Son, 'Development of Agricultural Production Systems in the Mekong Delta', in V. T. Xuan and S. Matsui (eds), *Development of Farming Systems in the Mekong Delta* (Ho Chi Minh City: JIRCAS & CLRRI, 1998).
7. An estimated 1,700 species of fish inhabit the Mekong water. See MRC, *Local Knowledge in the Study of River Fish Biology: Experience from the Mekong* (Phnom Penh: Mekong River Commission, Mekong Development Series No. 1, 2001). The total annual catch of the lower basin alone is conservatively estimated at 1.6 to 1.8 million tonnes. See J. G. Jensen, *MRC Programme for Fisheries Management and Development Cooperation, Annual Report, April 2000–March 2001* (Phnom Penh: Mekong River Commission, 2001).
8. MRC, *Fisheries in the Lower Mekong Basin: Status and Perspectives* (Phnom Penh: Mekong River Commission, MRC Technical Paper No. 6, 2002).
9. Öjendal, *Sharing the Good: Models of Managing Water Resources in the Lower Mekong River Basin*.
10. In 1954, the Indo-Chinese states, Cambodia, Laos and (North and South) Vietnam received their formal independence.
11. D. E. Weatherbee, 'Cooperation and Conflict in the Mekong River Basin', *Studies in Conflict & Terrorism*, 20, 2 (1997), pp. 167–84.
12. Even after the ouster of the Khmer Rouge regime, the new government was not recognized by Thailand and was blocked from participating in the Interim Mekong Committee during the 1980s.
13. Green Cross International, *National Sovereignty and International Watercourses* (Geneva: Green Cross International, 2000), p. 90.
14. H. Hori, *The Mekong: Environment and Development* (Tokyo: The UNU Press, 2000).
15. *International Herald Tribune*, 11 March 2002.
16. A. M. Chee, *Political Structure and Public Policy Conflict Management: A Comparative Study of Thailand and Malaysia* (Uppsala: Uppsala University Programme of International Studies Masters Thesis, 2003).
17. The Pak Moon Project was funded with a 23 million US dollar loan from the World Bank in 1991 (13% of the total cost). This World Bank loan was to help Thailand meet its growing demand for power needed to sustain its economic growth. This run-of-the-river dam is 17 metres high and 300 metres long and produces 136 megawatts of hydropower.
18. *Bangkok Post*, 5 May 2001.
19. Ibid., 10 February 2002.
20. Ibid., 2 December 2001.
21. Ibid., 19 June 2002.

22. M. Osborne, *The Mekong* (Sydney: Allen & Unwin, 2001), p. 138.
23. Ibid., p. 153.
24. *Bangkok Post*, 26 February 2002.
25. *The Nation*, 9 July 2002.
26. Ibid., 19 May 2002.
27. *Bangkok Post*, 2 February 2002.
28. In November 2002, the opponents of this project received support from an unexpected quarter: Thailand's army. The military is worried that the riverbank erosion may influence the country's boundary with Laos, which has never been properly delineated (*Financial Times*, 20 November 2002).
29. *The Nation*, 9 July 2002.
30. *Bangkok Post*, 21 April 2002.
31. *The Nation*, 9 July 2002.
32. *The Cambodian Daily*, 29 April 2002.
33. Irrawaddy dolphin (*Orcaella brevirostri*) is included on the IUCN Red List of Endangered Species.
34. MRC, *Local Knowledge in the Study of River Fish Biology: Experience from the Mekong*.
35. Hori, *The Mekong: Environment and Development*.
36. Jensen, *MRC Programme for Fisheries Management and Development Cooperation*.
37. Öjendal, *Sharing the Good: Models of Managing Water Resources in the Lower Mekong River Basin*, p. 21.
38. *Bangkok Post*, 15 February 2002.
39. J. Öjendal and E. Torell, *The Mighty Mekong Mystery – A Study on the Problems and Possibilities of Natural Resources Utilization in the Mekong River Basin* (Stockholm: Sida, 1997).
40. MRC, *Fisheries in the Lower Mekong Basin: Status and Perspectives*.
41. In 2000, floods took the lives of 800 people, as well as causing more than 400 million US dollars damages by washing away infrastructure such as bridges (*Viet Nam News*, 24 April 2002).
42. *Beijing Time*, 30 June 2002.
43. *The Nation*, 14 June 1996.
44. Öjendal and Torell, *The Mighty Mekong Mystery – A Study on the Problems and Possibilities of Natural Resources Utilization in the Mekong River Basin*, p. 62.
45. Detailed information about the Mekong River Commission can be obtained from its official website: http://www.mrcmekong.org/
46. This dam building agenda of the Commission can also potentially create problems for the rice growing regions in the downstream, particularly Vietnam and Cambodia. See N. Kliot, D. Shmueli and U. Shamir, 'Institutions for Management of Transboundary Water Resources: Their Nature, Characteristics and Shortcomings', *Water Policy*, 3 (2001), pp. 229–55.
47. N. Badenoch, *Transboundary Environmental Governance* (Washington DC: World Resources Institute, 2002), p.6.
48. M. Nakayama, 'Mekong Spirit as an Applicable Concept for International River Systems' in *Water Security for Multinational Water Systems – Opportunity for Development* (Stockholm: SIWI Report 8, 2000), p. 62.
49. *Beijing Time*, 30 June 2002.
50. P. Holtsberg, *Sustainability in Water Management: Conflict and Cooperation in the Mekong River Basin* (Uppsala: The Uppsala University Programme of International Studies Masters Thesis, 2002).
51. A. D. Usher, 'Damming the Theun River, Nordic Companies in Laos', *The Ecologist*, 26, 3 (1996), p. 88.
52. *Financial Times*, 20 November 2002.

5

Southern Africa and its Shared Rivers: The Orange, the Limpopo, the Okavango and with Special Emphasis on the Zambezi[1]

The Southern African Development Community (SADC) comprises currently 14 member states; Angola, Botswana, Democratic Republic of Congo, Lesotho, Malawi, Mozambique, Namibia, South Africa, Swaziland, Tanzania, Zambia and Zimbabwe, and two island states in the Indian Ocean, Mauritius and Seychelles. The SADC has a total land area of 9.3 million square kilometres. The use of water is the fundamental cornerstone of the foundation for the economic development and social life in Southern Africa. The region is highly dependent on water resources and extremely vulnerable to water scarcity.[2] In Southern Africa, the availability and demand for water is unevenly dispersed on the sub-national, national and regional level. The available technical and social arrangements to address the water scarcity situation are not sufficient to comply with the emerging situation. The mis-match between the supply and demand of water in most of the countries in Southern Africa is becoming increasingly urgent. Moreover, many countries do lack technical and economic ability to manage their water resource base. Zambia, which is one of the most well-endowed countries in the region in terms of water availability, suffers from acute local water scarcity problems owing to its failure in storage and distribution.[3] Large-scale careless pollution of water is also responsible for water scarcity in this region.[4]

Despite the numerous river systems in the area, Southern Africa is one of the world's most water scarce regions. The region suffers from extreme variations in temporal and spatial rainfall. Rainfall in the SADC region, which is generally arid and semi-arid, is very variable and often unreliable both in time and space. Long droughts that are interrupted by severe floods are increasingly becoming critical. In the SADC region, an average of about 65 per cent of the precipitation evaporates soon after it has fallen. Growing population and urbanization increase further water scarcity and pollution. Increased agricultural activities and industrialization raise the importance for water storage and hydropower.

In the Southern African region, the major water using sector is agriculture (to a large extent irrigated agriculture), which uses more than 60 per cent of the water withdrawn. Zimbabwe uses almost 80 per cent of its water for agricultural purposes. The share for agriculture in Malawi and Mozambique is also higher. In the independence period, countries in the region have witnessed dramatic expansion of water allocation and groundwater exploitation for the provisions of agricultural needs in rural areas. Owing to urban expansion, domestic and industrial sectors are currently the most increasing water use sectors in the region. In 1990, 17 per cent of the total water use in South Africa was for urban and domestic purposes. In Botswana it was even 32 per cent of the total water use in 1992.

Table 5.1 Sectoral Water Withdrawals by SADC States

Country	Data year	Total annual withdrawals (cu km)	Domestic withdrawals	Industrial withdrawals	Agricultural withdrawals
Angola	1987	0.48	14	10	76
Botswana	1992	0.11	32	20	48
Lesotho	1987	0.05	22	22	56
Malawi	1994	0.94	10	3	86
Mozambique	1992	0.61	9	2	89
Namibia	1990	0.25	29	3	68
South Africa	1990	13.3	17	11	72
Swaziland					
Tanzania	1994	1.17	9	2	89
Zambia	1994	1.71	16	7	77
Zimbabwe	1987	1.22	14	7	79
DRC	1994	0.36	61	16	23

Source: WRI, *World Resources, 2000–01* (Washington DC: World Resource Institute, 2001), p. 277.

As can be seen from Table 5.1, the current allocation of water still favours irrigated agriculture in the region. However, this form of water use leads to severe waste due to inefficiency and high state subsidies. In some cases, water is virtually free. There is also widespread water pollution, which has affected the overall quality and quantity of the resource for the downstream users as a result of unsustainable agro-industrial practices.[5]

Southern Africa's landscape, like the rest of Africa, is dominated by international rivers. The lack of respect of the colonial powers for the natural and ethnic boundaries is the primary reason for it. Rivers became convenient means for demarcating state borders in the colonial policy of the settlers. As it can be seen in Table 5.2, there are at least 15

Table 5.2 Shared River Basins in Southern Africa

River basin	Area (sq km)	Length (km)	No. of riparian countries	Basin countries
Buzi	31,000	250	2	Mozambique, Zimbabwe
Cunene	106,500	1,050	2	Angola, Namibia
Cuvelai	100,000	430	2	Angola, Namibia
Pungwe	32,500	300	2	Mozambique, Zimbabwe
Rovuma	155,500	800	2	Mozambique, Tanzania
Save	92,500	740	2	Mozambique, Zimbabwe
Umbeluzi	5,500	200	2	Mozambique, Swaziland
Incomati	50,000	480	3	Mozambique, South Africa, Swaziland
Maputo	32,000	380	3	Mozambique, South Africa, Swaziland
Limpopo	415,000	1,750	4	Botswana, Mozambique, South Africa, Zimbabwe
Okavango	570,000	1,100	4	Angola, Botswana, Namibia, Zimbabwe
Orange	850,000	2,300	4	Botswana, Lesotho, Namibia, South Africa
Zambezi	1,400,000	2,650	8	Angola, Botswana, Malawi, Mozambique, Namibia, Tanzania, Zambia, Zimbabwe
Congo	3,800,000	4,700	9	Angola, Burundi, Cameroon, Central African Republic, Congo, DRC, Rwanda, Tanzania, Zambia
Nile	2,800,000	6,700	10	Burundi, DCR, Egypt, Eritrea, Ethiopia, Kenya, Rwanda, Sudan, Tanzania, Uganda

Source: G. Nhamo, 'SADC Region Committed to Sharing Water', The Zambezi, 1, 1 (1998), p. 8.

international rivers in the SADC region. Traditionally, these international river systems have been unilaterally exploited within national boundaries or they have been shared with the help of bilateral or multilateral agreements focusing on a single issue, e.g. irrigation schemes, hydropower or urban water supply. In recent years, there have been some attempts to rationalize and co-ordinate the supply and demand of water at the regional level.

Among all the international rivers of Southern Africa, the major ones are: the Orange, Limpopo/Save, Okavango, Zambezi, Zaire/Congo and Nile. All these rivers originate in uplands and mostly run through the drylands before meeting the sea. Seasonal and annual flow variations in these rivers are very large. Thus, any developmental activities in the upstream affect the runoff of the river in the downstream. The Nile River sharing issue has been discussed in detail in Chapter 3 of this book. In the Southern African region, Tanzania shares only a very small part of the Nile basin, which actually stretches northwards to the Mediterranean Sea. The Congo River has been excluded from an elaborate discussion because this river has remained almost unexploited owing to political instability in its main riparian country, Congo. Moreover, the Congo basin covers rather much of Central Africa, though Tanzania, Zambia and Angola have some shares of it.

THE ORANGE RIVER

The Orange River is the most over-developed river in the region, which is shared between Lesotho, South Africa, Namibia and Botswana. This river, originating in Lesotho, moves in a south-westerly direction and forms a border between South Africa and Namibia before reaching the Atlantic.[6] The Orange River, with its main tributary the Vaal, carries almost 20 per cent of the river flow in South Africa.[7] Though the Orange still continues to flow all through the year, the runoff has been reduced considerably due to upstream abstraction schemes.[8] In this river, there are 24 large dams in South Africa, 5 in Namibia and 2 in Lesotho. However, the construction of these dams in Lesotho, as part of the Lesotho Highlands Water Project, is the most controversial.

The Kingdom of Lesotho is surrounded by South Africa. Its mountains are the source of the Orange (Senqu) River. However, this river is the major provider of water to the industrial region of South Africa, the Gauteng province. The hydrology of the river has been changed in several ways to meet South Africa's increasing demand for water. South Africa has undertaken several water transfer schemes in this basin within its own territory, and it has had its eye for a long time on developing the river resource in Lesotho and diverting it to its own territory. It has also contemplated for a long time its intention to divert the Orange River water northwards to reach its industrial belt of Johannesburg.[9] After giving its support to a military coup against Lesotho's tribal chief's government in 1986, the South African apartheid regime was finally able to get the new government's agreement to its water diversion schemes. South Africa was also able to get a no objection certificate from Namibia, which is at the bottom end of the Orange River, before beginning the construction of the project.[10]

This Lesotho Highlands Water Project (LHWP) is designed to build six dams, two hydropower stations, three pumping stations and 225 kilometres of tunnels through Drakensberg watershed that divides the Vaal River from the Orange River catchment.[11] The construction work began in 1988, and all four phases are scheduled to be completed by the year 2017. This 30 years of construction will cost 8 billion US dollars. The LHWP is the single largest infrastructure development in Africa today.[12] The construction of Katse and Mohale Dams have already been completed. At 186 metres, the Katse Dam is the highest dam in Africa. These two projects are expected to enable Lesotho to export two billion cubic metres of water per year to South Africa. Simultaneously, these projects generate hydroelectric power for both Lesotho and South Africa. Phase 2 of the LHWP involves the construction of the Mashai Dam, which is supposed to be completed by 2008. In Phase 3, Tsoelike Reservoir will be constructed, and in the final Phase 4, the construction of Ntoahae Reservoir will be undertaken. South Africa aims to save on the capital and operational cost of transferring the water from the Orange River to the Vaal River. In its return, for the next 50 years, South Africa will pay royalties to Lesotho and after that period, the deal will be renegotiated.[13]

The LHWP seriously threatens to deprive a large number of population from their source of livelihood by enclosing communal grazing land, using agricultural fields to build roads, transmission lines and other infrastructures. The socioeconomic impacts of the LHWP are many and varied. Furthermore, the large-scale water diversion in the upstream is bringing adverse environmental impacts in the downstream areas.[14] The LHWP is a joint project involving Lesotho and South Africa. South Africa needs water and Lesotho is more than willing to sell its water to augment its dwindling revenue. However, according to Matlosa, there are five possible areas of conflict between two riparian countries: compensation; resettlement; renegotiations of the treaty; implementation of other phases of the project; and implications of political instability in Lesotho for the LHWP.[15]

Since 1987, South Africa and Lesotho have formed a Joint Permanent Technical Commission (JPTC) to facilitate sharing of Orange River water and the management of the LHWP.[16] In 1992, South Africa and Namibia came to an agreement to establish the Permanent Water Commission (PWC). With the Namibian initiative, all the four basin states decided in 2000 to establish the Orange-Senqu River Commission (ORACOM) after years of negotiation. The ORACOM aims to facilitate the sharing of the information and co-ordination over the water development projects among the basin states. In spite of Lesotho's demand, South Africa has not agreed for the ORACOM to supersede the bilateral treaty which governs the LHWP.[17] However, the LHWP's future impact on the downstream water flow is not the only problem for a basin-based cooperation. The further water diversion schemes in the basin, particularly by South Africa, raises the possibility of future water related tensions in the region. The thirst of South Africa has not been quenched with the LHWP. It is now conducting an investigation to explore the possibility of transferring more water into the Vaal River system from the eastward flowing rivers of the Drakensberg Mountains. While water can be directly transferred from the Tugela River to the Vaal River, water from the Umzimvubu River is planned to be transferred via the Tugela or the Orange River to the Vaal River system. With increasing water demand, the development of these schemes is a distinct possibility in the near future.

The Limpopo River originates in South Africa near Johannesburg as the Crocodile River. It moves north-westwards to the border with Botswana and continues in a north-east direction, first becoming the border between South Africa and Botswana and then between South Africa and Zimbabwe, and finally moving into Mozambique.[18] Near the city of Xai-Xai, it empties itself into the Indian Ocean. Several other tributaries, including Shashe, originate from Botswana. Another important tributary, the Elephants River (also known as Transvaal River) originates from Johannesburg and joins the Limpopo River in Mozambique. The Limpopo basin covers an area approximately 415,500 square kilometres and is shared among the four riparian states: Botswana, Mozambique, South Africa and Zimbabwe.

The Limpopo River basin has an average annual precipitation of 520 millimetres, while the potential evaporation is mostly in the order of 2,000 millimetres. Average runoff of the river is 5,500 million cubic metres, which is small in comparison to other major river basins in the region. The water availability of the river is mainly dependent on seasonal rainfall. There are no dams on the mainstream of the river, but the tributaries in South Africa and Botswana are so dammed and exploited that they have very marginal contribution to the downstream flow. Flow in the Lower Limpopo comes primarily from Zimbabwean tributaries. The Limpopo River, which was initially a perennial river in Mozambique, now-a-days due to upstream withdrawal, can actually fall dry for up to eight months per year.[19]

In the upper catchment of the Limpopo basin, Botswana has constructed major dams like the Shashe and the Letsibogo Dams to meet the increasing water demand in its urban centres. A recently commissioned north-south water carrier pipeline is supplying water to the capital Gaborone. Similarly in South Africa, major dams have been constructed in the Limpopo tributaries to provide water to Johannesburg and also several small dams to support irrigated agriculture. The Limpopo River is also the major source of irrigation in Zimbabwe. This river system has become the site for 44 large dams (4 in Botswana, 28 in South Africa, 11 in Zimbabwe and only 1 in Mozambique) in order to supply drinking water to urban areas as well as to support mining, industry, agriculture and hydropower generation. In the downstream Mozambique, Limpopo runs dry most of the year, but in the rainy season, together with the Save and Zambezi rivers, it becomes a major cause of flooding.

Due to increasing water scarcity in Southern Africa, the Limpopo River basin needs to be managed in a co-ordinated way among the basin countries. Deforestation and unsustainable agricultural practices lead to high siltation rates, which decrease the lifespan of dams. Agricultural and industrial waste has also adversely affected the quality of Limpopo water in recent years. South Africa has bilateral arrangements with Botswana and Mozambique over the sharing of the Limpopo water. For some time now, there have also been some initiatives to establish basin-based cooperation. In 1986, all the riparian states had agreed to establish the Limpopo Basin Permanent Technical Committee (LBPTC). The Committee, which was envisioned to play an advisory role over the basin development issues, failed to function for almost a decade. After the end of apartheid in South Africa, the LBPTC met for the second time in Pretoria. Besides reactivating the organization, the basin states also agreed to conduct a joint hydrological study of the river. In 1999, the joint study came up with a series of crucial recommendations, and since then, the emphasis has been to establish the Limpopo River Commission.[20]

The Limpopo River basin wavers between becoming a flashpoint for regional conflict or a model for regional cooperation. Several factors influence the direction in which this basin will follow. With the increasing demand, instead of putting greater emphasis on controlling consumption of the water, the states are opting for further river infrastructure development options. These actions are certainly going to bring crisis to the basin in the near future.

THE OKAVANGO RIVER

The Okavango River rises in the Angolan highlands. Fed by subtropical storms, the Cubango River originates in central Angola, flows through Namibia as the Kuvango River and finally enters Botswana as the Okavango River at Mohembo in the North, where it forms the world's largest inland delta system. This Okavango Delta, a large swamp area, spreads up to 15,000 square kilometres, which provides sustenance to tens of thousands of people. At the time of the high flood, a spillway joins the delta to the Chobe River in the Zambezi basin. From the foothills of the Angolan highlands to the Okavango Delta, the Okavango River is like a 'linear oasis' in an arid region where it plays an essential economic and ecological role.[21]

The Okavango River basin is one of the larger basins in Southern Africa. Nearly 150 cubic kilometres of water flow into the system annually. However, the evaporation in this basin is as high as 95 per cent.[22] Though Angola is the upstream contributor and holds larger potential in terms of water resource development, its intra-state instability has been responsible for its lack of interest and capability in this regard.[23] In Botswana, Okavango together with the Chobe River is the largest source of perennial surface water. Moreover, the Okavango Delta is an important source of subsistence fisheries, herding and farming, as well as a source of tourist industry. A large part of Namibia receives water supply from the Okavango River. Namibia withdraws water from the Okavango River for its domestic and irrigation use in its north-eastern part. Water scarcity coupled with severe droughts make Namibia highly dependent on the Okavango system.

The Okavango River basin has regularly been described as conflict prone. Very little development has taken place in the upper reaches of the basin due to long-running civil war in Angola. The Angolan government has proposed more than ten dams at the headwaters of the Okavango, but owing to internal problems, these plans have not been implemented. If the present peace process succeeds, one of the unfortunate dividends of it can be the development of the upper basin, which not only will negatively impact the ecological life of the Okavango system, but it may exacerbate the water sharing conflict among its riparian countries.

The increased water scarcity in two other riparian countries, particularly in Namibia, has resulted in large water abstraction schemes.[24] In the 1980s, the Botswana proposal of the Southern Okavango Integrated Water Development Projects, in order to meet the increasing demand for irrigation, urban water consumption and mining, created a huge international uproar. Local groups received support at the international level to oppose this proposed project on the ground of its adverse environmental implications. The Government of Botswana was forced to put the plan on hold, although it still has similar plans of water extraction from the basin.[25] In the lower reaches of the river, a limited water development infrastructure has been undertaken. The significant one is Mopipi Dam, which provides water to the Orapa Diamond Mine and a limited volume of water for irrigation purposes to the Shakawe area in Botswana.

In Namibia, a small dam has been built on the Omatako River, from which water is diverted to the Okahanja-Windhoek complex for domestic and industrial purposes. Since Namibian independence in 1990, the capital city Windhoek has experienced extremely high population growth. The industrial and commercial interest has also increased water demand in the capital region. After years of insufficient rainfall, Namibia came up with a scheme called the Eastern National Water

Carrier (ENWC), to divert water from Okavango to its drought-stricken capital. In both Namibia and Botswana, there was strong public opposition to the project. The proposed ENWC scheme is seen as having the potential to negatively affect the tourism industry on the Namibian side of the river.[26] Botswana's opposition to the project is much more serious in nature. The plan to abstract 20 million cubic metres of water per year by Namibia is being challenged by Botswana on the grounds that it will directly affect the livelihoods of 50,000 to 70,000 people who are dependent on the flooding water. Thus Botswana considers Namibia's plans as a threat to its national security.[27] A large number of international groups support Botswana on ecological grounds. Thanks to Botswana's persuasion, UNESCO has declared the Okavango Delta as a Ramsar Site in 1997.[28] Owing to international pressure and also a good rainfall in the latter part of the 1990s, Namibian plans to build the pipeline have been put on hold. Despite serious objections from Botswana, Namibia is considering proceeding with the plans. However, an agreement has been reached between the disputing riparian countries to maintain information flow and share feasibility studies of the project.

Botswana and Namibia had set up the Joint Permanent Water Commission in November 1990 as a bilateral initiative immediately after the independence of Namibia. Subsequently, all three riparian countries came together and formed the tripartite Permanent Water Commission on the Okavango River (OKACOM) in 1994. The OKACOM is being supported by the Global Environmental Facility (GEF) for environmental protection and sustainable management of the river. It is struggling to formulate an integrated water management strategy for the whole Okavango basin. The basins states have not yet reached agreement on the issue of exactly what constitutes their share of the available water. Moreover, there is also dissension over the shape of institutional structure that will regulate the day-to-day management of the Okavango River water resources. However, the OKACOM has been functioning for the last ten years in spite of the Kasikili/Sedudu island dispute and the ENWC pipeline controversy.

The ownership of a small island in the Chobe River has been a long-standing dispute between Botswana and Namibia. The island is known as 'Sedudu' in Botswana and 'Kasikili' in Namibia. After a long period of protracted debate and occasional threats of military action, both the disputing countries in May 1996 jointly submitted their cases to the International Court of Justice in The Hague. The International Court of Justice ruling came in 1999, which settled the Kasikili/Sedudu island dispute in Botswana's favour. This has been able to improve the bilateral relationship. However, it is too early to predict the end of the conflict in the river basin. Another cycle of drought may force Namibia to secure a strategic supply of water for its economically and politically important Windhoek area and this action might lead to another round of hostility between the two neighbours. Furthermore, the Angola factor cannot be overlooked. Angola is water rich and the upper reaches of the Okavango basin have not been developed yet. There is very little irrigated agriculture in the Angolan part of the Okavango basin.[29] If the peace process becomes successful and normalcy returns to Angola, the country may move ahead in implementing its proposed water development schemes on the river and that may rekindle the water dispute in the basin.[30]

THE ZAMBEZI RIVER

The Zambezi is Africa's fourth largest river system, after the Nile, Congo and Niger Rivers. It passes through eight countries in Southern Africa before running into the Indian Ocean. It is the largest African river to flow into the Indian Ocean. The Zambezi River basin covers the territories of eight countries: Angola, Botswana, Malawi, Mozambique, Namibia, Tanzania, Zambia and Zimbabwe. Within these countries a large number of different peoples and sub-groups build much of their social and economic life around the river. The Bundu people of Zambia believe that the Zambezi River has a spirit called Nyami Nyami. This spirit brings them water to grow crops and fish to eat so they call the river 'the river of life'. The population of the basin is currently estimated to be around 40 million, representing about 20 per cent of the total SADC population. The basin is generally semi-arid or arid, with the annual rainfall averaging between 600 and 1,200 millimetres. Lack of water is regarded as the main constraint for agricultural production in all but 8 per cent of the arable land in this river basin.[31]

As we see in Table 5.3, Zambia is the largest contributor to the Zambezi basin area, but it is Malawi that is completely dependent upon basin surface water resources. Almost 90 per cent of the population of Malawi live in the basin. Besides Malawi, a large part of the population in Zambia (70 per cent) and Zimbabwe (72.1 per cent) are dependent upon the Zambezi water.[32] Angola, Namibia and Botswana have small proportions of their populations within the basin, but because of the future water demand, they still have a strong interest in the basin management. Mozambique, which is the farthest downstream riparian, also fears to lose most by upstream water diversion.

Areas of Conflict

In the 1950s, Northern Rhodesia (now Zambia), Southern Rhodesia (now Zimbabwe) and Nyasaland (now Malawi) cooperated to construct

149

Map 4 The Zambezi River

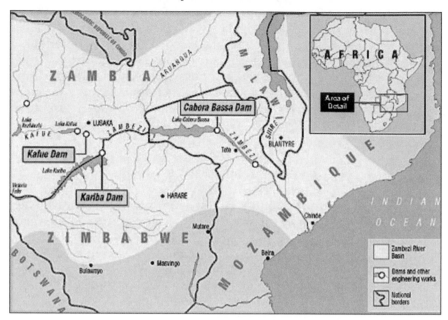

Table 5.3 Statewise Share of the Zambezi River Basin

Country	Total area of country ('000 sq km)	Area of country in basin ('000 sq km)	As % of total area of country (%)	As % of total area of basin (%)
Zambia	753	540	71.8	40.6
Zimbabwe	391	251	64.3	18.9
Angola	1,241	145	11.6	10.9
Mozambique	799	140	17.5	10.5
Malawi	119	118	100	8.9
Botswana	582	84	14.4	6.3
Tanzania	945	27	2.9	2.1
Namibia	824	24	2.9	1.8

Source: R. Hirji and D. Grey, 'Managing International Waters in Africa: Process and Progress', in S. M. A. Salman and L. B. de Chazournes (eds), *International Watercourses: Enhancing Cooperation and Managing Conflict* (Washington DC: World Bank Technical Paper No. 414, 1998), p. 88.

the Kariba and Kafue Dams in the Zambezi River basin. This, however, did not lead to the formation of a basin-based organization to manage the river water resource. At the time of construction of the Kariba Dam, both banks of the Zambezi River belonged to the British colony Rhodesia. With time, Zambia and Zimbabwe gained their independence and in 1987, they formed the Zambezi River Authority (ZRA) in order to obtain the most possible benefits from the Zambezi. To govern the ZRA, both countries established a Council of Ministers. The ZRA's mandate only covers that section of the Zambezi River that forms the common border between Zambia and Zimbabwe. The resources of the ZRA have been devoted largely to the operation and maintenance of the Kariba Complex. Despite these limitations, the ZRA is an example of cooperative management of the shared rivers.[33] The annual budget of the Authority is equally shared between two riparian countries and the size of their share of the power is determined according to their contribution to the total construction cost.

Zimbabwe withdraws water from the Zambezi River for its Huangwe thermal station despite the fact that Zambia has surplus hydropower. The people in the Gwembe Valley in Zambia are not happy as it was they who were displaced by the Kariba Dam and have not received any benefit from it. The southern region of Zambia is opposing any water concession to Zimbabwe. The sharing of the Kariba Lake has also been the source of tension between the two countries. In the Zimbabwean part, tourism and commercial fishing are promoted while the Zambian side is primarily used for artisan fishery.[34] There is also tension over the Zambezi River resources due to Zimbabwe's plan to pipe water from Zambezi (The Matabeleland Zambezi Water Project) to its drought affected second city, Bulawayo. The water transfer to urban centres has not only brought tension with Zambia, it has also created opposing actors inside Zimbabwe. Sharing of the water has brought tensions between urban and rural people, big (predominantly white) farmers and small (predominantly black) farmers.

The intensification of irrigated agriculture in Zimbabwe has reduced the water supply to downstream Mozambique. The threat to Mozambique's water supply is not only limited to Zambia or Zimbabwe's water diversion from Zambezi. The regular droughts and growing water scarcity have prompted many riparian countries to plan for water abstraction projects at the national as well as local levels. Among these upstreamers, the major ones are Namibia, Botswana and Malawi. South Africa, a non-riparian state, also has a large water diversion plan, the Zambezi Aqueduct, to meet its water scarcity situation. South Africa intends to withdraw water over 1,200 kilometres from the Zambezi River at Kazungula through Botswana to Pretoria. The implementation of these proposed water diversion projects can potentially disturb the continuing water-sharing arrangement in the Zambezi basin, and also may lead to population displacement which can spill over the border and create conflicts.

Threats to equitable sharing of the Zambezi water are due to drought driven water scarcity, growing population and economic and political development in the region.[35] In many cases, development objectives of different countries are based on mutually exclusive claims for water from the Zambezi basin. The proposed Batoka Gorge hydroelectric project is among them. Zimbabwe favours this project for hydropower, but the plan faces opposition from Zambia. Most of the riparian countries have some sort of plan for large-scale water withdrawal from the Zambezi. In the East Caprivi region of Namibia, tourism facility operators' refusal to the fishing community from Namibia and Zambia of access to the river, has already been a source of tension between the two groups. Namibia and Botswana are engaged in a conflict over the Sidudu island in the Chobe/Caprivi wetlands, which is part of the basin. In the lower part of the basin, the use of water and related resources of the Shire River has been the source of conflict between Malawi and Mozambique. In spite of the presence of several international as well as localized conflicts, there have been several efforts for increased cooperation among the basin countries to develop Zambezi on a multi-lateral basis.

Moving Towards Cooperation

Several projects are being undertaken for improved cooperation among the Zambezi basin countries. International and bilateral treaties and SADC guidelines are being used to devise ways of sharing and managing Zambezi water. Coinciding with the formation of the ZRA, the Zambezi Action Plan (ZACPLAN) was drawn up in 1987 by the Zambezi basin states with UNEP support. In the same year, this ZACPLAN was adopted by SADC as a part of its Programme of Action. It aims to ensure sustainable utilization of Zambezi water resources within a sound and balanced environment. The action plan expects to contribute the development of environmental legislation both at national and regional levels. Besides environmental impact assessment and supporting measures such as an information and education programme, the action plan also aims to create mechanisms for prevention or resolution of conflicts over water uses. The aims of the ZACPLAN have been manifested into 19 projects, which are called ZACPROs. The ZACPROs are grouped into two categories. The first eight ZACPROS have been put in Category 1, which is given highest priority, mainly emphasizing water resource monitoring and planning. The rest of the ZACPROs are put in Category 2, which focuses on environmental conservation issues.

The small SADC Secretariat is the implementing agency of the ZACPLAN. However, initially the executive and co-ordination function was assigned to the Sector Coordinator for Soil and Water Conservation and Land Utilization (SWCLU) in Lesotho, which was later transformed into Environment and Land Management Sector Unit (ELMS). Since 1996, the SADC Water Sector has taken over the responsibilities of the ELMS.

The involvement of a large number of actors in this scheme has posed problems in execution. Moreover, ZACPLAN is heavily dependent upon external funding. The riparian states have given full political and moral support, but when it comes to financial support, the commitment is absolute minimal.[36] With the support of UNEP and Nordic countries, the ZACPRO 1, 2, 5 and 6 have been fully or partially implemented. The implementation of the ZACPRO 2 started in 1991, which developed regional legislation and provided the basis for the SADC Protocol on Shared Watercourse System, which was signed in 1995. The ZACPRO 6 is involved to establish the legal and institutional framework and proposes the establishment of a river basin commission (ZAMCOM). A draft agreement in this regard is being discussed, but has not been signed yet by the riparian countries. The major obstacle for the implementation of ZAMCOM is the disagreement among the basin countries over deciding what is the reasonable and equitable utilization of the shared water.

In spite of all these efforts and external support, the Zambezi River basin has not yet experienced the establishment of a River Basin Authority with the participation of all the riparian countries. The real problem is strong national interests over basin-wide interests. To maximize the utilization of the Zambezi water, there is a certain need for the establishment of ZAMCOM. Of course, the establishment of this inter-governmental organization will not be able to resolve all the conflicts, but it will certainly help to reduce the water-related tensions and promote basin-based cooperation. Establishment of a river basin organization on Zambezi will be instrumental in sharing information among basin countries and may bring further international collaboration and external assistance. The basin-based cooperation on Zambezi can bring all riparian countries benefits greater than what they could have achieved through their purely state-centric development.

FINDING A REGIONAL APPROACH

SADC region includes numerous international river basins. A major step towards the better management of the regional river has been taken up by the South African Development Community (SADC). In 1995, the

SADC member states signed a protocol establishing basic principles for the sharing of the region's water resources. The 1995 SADC Protocol on Shared Water Course Systems declares respect for the principle of equitable utilization and aims to promote exchange of information, to maintain balance between development and protection of environment.

In November 1995, a meeting of regional water ministers was convened by SADC at Pretoria to explore opportunities for greater cooperation. The Pretoria meeting led to the establishment of a Water Sector within SADC in August 1996. Among other functions, this Water Sector has the role of facilitating and stimulating cooperation among the riparian countries over the shared water resources. Its institutional arrangement consists of a Sectoral Committee of Ministers, a Sectoral Committee of Senior Officials (meeting once a year), a Sector Coordinating Unit (based in Lesotho) and Technical and other sub-committees. The mandate of the Water Sector is limited, and it lacks any authoritative instruments of enforcement. In August 2000, a revised Protocol on Shared Watercourses was signed by 13 SADC member states in Namibia. Articles 3, 4 and 5 of the Protocol prescribe the formation of river basin organizations and Article 7 bestows the power of dispute adjudication to the SADC tribunal. The Revised Protocol incorporates several key provisions from the 1997 UN Convention on the Law of the Non-navigational Uses of International Watercourses. Moreover, it also empowers existing SADC institutions to implement the terms of agreement and resolve potential conflicts.

The most important aspect of the protocol and establishment of the Water Sector is the spirit in which the SADC member states agreed to manage and utilize the shared water systems in an environmentally sustainable manner. At the basin level, SADC countries have negotiated several bilateral and multi-lateral agreements and established river commissions and institutions to manage their shared rivers. However, the elements of sovereignty and achieving self-sufficiency among these newly independent states are the major obstacles for greater regional cooperation. The large economic disparity among the member states also poses an obstacle for effective regional cooperation on water systems.

Southern Africa is a water scarce region. The declining population growth rate in the region, mainly due to the HIV/AIDS pandemic, has to a certain extent stopped the rapid downward slide to the per capita water availability. But the water situation is still precarious. Nearly 70 per cent of the region's surface water is shared between two or more states.[37] It is estimated that in two decades, three to four economically powerful countries in the region will face water shortages in the absence of appropriate water management.[38] The adoption of the supply management strategy only to address the water scarcity in the region is not enough. Several big dam projects, which the countries in the region have constructed to increase the supply of water, have also been the source of bilateral disputes. To meet the growing demand, there is a need to minimize water use, particularly in the agricultural sector which uses water most. Unless, the member countries of the SADC agree on a common framework of their water-use priorities, the sharing of the river water may eventually lead to heightened friction and open hostility in some of the international river basins in this region.

NOTES

1. This chapter has used certain parts of the author's earlier work: A. Swain and P. Stalgren, 'Managing the Zambezi: The Need to Build Water Institutions', in D. Tevera and S. Moyo (eds), *Environmental Security in Southern Africa* (Harare: SARIP, 2000), pp. 119–38.
2. M. M. Khosa and C. Mupimpila, 'On Global Security: A Suggested Interpretation for Southern Africa', in J. Whitman (ed.), *The Sustainability Challenge for Southern Africa* (London: Macmillan, 2000).
3. A. Turton, 'Precipitation, People, Pipelines and Power: Towards a Political Ecology Discourse of Water in Southern Africa', in P. Scott and S. Sulivan (eds), *Political Ecology: Science, Myth and Power* (London: Edward Arnold, 2000), pp. 132–53.
4. J. Lundqvist, 'Avert Looming Hydrocide', *Ambio*, 27, 6, (1998), pp. 428–33.
5. L. Swatuk, 'The New Water Architecture in Southern Africa: Reflections on Current Trends in the Light of Rio + 10', *International Affairs*, 78, 3 (2002), pp. 507–30.
6. The dunes of the Kalahari Desert have now blocked the passage of the Molopo tributary, thus Botswana is not able to contribute to the runoff of the Orange River.
7. See M. S. Basson, P. H. van Niekerk and J. A. van Rooyen, *Overview of Water Resources Availability and Utilization in South Africa* (Pretoria: Department of Water Affairs and Forestry, 1997).
8. J. Pallett (ed.), *Sharing Water in Southern Africa* (Windhoek: DRFN, 1997).
9. The history of planning to transfer water from Lesotho to South Africa is traceable to British colonial rule in the 1950s, when the colonial administrators had made some attempts to develop water management schemes. See P. Vale and K. Matlosa, 'Beyond the Nation State: Rebuilding South Africa from Below', *Harvard International Review*, 17, 4 (1995).
10. Formally Lesotho had approached the UN Council for Namibia in New York (Namibia was then under South African occupation) for a no objection statement in the middle of the 1980s. This was to fulfil the World Bank's condition for financing the LHWP. See R. T. Mochebelele, 'Good Governance and the Avoidance of Conflicts: The Lesotho Highlands Water Project Experience', in Green Cross International, *Water for Peace in the Middle East and Southern Africa* (Geneva: Green Cross International, 2000), pp. 107–11.
11. Pallett, *Sharing Water in Southern Africa*.
12. The cost of the project is almost 800% of Lesotho's gross national product (GNP).
13. The supporters of the LHWP argue that the deep gorges in the Lesotho highlands provide excellent sites for the dams and their reservoirs. The head difference between the highlands and the Gauteng region helps better gravity flow of water from the reservoirs to the Vaal River system. Moreover, the regime in Lesotho justifies the project on the basis of their own national interest on the ground that more

than half of the labour force from Lesotho working in South Africa are employed in the Gauteng province only.

14. K. Horta, 'The Mountain Kingdom's White Oil: The Lesotho Highlands Water Project', *The Ecologist*, 25, 6 (1995), pp. 227–31; K. Horta and S. Coverdale, 'Dams & Distress for Kingdom in the Sky', *People & the Planet*, 5, 3 (1996), pp. 24–5.

15. K. Matlosa, 'The Lesotho Highlands Water Project: Socio-Economic Impacts', in D. Tevera and S. Moyo (eds), *Environmental Security in Southern Africa* (Harare: SARIP, 2000), pp. 175–86.

16. In 1999, the JPTC changed its name to the Lesotho Highlands Water Commission (LHWC).

17. A. Turton, 'An Overview of the Hydropolitical Dynamics of the Orange River Basin', in M. Nakayama (ed.), *International Waters in South Africa* (Tokyo: UNU Press, 2003), p. 149.

18. Though the basin is shared among four countries, the Limpopo River is extremely important for the eastern part of Botswana as it is one of the major sources of surface water.

19. Pallett, *Sharing Water in Southern Africa*.

20. A. E. Mohamed, 'Joint Development and Cooperation of International Water Resources', in M. Nakayama (ed.), *International Waters in South Africa* (Tokyo: UNU Press, 2003), p. 221.

21. P. J. Ashton, 'The Search for an Equitable Basis for Water Sharing in the Okavango River Basin', in M. Nakayama (ed.), *International Waters in South Africa* (Tokyo: UNU Press, 2003), p. 167.

22. A. Mutembwa, 'Towards a Sustainable Water Management Strategy for Southern Africa', in J. Whitman (ed.), *The Sustainability Challenge for Southern Africa* (London: Macmillan, 2000).

23. Virtually no development has taken place in the upper catchment of the Okavango basin since civil war started in Angola in 1975.

24. P. J. Ashton, 'Water Security for Multinational River Basin States: The Special Case of the Okavango River Basin', Paper presented at the SIWI Seminar on Water Scarcity for Multinational Water Systems – Opportunities for Development, Stockholm, 14–17 August 2000.

25. P. H. Gleick, *The World's Water: The Biennial Report on Freshwater Resources 1998–1999* (Washington DC: Island Press, 1998).

26. P. J. Ashton, 'Potential Environmental Impacts Associated with the Abstraction of Water from the Okavango River in Namibia', Paper presented at the Annual Conference of the Southern African Association of Aquatic Scientists, Swakopmund, Namibia, 23–26 June 1999.

27. L. Swatuk, 'Environmental Cooperation for Regional Peace and Security in Southern Africa', Draft Chapter Prepared for the Project on Environmental Cooperation and Regional Peace (Washington DC: The Woodrow Wilson Centre, 1999).

28. The Ramsar Convention is formally known as the 'Convention on Wetlands of International Importance, especially as Waterfowl Habitat'. Named after the Iranian town where the Convention was first adopted in 1971, it has now over 74 signatories.

29. FAO, 'Irrigation Potential in Africa: A Basin Approach', *FAO Land and Water Bulletin*, 4 (1997).

30. See K. Akerfeldt, *Transboundary Water Sharing: Cooperation and Conflict in Managing Freshwater Resources in Southern Africa* (Uppsala: Uppsala University Programme of International Studies, Masters Thesis, 2001).

31. Swain and Stalgren, 'Managing the Zambezi: The Need to Build Water Institutions'.

32. See M. Chenje (ed.), *State of the Environment Zambezi Basin 2000* (Maseru/Harare/Lusaka: SADC/IUCN/ZRA/SARDC, 2000).

33. Although both these countries have some agreement over the operation of the Kariba Dam, they have been involved in a protracted conflict over the building of Batoka Gorge Hydroelectric project on the upstream of Lake Kariba. Zimbabwe favours the speedy implementation of the project in the hope of gaining hydropower, but for Zambians this is not of high priority.

34. T. M. Chiuta, 'Shared Water Resources and Conflicts: the Case of the Zambezi River Basin', in D. Tevera and S. Moyo (eds), *Environmental Security in Southern Africa* (Harare: SARIP, 2000), pp. 139–55.

35. M. Chenje and P. Johnson (eds), *Water in Southern Africa* (Harare: SADC/IUCN/SARDC, 1996).

36. F. I. Aasand, T. A. Kammerud and J. M. Trolldalen, *Challenges in Management of Shared Water Basins – Zambezi River Basin in Southern Africa and Implementation of ZACPLAN* (Oslo: CESAR, 1996).

37. WSCU, *Regional Strategic Action Plan for Integrated Water Resources Development and Management in the SADC Countries 1999–2004* (Maseru, Lesotho: Water Sector Coordinating Unit Summary Report, 1998).

38. P. P. Zhou, *Issues Paper on Shared Water Resources* (Regional Centre for Southern Africa, RAPID Paper, 1997).

6

Sustaining Water Agreements and Maturing Cooperation[1]

In most parts of the world competition among water users is rising as people demand more and more from limited water resources. Particularly in Asia, Africa and the Middle East, the demand for water is rapidly overtaking the existing supply. As the major rivers of these regions are shared by two or more countries, disputes over the sharing of the water are becoming increasingly contentious. Tensions over decreased water supplies are emerging in these areas, which face population pressures, rapid urbanization and pressing development needs. Global climate change may further complicate the situation.

Water not only brings conflict, it can also play its part to promote peace. In the face of mutual dependence on the same fresh water resource, the withdrawal or pollution by one riparian state can potentially not only lead to disputes but also bring cooperation in the basin. In most of the international river basins, competing and disputing riparian countries are now moving towards cooperation. Nearly 150 water-related treaties have been signed in the last century. Growing competition over the river waters has resulted in these cooperative sharing arrangements. As has been discussed in earlier chapters, in the face of growing water scarcity, sharing agreements have been signed in most of the rivers in Asia, Africa and the Middle East.

In the 1990s, there have been riparian agreements on the Zambezi, Okavango, Limpopo, Mekong, Jordan, Mahakali and Ganges rivers. The existing agreements on the sharing of the Nile, Indus, Orange and Euphrates-Tigris River water have been going through severe stress, but they are still holding up. Usually, the riparian countries have agreed to settle their dispute over the quantity issue when there is a hope for the further exploitation of the river resource.

AGREEING TO EXPLOIT

The contending riparian states are more likely to reach an agreement over the quantity allocation, when there is a substantial amount of unused water left in the river. The hope and expectation to control the 'unused' portion of the river water, help the countries to come together to acquire the profit. Agreement on the Indus River system became a possibility in 1960 between two traditional rivals, India and Pakistan because nearly 80 per cent of the river water was running to the Arabian Sea unused by both the basin countries. Of course it took nine long years for the World Bank to bring both the riparian countries into agreement, but it became possible when there was scope for exploiting water resource further with the help of mega projects.

The approach of the 1960 Indus River Agreement was to increase the amount of water available to the two parties. This future prospect persuaded the two countries to share the flow and agree to the settlement. Partition of the rivers was more acceptable to the countries than joint management and both countries got into the business of water exploitation of their respective shares with the help of the 'Indus Basin Development Fund' administered by the World Bank. In recent years, the water scarcity has become severe in the Indus basin. Both India and Pakistan have almost developed the capacity to get the maximum use of the Indus water system. The water demand is increasing rapidly within their own territory. The ongoing projects in the upstream of the rivers on the Indian side may affect the water flow to Pakistan and that can bring difficulty to the Indus River Agreement. Water also figures prominently in the Kashmir dispute as the Indus and its tributaries pass through Indian controlled Kashmir on their journey from the Himalayas to the Arabian Sea. Any territorial compromise of India to settle the Kashmir dispute with Pakistan can affect the functioning of the 1960 Indus River Agreement.

In 1959, Egypt and Sudan reached an agreement on the sharing of the Nile River. This 1959 Agreement also became possible due to the large amount of runoff that remained unallocated by the 1929 Agreement. From the newly calculated runoff of 84 billion cubic metres of water at Aswan, Egypt got the right to use 55.5 billion cubic metres and 18.5 billion was allotted to Sudan. The Lake Nasser created by the High Aswan Dam is one of the largest man-made lakes in the world. Without the Aswan, Egypt would undoubtedly have been in serious economic difficulties. The water reservoir has brought significant increase in the welfare of the country due to the supply of reliable and adequate water for irrigation, municipal and industrial use. However, with increasing water demand in the upstream and less availability of unused water, the river has already become a source of serious dispute among the major riparian countries. Ethiopia, the upstream nation which supplies most of the water to the Nile, now demands its legitimate share. Without addressing the genuine needs of Ethiopia, the World Bank promoted Nile Basin Initiative cannot move forward.

The increasing riparian demand has also raised doubts about the continuation of the existing water-sharing agreements on the Euphrates-Tigris River system. Turkey and Syria signed a bilateral agreement in 1987 to share the Euphrates River. In spite of bilateral tension, the possibility of future river water exploitation at the national level brought both the riparian countries to opt for this arrangement. Since the 1960s, Turkey and Syria have plans for several large-scale water projects over the Euphrates-Tigris. Turkey is busy with its massive South-eastern Anatolia (GAP) Project on the Euphrates-Tigris system. Syria is also building a series of dams on the river. However, the increasing water withdrawal in the 1990s by Turkey with the help of the ongoing GAP has not only strained relations between Turkey and Syria but also Syria's relations with Iraq. The 1990 Agreement between Syria and Iraq at Tunis, regulating allocation of water at the point where the Euphrates leaves Syria, allots 58 per cent to Iraq and 42 per cent to Syria. With the decreasing runoff from the Turkish side, Syria is opting to reduce the water supply to Iraq. Thus, the GAP has already become a source of common concern for Syria and Iraq, and also a serious future threat to the bilateral water-sharing agreements between Turkey and Syria and also between Syria and Iraq.

The hope for further exploitation has not only brought agreements on the Indus, Nile or Euphrates-Tigris in the past; it has also facilitated agreements in recent years over some other shared river basins. The 1995 Agreement signed among the Lower Mekong basin countries became a possibility as the slow-flowing Mekong River provides a lot of potential for further exploitation. The Mekong River consists of six riparian states. However, under the Cold War politics, combined effort to exploit the river was promoted during the 1950s among the four lower basin countries. In 1995, a new statute was signed by the same four lower riparian countries, giving birth to the Mekong River Commission. This new initiative was possible due to the support from the UNDP and the Asian Development Bank. With the help of international funding and assistance, lower riparian countries aim to further exploit the river water for hydropower and irrigation. However, the non-inclusion of upper riparian states – particularly the absence of China – may soon become a spoiler in this cooperative effort to harness the river.

The Zambezi River basin is another example of riparian cooperation due to hope for future exploitation. The riparian countries have several plans for large-scale withdrawal from the Zambezi. In spite of individual water withdrawal plans, there are some signs of cooperation among the basin countries to develop Zambezi on a joint basis. Several initiatives are being undertaken for improved cooperation, not only in the Zambezi basin, but also in other shared river basins in Southern Africa. The South African Development Community is in the forefront of formulating a regional policy for the further development of the shared river systems.

The agreements between Israel and Jordan over the Jordan water in 1994 and between India and Nepal over the Mahakali water in 1995 are other examples of the riparian desire to exploit the rivers. The water scarcity in all these river basins has brought the riparian countries to come to the negotiation table rather than waging war against each other. The possibility of further extraction of water resources has been the attraction for the negotiated settlement. However, there are very few international rivers left, which can provide a certain hope for feasible further exploitation. Most of the rivers have been exploited to a large extent; a few other feasible water projects bear massive economic and environmental cost. Local politics and environmentalists have also brought difficulty to the engineering solution to the water scarcity problem. When there is not enough water in the river to meet the demands of the contending riparian states, and almost all the feasible water projects on the river have been already undertaken, then to reach an agreement over the sharing dispute, India and Bangladesh have taken the help of manipulating the river runoff data. The Agreement between India and Bangladesh in 1996 over the sharing of the Ganges River is one of the examples of this ingenuity.

However, allocated water in almost all of these sharing agreements is unable to meet the increasingly growing demand. The time has come to realize the fact that addressing the supply side alone cannot find a lasting solution to the quantity question of the sharing of international rivers. Thus, the water-sharing issue needs to be addressed from the demand side as well. For the appropriate and competent management of shared fresh water systems, it is vital to build institutions at the basin level. Some of the international organizations and legal principles are aiming at providing guidelines for the basin-based arrangements that should emerge.

INTERNATIONAL ORGANIZATIONS AND LEGAL PRINCIPLES

There are numerous organizations and legal principles at the international level that affect the management and development of water resources. In the 1990s, some important legal and institutional changes have taken place. Two new international water organizations have been created, along with the adoption of the Convention on the Law of the Non-Navigational Uses of International Watercourses by the United Nations General Assembly.

International Organizations

The World Water Council (WWC) and the Global Water Partnership (GWP) are two major international 'water' institutions, which have been established in the 1990s. The WWC, created in Dublin in 1992 and with its Secretariat in Marseilles, aims to promote an awareness of water issues and works in favour of efficient, sustainable conservation and management of fresh water. This non-governmental non-profit organization provides an independent forum for exchanging views and information, for sharing experiences and concerns, and for recommending actions on water management. The WWC aims to be 'the world's water-policy think-tank'. Its main activities have focused on holding international meetings, the series of World Water Forums.[2] While the WWC is essentially a forum for discussion working on raising awareness of proper water resource management, the GWP comprises organizations with financial powers to implement various programmes.

In August 1995, the World Bank and the United Nations Development Programme (UNDP) proposed the creation of this organization and it is open to all parties involved in water resource management including governments, international agencies and multilateral banks. The GWP brings together a large number of organizations including aid agencies in an informal partnership. It is not a donor agency, but a network with a shared vision of water management and development. It promotes integrated programmes at the regional and national levels and helps capacity building and sustainable investment across national boundaries. Its Secretariat is located in Stockholm.

These global initiatives to address the issue of fresh water have brought the international fresh water sharing problem to the fore. There have also been numerous individual attempts, for instance by the Global Environmental Facility (GEF), World Bank, UNDP, UNEP, Food and Agricultural Organization (FAO), and World Meteorological Organization/United Nations Educational, Scientific, and Cultural Organization (WMO/UNESCO) to find ways of successfully sharing the international watercourses among states. Moreover, thanks to the efforts of the annual Stockholm Water Symposium and International Water Resources Association, and the establishment of a powerful World Commission for Water in the Twenty-first Century, water has recently become a priority issue in the international political agenda. Significant new fresh water initiatives were one of the highlights of the World Summit on Sustainable Development in Johannesburg in August 2002.

International Water Law

Besides providing institutional support for the fresh water resource management, there is an ongoing move towards establishing a common legal framework for the sharing of international watercourses at the global level.

There have been numerous unsuccessful attempts in this century to establish an international legal framework to manage the international rivers. In the first part of this century, the Territorial Sovereignty Doctrine (absolute sovereignty over waters flowing within a country) and the Natural Water Flow Approach (the river belongs to all the riparian states) came up in addressing the issues over the sharing of international rivers. Unfortunately, neither the territorial sovereignty, nor the natural water flow approach provided a solution as they were based on an individualistic and anarchical conception of international law. None of these theories offered a long-term resolution of the conflicting interests of the upper and lower riparian states of an international river. The failure of these two legal approaches led some to think of sharing the rivers on an economic basis. It also led to the preaching of Community of Interest/Optimum Development approach. According to this approach, the whole river basin is regarded as an economic unit irrespective of state boundaries, and the waters are vested in the community of the users or divided among the co-riparians.

Under an integrated programme of development of a river, dam and other water development works are to be located at optimal locations and the benefits accruing from them are to be used by the riparian states in need of those benefits. This joint approach includes joint planning, joint construction, joint management and sharing of expenditure on construction and maintenance. The idea of single basin approach is attractive to economists and water engineers because it allows them to consider the international rivers as single hydrological units and plan accordingly. However, there are many difficulties involved in sorting out the externalities among the various riparian nations. The regulation and management of international river basins with so much concentration of power in the hands of non-political commissions is an exception rather than the rule in the inter-state practice. Owing to obvious limitations in states agreeing to joint development, not many examples are found of this approach.

All these above mentioned approaches were adopted and implemented in individual cases, and due to their various limitations could not be upgraded as an acceptable international practice. In the absence of any law to regulate international rivers, the International Law Association (ILA) have made several attempts since 1956 to establish 'principle of equitability' in sharing the international river water. The 'principle of equitability' departs from the approach that advocates maximum benefit accruing to all the riparians, keeping in mind their economic and social needs. During its 52nd Conference in 1966 at Helsinki, the ILA decided on the Helsinki Rules for International Watercourses, which emphasize that an existing use of a river would have to give way to a new use in order to reach an equitable apportionment of shared water resources, though the new user would have to pay compensation.

In 1970, Finland introduced a resolution in the UN General Assembly on laws for international watercourses. This resolution suggested that the Helsinki Rules should be considered as a model for sharing international rivers. The Sixth Committee of the UN discussed this proposal, and there was near consensus on having an international watercourse law. Objections surfaced, however, against the acceptance of the Helsinki Rules. The voices against the Rules came mostly from a number of upstream nations around the world. The resolution to refer to the Helsinki Rules as a model was convincingly defeated by 41 votes to 25 (32 abstentions). The voting pattern was completely different from the then usual practice of voting on the basis of global political alignment. In this case, upstream countries voted against downstream countries. After deleting the reference to the Helsinki Rules, the resolution was passed with overwhelming majority. While noting that 'the use of international rivers and lakes is still based on general principles and rules of customary law', the UN General Assembly recommended that the International Law Commission (ILC) should '... take up the study of the law of the non-navigational uses of international watercourses with a view to its progressive development and codification ...'.[3]

After being directed by the UN General Assembly Resolution in 1970, the International Law Commission first undertook the task of defining the scope of the term 'international watercourse' and applicability of the drainage basin concept. In 1976, the ILC agreed to use the term 'international watercourse' instead of contentious terms such as 'international drainage basin' or 'international watercourse system'. After years of wrangling, in 1991, the ILC sent its Draft Report concerning the Law of the Non-Navigational Uses of International Watercourse to the Secretary General of the United Nations on which the member states were asked to comment. The Draft law was based on two fundamental ideas. As is the case in the Helsinki Rules, its Article 5 said, 'Watercourse States shall in their respective territories utilise an international watercourse in an equitable and reasonable manner.' But, at the same time, Article 7 of the Draft stipulated that 'Watercourse States shall utilise an international watercourse in such a way as not to cause appreciable harm to other watercourse States.' However, to some, the injunction of not causing appreciable harm held force as an imperative prohibition in absolute terms, the right to equitable sharing.[4]

The suggestions from Germany and USA persuaded the ILC in its 46th session in 1994 to replace the word 'appreciable' with 'significant' while adopting the final text of a set of 33 draft articles on the law of the non-navigational uses of international watercourse.[5] While doing this cosmetic change to avoid the definitional problems, the new text also gave priority to the equitable use in case it conflict, causing significant harm to a prior user. The burden of proof to establish that a use is equitable and reasonable lies with the state whose use of the watercourse is causing significant harm. Finally, after 25 years of deliberations, the ILC submitted its draft on 'Convention on the Law of the Non-Navigational Uses of International Watercourses' in 1996 to the UN General Assembly, which adopted it on 21 May 1997.[6] The draft resolution was sponsored by Antigua and Barbuda, Bangladesh, Bhutan, Brazil, Cambodia, Canada, Chile, Denmark, Finland, Germany, Greece, Hungary, Italy, Japan, Lao People's Democratic Republic, Liechtenstein, Malaysia, Mexico, Nepal, Netherlands, Norway, Portugal, Republic of Korea, Romania, Sudan, Sweden, Syria, Tunisia, United Kingdom, United States, Uruguay and Venezuela. The 37-article Watercourses Convention and its 14-article annex governs the non-navigational uses of international watercourses, as well as measures to protect, preserve and manage them. Viewed as a framework Convention, it addresses such issues as flood control, water quality, erosion, sedimentation, saltwater intrusion and living resources. The Assembly adopted the draft resolution (document A/51/L.72) by a recorded vote of 103 in favour to 3 against, with 27 abstentions (for the full text of the Convention, see the Appendix).

A number of states who abstained or voted against the text drew attention to a lack of consensus on several of its key provisions, such as those governing dispute settlement. Their reservation regarding the draft was also on their perceived lack of balance in its provisions between the rights and obligations of the upstream and downstream riparian states. They also expressed concern that the Convention had deviated from the aim of being a framework agreement.

By having both the principles of 'equitable utilization' and 'not to cause significant harm' in the text, the UN Convention was able to obtain a majority support in the UN General Assembly. However, the major problem may arise while defining the equitable and reasonable shares for the riparian states. The reasonable share or equitable use expresses respect for a riparian's sovereign right within its territory, but restricts its uses to ensure reasonable share for the other riparians. What is equitable sharing is not an easy question to determine. In practical terms, there is a need of using a non-involved third party to determine the equitability in the distribution of water resources. Article 33 of the

Table 6.1 Voting in the General Assembly for the Adoption of Convention on the Law of the Non-navigational Uses of International Watercourses

In favour	Albania, Algeria, Angola, Antigua and Barbuda, Armenia, Australia, Austria, Bahrain, Bangladesh, Belarus, Botswana, Brazil, Brunei Darussalam, Burkina Faso, Cambodia, Cameroon, Canada, Chile, Costa Rica, Côte d'Ivoire, Croatia, Cyprus, Czech Republic, Denmark, Djibouti, Estonia, Federated States of Micronesia, Finland, Gabon, Georgia, Germany, Greece, Guyana, Haiti, Honduras, Hungary, Iceland, Iran, Ireland, Italy, Jamaica, Japan, Jordan, Kazakhstan, Kenya, Kuwait, Lao People's Democratic Republic, Latvia, Lesotho, Liberia, Libya, Liechtenstein, Lithuania, Luxembourg, Madagascar, Malawi, Malaysia, Maldives, Malta, Marshall Islands, Mauritius, Mexico, Morocco, Mozambique, Namibia, Nepal, Netherlands, New Zealand, Norway, Oman, Papua New Guinea, Philippines, Poland, Portugal, Qatar, Republic of Korea, Romania, Russian Federation, Samoa, San Marino, Saudi Arabia, Sierra Leone, Singapore, Slovakia, Slovenia, South Africa, Sudan, Suriname, Sweden, Syria, Thailand, Trinidad and Tobago, Tunisia, Ukraine, United Arab Emirates, United Kingdom, United States, Uruguay, Venezuela, Vietnam, Yemen, Zambia
Against	Burundi, China, Turkey
Abstaining	Andorra, Argentina, Azerbaijan, Belgium, Bolivia, Bulgaria, Colombia, Cuba, Ecuador, Egypt, Ethiopia, France, Ghana, Guatemala, India, Israel, Mali, Monaco, Mongolia, Pakistan, Panama, Paraguay, Peru, Rwanda, Spain, United Republic of Tanzania, Uzbekistan
Absent	Afghanistan, Bahamas, Barbados, Belize, Benin, Bhutan, Cape Verde, Comoros, Democratic People's Republic of Korea, Dominican Republic, El Salvador, Eritrea, Fiji, Guinea, Lebanon, Mauritania, Myanmar, Niger, Nigeria, Palau, Saint Kitts and Nevis, Saint Lucia, Saint Vincent and the Grenadines, Senegal, Solomon Islands, Sri Lanka, Swaziland, Tajikistan, The former Yugoslav Republic of Macedonia, Turkmenistan, Uganda, Zaire, Zimbabwe

Note: Belgium is recorded as having abstained in the vote on adoption of the Convention on the Law on Non-navigational Uses of International Watercourses. The representative of Belgium subsequently informed the Secretariat that he had intended to vote in favour.

Convention, however, prescribes a time-taking procedure to settle the dispute in the absence of an applicable agreement among the riparian states.

However, for this Convention to be legally binding it needs to be signed and ratified by 35 countries. This ratification process is moving along at a very slow pace, which has raised the fear that the Convention may not be ratified by enough countries to enter into force. Many governments are finding it either too strong or too weak, with positions often coinciding with whether the nation is upstream (too strong) or downstream (too weak) in international basins. In the beginning, the Convention remained open for signature till 20 May 2002. In that period, the Convention was signed by 13 countries (Ivory Coast, Finland, Germany, Hungary, Jordan, Lebanon, Luxembourg, Norway, Paraguay, Portugal, South Africa, Syria and Venezuela) and got ratified by six countries (Finland, Jordan, Lebanon, Norway, South Africa and Syria) only.

Even if this Convention gets ratified by member states and becomes a legal framework, it will not be sufficient to address the problem of water sharing in different parts of the world. The sharing of international fresh waters among the riparian countries in different geographical regions is a problem of huge dimension. Complex water disputes can only be solved by cooperation and compromise, not by a strict insistence on rules of law.

WATER AVAILABILITY AND ITS REGIONAL VARIATION

Water availability is highly erratic in different regions of the world. More than 80 per cent of the total global runoff is concentrated in the northern temperate zone, which houses a relatively small population. In the tropical and arid areas, where most of the world population lives, the situation is complicated by scarcity as well as by the uneven distribution of water. The problem of these water-short countries in the South is manifold. They have intermittent wet and dry seasons and the main part of the year is often dry. Recurrent drought years are part of their climate. The soils in these countries are vulnerable to being impenetrable, which leads to faster land desiccation. The re-charge of their aquifers and rivers is low since most rainfall evaporates.

The world's population is now increasing by about 90–100 million people every year. The population growth of most of the developed countries is nearly stable or declining. As the World Bank Report states, 95 per cent of future growth will take place in the developing countries of Africa, Asia and Latin America. This high population growth in the developing countries multiplies pressure on fresh water. With each passing day, the gap between the needs of the growing population in these regions and the diminishing fresh water resources widens. Due to current population projection, the per capita water supply is projected to decline at a much faster rate in the developing countries than their developed counterparts. The increasing urbanization in the developing world is also placing great stress on its meagre water resource. While the urban population is growing by only 0.8 per cent per year in the developed countries, the growth rate in the developing regions is 3.6 per cent. The need for water is not only dependent on population or urbanization but it also varies from region to region on the basis of the major economic activities.

There is traditionally high consumptive use of water in the agricultural sector. Not only do the developing countries have a lesser share of the water resources, but their agro-based economy also needs and consumes more water. In major agrarian economies of countries like India and Egypt, water used for agricultural production still accounts for more than 80 per cent of their total water use. In the developed industrialized countries, the water use for agriculture sectors is less than half of such estimates.

Water used in industrial sectors poses a different problem. The water which is used for industrial purposes comes back to its source after cooling the plant, so the cause of concern is not the increasing volume of water withdrawn, but the discharge of heated and polluted water back to the system. The large-scale industrial use of water leads to the problems of water quality. In most of the developed countries, where the per capita water availability is somewhat plentiful, the water supply is polluted by various human activities. The water quality not the quantity is the major environmental issue in many of the northern countries.

Water is irreplaceable – so, the problem of its reduced quantity cannot be easily solved. Water, unlike many other natural resources, is not easy to transport from one region to another to address the distribution problem. One of the lessons brought back by American forces from the Persian Gulf in 1991 was the tremendous logistics needed to bring water to half a million soldiers operating in an arid environment.[7] This experience also contributed to a large extent in the planning and executions of coalition attacks against Iraq in 2003. It is gradually getting more difficult to take advantage of the mobile character of water and flow it from one region to another with the help of canals or pipelines. A number of major river diversion schemes in many parts of the world are not being implemented owing to political-environmental reasons. Some of the deepest divisions are gradually taking place between people near to the original source of water and the diversion beneficiaries. Like the building of large dams, water diversion has become unpopular and the fear of popular protest is dithering the government planners in further executing these schemes.

The popular perception regarding the value of river water varies significantly from one region to another. In general, urban users of water are willing to pay more for their water supplies than a farmer using water for irrigation purposes. In most parts of the industrial north, river water is merely an economic commodity and its use can be decided primarily on economic consideration. Accruing optimal benefits from river water is the rule of the game. However, in some regions, rivers are much more than that: they are sacred and worshipped as God. It becomes further difficult to price the water of these rivers as it is considered as the gift of God. The principle that may be adopted to effect a cooperative arrangement over the water of the Rhine may be simply not discernible to a Hindu Indian in getting his agreement to share the sacred water of the river Ganges with a Muslim Bangladeshi. This highly nationalistic value is also attached to the waters of river basins in the Middle East.

The United Nations inter-regional seminar held in Dakar in 1981 addressed the question of a standard or ideal approach to joint river basin arrangement. Due to the presence of unique characteristics in each and every river basin, it concluded '... the golden rule is that there does not exist any golden rule. It is necessary to adopt an ad hoc solution for each river basin.'[8] In the presence of strong regional variance over the availability, need and perception of fresh water, establishing an internationally acceptable legal principle to share the common rivers may not itself bring the solution. There is no harm in obtaining a common agreement among the nation-states over the sharing of international rivers; rather it may help to diffuse the conflicts at a certain level. However, it needs to be emphasized that a universal legal framework may not be able to efficiently handle the specific problems arising out of sharing disagreements over international rivers in various regions of the world. The hydro-politics on an international river basin is closely related to that region's geostrategic thinking. Every river basin has its own long history of water use and sharing – consistent with the region's culture and tradition. The riparian countries have their own clearly shared social and economic interdependencies. Thus, the water-sharing issues over an international river need to be addressed seriously in a regional framework. The existing regional organizations in different parts of the world may be encouraged to strengthen their institutional mechanism to deal with common water problems.

The water management institutions besides providing reliable mechanism for long-term visions need to be flexible to react to short-term occurrences. The regional bodies can be potentially more flexible to respond to the water flow fluctuations in their trans-boundary rivers than an international outfit. These organizations may also be inherently capable of handling the peculiar attributes involved with the river water sharing in their own respective regions. Building institutions to facilitate sharing of the fresh water resource in the regional framework may take time. The ongoing sharing of hydrological, meteorological, and other relevant kinds of data and information among the regional members may build the grounds for establishing joint institutional mechanism. Regional agreements on allocation and sharing are not absolute as they continue to evolve after establishment of initial cooperative institutions. These institutions, however, can provide a secure context for negotiation.[9]

The European Union has led the way in this regard. The EU, with its range of directives on water management and protection, is working towards sustainable management of European water. The EU Water Framework of Directive (EUWFD) of 2000 has adopted the principle of looking at water in a holistic way, where the resources are linked to the uses, the terrestrial environment, the aquatic environment and finally to development and human health. It is part of the 'acquis communautaire' that applicant countries need to implement. Since 1986, the cooperation in the Rhine basin has been a success story, thanks to the combination of political motivation and realistic target. In the Danube basin, cooperation is limited, but some positive changes have recently been witnessed after the application of some riparian countries to join the EU.

The EUWFD emphasizes the following: (1) The best model to manage the river water is according to the natural geographical and hydrological unit, instead of according to administrative or political boundaries; (2) Protection of all waters (aquatic ecology, unique and valuable habitats, drinking water sources and bathing water) by a set deadline; (3) Co-ordinating the number of measures taken at Community level to address a particular pollution problem; (4) Combined approach of emission limit, values and quality standards; (5) Public participation which is crucial to keep waters clean as it helps to balance the interest of various stakeholders and facilitates enforceability; (6) EUWFD repealed seven old directives on exchange of information on fresh water quality, the fish-water, the shellfish water and ground water, etc.; and, (7) Adequate water pricing to act as an incentive for the sustainable use of water resources.

EUWFD is an admirable document but the specific actions to achieve 'good status' are the responsibility of the competent authorities at all levels. The implementation of this directive poses various challenges. However, taking over ten years to develop, the new EU Water Framework Directive is the most significant legal instrument in the water field to emerge from Brussels for some time and will have a profound effect on how water is managed in Europe. NAFTA in North America has the economic potential to follow the path of the European Union in managing their respective shared fresh water resources. The expensive nature of the EU directives, however, brings apprehension for their implementation by the regional outfits of the developing countries, particularly in Asia, Africa and the Middle East. But at the same time, it also shows that a regional organization can effectively manage and develop the shared fresh water resources in its own region. In the South, the Southern African Development Community (SADC) has been the first regional organization to take up this challenge seriously.

Signing of agreements on water sharing may be easy, but the real problem is how to keep the agreement working. Agreements need to stand the test of time. An agreement can positively contribute to peace and cooperation in the basin by addressing the future water needs of the riparian countries. Thus, it is not only that we need agreements on international water systems, we also need the agreements to be sustainable, lasting and progressive. For the appropriate and competent management of shared fresh water systems, it is vital to build upon institutions at the basin level.

The problems associated with establishing cooperative management around a common river water resource can be analysed as so-called social dilemmas.[10] This refers to a situation whereby interdependent actors have free access to the fresh water resources of the river. All these actors face choices given that the maximization of short-term self-interest yields an outcome which leaves all participants worse off than if cooperation had been established. Thus, establishing and maintaining sustainable water management demands measures, which can overcome this dilemma.

It has been commonly suggested that there are two types of solution for establishing and maintaining social cooperation over a common property resource: the first builds on the use of the executive power of an external political authority, such as the apparatus of a nation-state or a political actor in the international community; the second solution draws on the mechanism of self-interest, profit maximization and property rights, incorporated in a market economy. It would seem that neither state nor market-based solutions guarantee durable and sustainable solutions to international river water management, particularly in the developing world. Thus, there is a need for a more comprehensive approach to the management of international rivers, which can incorporate, as well as complement, the two above strategies. Considering the complexity of the task, the solution to this social dilemma requires the participation of all actors, state and non-state, who are in some way physically linked to the common international rivers.

The interdependence of individual actors in the river basin catchment areas can be seen as a problem of appropriation of a common water resource. Cooperation among river water 'appropriators' involves costs and benefits that are much more difficult to estimate and harder to grasp for their users than their present, short-term, individual utility-maximizing behaviour. Therefore, there is a need to achieve a sustainable regime which can be seen as legitimate and binding by those concerned. This regime should consist of institutions, i.e. of principles, norms and regulations which cumulatively affect the actions taken and outcomes obtained in using river water.

International River is a Single Unit

An international river does not, as per definition, confine itself into national boundaries. The shared rivers should be treated as single units for the maximum utilization of their resources. The development of river water occurs most optimally on the basin-wide level. The whole river basin should be regarded as an economic, ecological and political unit irrespective of state boundaries and the waters are vested in the community. Under an integrated programme of development of a river, water projects are to be located at the best available locations. Further, notwithstanding geographic divisions along political lines, a management solution involving a wide range of basin-based riparian countries can bring mutual benefits, such as the right to submerge upstream land in return for availing hydropower or supply of water to one state and electricity to another. The benefits of these projects should be allocated taking into account the needs of riparian countries as well as who has made the sacrifices to realize these projects. This approach includes joint planning, joint construction, joint management and joint cost sharing. The regulation and management of an international river basin should be entrusted to an independent body outside the political control of any single riparian.

To facilitate the participation of all the riparian countries in a meaningful joint endeavour and treating the basin as a single unit outside the control of individual states, the nation-states are required to be flexible in their approach. The flexibility is central to successful negotiation of agreement among the riparian states in building basin-based institutions on international rivers. Generally, the sharing issues of international rivers are commonly handled by foreign ministry officials rather than being given to bureaucrats and technocrats in a water resource ministry.[11] Foreign ministry officials are usually unable to understand the water issues, which brings lack of interest and leads to relatively long negotiations and unsuccessful resolutions. Understanding of the problem is necessary for the negotiators to find the ways and means for the conflict management and mutual cooperation. The source of the international river sharing is a highly complex issue as it encompasses such diverse disciplines as ecology, economics, social psychology, religion, cultural anthropology, engineering, hydrology and geopolitics.[12] For a regular diplomat, it is not easy to grasp the complexity of the issues involved. Water resource management in general and sharing of international rivers in particular, is also a continuously changing process. There is a need for the national negotiators coping with, and adjusting to such changes as well as understanding conceptual, methodological and institutional shifts.

Political interest by the leaders of river basin countries may help to overcome much bureaucratic red tape in order to reach a common understanding. There is a growing public awareness about the importance of water resources. Common incentives and reciprocal disadvantages should be projected effectively by the state and leadership in order to calm down the emotional aspects in the water-sharing issue. Without popular support, it is difficult to implement any river basin arrangement even if it can be reached at the top.

Rational Use of Water in the Basin

Most parts of Asia, Africa and the Middle East are exposed to water stress or even water scarcity. The adoption of the supply management strategy only to address the water shortage in the region is not enough. To meet the growing demand, there is a need to minimize water use, particularly in the agricultural sector which uses the water most. This can be achieved in two ways: by ceasing to export 'virtual water' and starting to import 'virtual water' in the case of water deficient regions. 'Virtual water' means the agricultural products that have been produced with large amounts of water.[13] Following these two principles – by stopping the production of water intensive agricultural products for export purposes and importing water intensive agricultural products from water abundant regions – would decrease water demands in the river basin. River basins may opt for a planned allocation of agricultural activities in their various regions in order to meet future demand for food. This is not possible without the establishment of basin-based institutions. These institutions may also help in innovating technical developments to facilitate a more efficient usage of the water in the basin. Affirmative actions can be taken to find new solutions, such as making efficient usage of the dew, and also irrigation without exposing the water to evaporation. Furthermore, endogenous knowledge on how water allocation has been dealt within societies that have experienced long periods of water shortage may also be useful.

The prevailing idea that water should be free and that the use of water in a particular economic or social activity could be pursued without concern is no longer acceptable. Water allocation, particularly of shared rivers, has become a challenge in the face of greater demand. To reduce the incompatibility on the water-sharing issue, the help of economic measures is very much needed. The pricing of the water will create quantity restrictions for the competing actors. It will force consumers to use water more efficiently than it would if there were no price tag on it.

In recent years, the construction of water projects has demanded greater investment. This is partly because the ratio of use to availability is high in most parts of the world and also because new sites for dams and storages are increasingly available only at greater economic and environmental cost. It is not only the construction of the projects, but the proper management of the water storage and its distribution that is needed for efficient use of water. The water distribution systems in Asia, Africa and the Middle East are not self-sustaining, because even if a price is charged for water, it has been kept very low. This huge cost-benefit difference has reduced the performance of many irrigation and water distribution systems.

The enactment of pricing the water is not sufficient in itself. There is a need to make effective institutional arrangements to collect the 'water tax'. In the state of Bihar in India, the government usually spends three times more money to collect the water revenue than the actual tax collected from the farmers. The law must be simple but strong enough to compel the people to pay their tax. Water Courts may be created to facilitate speedy justice on disagreement over water sharing and also disputes over water taxation. By strengthening institutions, a single chain of authority is required to carry out policy making, planning and management of water issues. Planning needs to be co-ordinated, making it strategic and holistic.

Pricing of the water is not a politically sound act for the policy makers in the South. For a politician, political interest is invariably more important than economics or environment. Taxing the water might cost the political leaders their major 'vote banks'. In Asia, Africa and the Middle East, farmers constitute the most important voting bloc. Thus, there is a need to distance politics from technical, economic and environmental criteria in decision-making. Greater awareness is needed about the water scarcity among the common people, which can help to de-politicize water pricing to a large extent. Moreover, with the price, people should be offered some tangible benefits. Reliable and timely water supply, universal applicability of the rules and regulations under a democratic and efficient system, and rational allocation of water among various competing sectors are some of the prerequisites for the smooth implementation of water pricing.

Building Basin-Based Institutions

The problems in the sharing of the river water resource stem mainly from a number of institutional deficiencies. Reforms of water-sharing institutions demand a will to address the situation in a coherent and comprehensive manner. This comprehensive approach needs to take into account social, environmental and economic objectives combined with decentralized management and distribution structures and fuller participation of all the water users.

Both the actual common resource constituted by the international river system as such and those seen as 'rightful' appropriators of water from the system should be clearly identified. The definition of the river system should include the tributaries and distributaries and be considered as a joint unit. Various groups, state or non-state, are using the water from the river system for their economic and social activities. In the absence of proper identification of these groups and the nature of their demand, it will be impossible to find a formula of sharing. Appropriation rules must restrict when, how, where and how much an appropriator can withdraw from the river. As Lundqvist and Gleick argue, the 'demand for water includes a combination of basic "needs" and larger set of "wants"'.[14] Basic needs for water must be identified and given priority. These allocation rules must include considerations of variations due to weather conditions and other local physical characteristics. Having a firm understanding of the supply and demand of the water resource, the rules of appropriation must be stated determining the rate of exchange between appropriation from the resource and provision to the common pool in terms of maintenance, resources and/or money.

In order to construct sustainable basin-based water management institutions to manage the international rivers, contextual considerations are of high importance. The complexity associated with sustainable management institutions does not only come from technical and geographic conditions. Of utmost importance is the consideration of the social and cultural institutions at hand. Recognizing the salience of contextual sensitivity in constructing a water management institution, one must not only consider incumbent formal institutions but also include a focus on the informal institutions. Policies recognizing this comprehensive understanding of contextual institutions in the region will be able to match enduring patterns of behaviour that have developed from the way people have organized as individuals, groups or classes to utilize and exploit scarce material and social resources.

All the riparian actors should participate in the formation and management of the river basin organization. Not only the states but also the non-state water users affected by operational rules must be eligible to participate as decision-makers in modifying the organization. The river is decisive for the physical survival of many of its users. The recognition as eligible decision-makers provides an essential democratic channel mitigating the construction and maintenance of the river management through the establishment of legitimacy and mutual trust. Local institutions cannot function effectively without popular participation by the management. The sustainable use of river water requires that users participate in all aspects of water policy and management in the basin.

In identifying the relevant actors participating in the management of the water resource one needs to move beyond pin-pointing actors at various institutional levels. Social groups, such as women and other less empowered groups, should be given special attention as they might have rightful claims on a specific treatment in relation to the common water resource. In particular, women's rights and roles should be considered as they often manage water-related activities such as irrigation and food production.

The maintaining of a river basin management regime requires a functional judicial framework. This framework should be characterized by mutual monitoring. Those who supervise and monitor appropriators' behaviour, and the condition of the river water, should be responsible to the appropriators, or could be the appropriators themselves. It facilitates opportunities to construct reciprocal trust and obedience through increasing the risk of social stigmatization if an actor defects from the regime rules. An international river basin counts among its principal core actors two or more nation-states and potentially numerous non-state actors. Given the potential multiplicity of organizational levels in an appropriate management regime the judicial framework must allow for the appropriator to establish local arenas to solve problems and resolve conflicts.

The need for networking judicial institutions requires a general political climate recognizing the right to organize in general and the jurisdiction of these judicial bodies in particular. Hence external political authorities should not challenge the appropriators' rights to set up their own institutions. Political authorities are also needed to act positively to build the human capacity which is necessary for the effective community participation in water management and institution. With the help of free flow of relevant information, providing training and education, and allowing for a vibrant civil society, the state can help in the capacity building of the water appropriators. Real long-term success in river basin management depends on the ability of the community to identify problems and formulate and implement policies and strategies.

These policy measures, national governments as well as the international community might be in a position to take, with a view to easing tension over shared water resources, facilitating cooperation among co-riparian states and, in the long run, avoiding tomorrow's potential conflict over the world's water. It is true that the measures proposed above would be far from easy to implement; some would prove highly difficult to put into place. For instance, halting the production of water-intensive agricultural products would necessitate a radical reform of an individual state's economic structure. Challenging as they may be, however, such comprehensive measures are of primordial importance: they represent the crucial core of initiatives aimed at overcoming the institutional deficiencies within existing international organizations and rules, in an effort to build and strengthen water-regulatory institutions both at the international and basin-wide levels. Only then will greater cooperation be possible.

External intervention and assistance can sometimes facilitate the negotiation of international river water agreements. The Indus River Agreement between India and Pakistan is one of the success stories of such external intervention. The World Bank played a significant role in bringing these two hostile countries to an agreement in 1960, to share and develop the Indus River. Currently, the Bank is involved in the Nile basin to establish a basin-based institution. The UNDP and the Asian Development Bank also played a significant role in bringing the four lower riparian countries of the Mekong River basin into a cooperative management framework. Where riparian countries have been able to establish cooperative arrangements, successful and sustainable development programmes follow.[15] The establishment of cooperative arrangements on shared river systems also bring further international collaboration and external assistance.

Due to resource constraints, riparian countries, particularly in Asia, Africa and the Middle East, have become increasingly aware of the costs of not cooperating. Water scarcity and a lack of financial resources are gradually encouraging the riparian countries to cooperate in order to achieve optimal benefits. In many cases, however, riparian countries in these regions are unable to establish institutional cooperative arrangements because of their concern regarding existing and future water rights. Mutual suspicion and uncertainties of reciprocal action obstruct constructive engagement. To overcome such obstacles, credible and impartial international assistance is required.

The change in attitudes of international financial institutions and bilateral aid programmes may provide incentives for existing and future basin-based cooperation. Many development agencies are already concerned with increasing water scarcity and have developed water resource strategies for foreign assistance. These organizations are required to be proactive in their approach. The international lending institutions and donor agencies might assume a facilitative role in encouraging early collaborative and participatory efforts among the basin states. Their financial resources could be used as incentives for riparian states to come together.[16] The basin-based institutional arrangement on shared rivers can bring all riparian countries greater benefits than would be achieved through state-centric development. With the proper institutional support, international rivers could potentially become the cornerstone of regional cooperation instead of being a source of fierce conflict.

There are several ways in which external support could help to prevent conflict and promote regional cooperation among riparian states.

The international community can especially play the role of facilitator of water resource sharing agreements. Riparian countries are often unable to establish institutional cooperative arrangements because of their mutual suspicion. To overcome such obstacles, the international community can provide international assistance to launch the process of cooperation. Gradually, this assistance will facilitate mutual trust and confidence among the basin riparian states in order to achieve collective action.

Formation of a River Basin Organization (RBO) may be actively encouraged by the international community as a pre-condition for financial and technical assistance. As constraints on the resource grow, the opportunity cost for not cooperating becomes more clear. The increasing scarcity of available fresh water per capita and lack of financial strength in the developing countries may gradually encourage the basin countries to cooperate in order to increase the benefit of shared water. Basin-based development of irrigation, hydropower, water diversion or flood control projects can provide riparian countries with greater net benefits than what they could have achieved through purely state-centric development.

Lack of resources usually affects the effectiveness of an RBO in the South. A strong and vibrant RBO is necessary to stipulate a set of clear rules and regulatory measures in the basin regarding water rights and environmental obligation. Moreover, in several cases, riparian countries have unequal access to data and information due to differing data accessibility and asymmetric competence to process data. This asymmetric information can be scientific and/or strategic. RBOs should be supported to maintain a functional information sharing framework, which can facilitate the smooth running of a river basin management regime. RBOs should be assisted to possess an early warning system and also a credible conflict management capacity. Besides technical and financial support, the international community can provide training in this regard.

In recent years, there has been a clear move towards establishing a common legal framework for the sharing of international watercourses at the global level. However, whether it will be able to address the issues over the sharing of specific international rivers remains questionable. The major problem may arise in defining the 'equitable use' and also, its conflict with the 'no-harm principle'. The international community may promote the idea of establishing an International Water Court.

Establishing a court like this will not only help to address the existing inconsistencies associated with water-sharing norms and doctrines, but it will also prevent individual basin states from going out of the basin-based framework and from taking advantage of their superior military or hydrological situation.

FACING THE FUTURE

Population growth results in a declining supply of fresh water per person. The Worldwatch Institute estimates that due to population growth only, the amount per capita water availability from the hydrological cycle will fall by 73 per cent between 1950 and 2050.[17] Rapid population growth and the strive for economic development has severely stressed natural renewable resources, so much so that fresh water is beginning to have a scarcity value and emotional intensity that exist for fossil fuel. Countries have already started to frame the issue of water scarcity in national security terms. Even the George W. Bush administration has started considering water an issue of national as well as global security.[18] However, framing the issue as a national concern by individual states will in most cases make it impossible to resolve the issue.[19] The sheer size and nature of this problem demands solutions that go beyond the purview of a particular state or government. Managing water effectively requires consideration of all the interacting actors.

Multi-lateral water basins are mostly governed by the bilateral arrangements. This has raised the concern of free riding behaviour. Decisions made by one riparian or some of the riparian states are likely to fail to serve the interests of non-participating riparian state(s) due to conflicting priorities of nations.[20] Thus, principles for comprehensive basin-based water management and planning must be adopted. In order to face the future, there is an urgent need for water allocation priorities and mechanisms to derive optimum benefit from the available water resource in the world.

Many regions are using virtually all of the river flow to meet their water demand. The Yellow River in China and the Nile River in Africa have very little water left when they reach the sea. Pressure is growing not only on the surface water, but also on the groundwater as well. Several major agricultural regions are extracting groundwater faster than it is recharged by rainfall. Due to this unsustainable practice, the water source might dry up or become too expensive to pump. It is not the water quantity alone; the poor quality of fresh water resource is also increasingly bringing hazard to a large portion of world population.

To meet the increased water demands, crucial decisions are needed to be taken about water and the way it is to be used. Rather than continuing to search for more and more water to meet anticipated demand, it is time to decide what to do with the amount that can be feasibly and sustainably developed. This perceptual change can help to avoid the 'water wars' and instead develop cooperation over the sharing of international rivers.

NOTES

1. This chapter has borrowed liberally from the author's earlier works: A. Swain, 'Sharing International Rivers: A Regional Approach', in N. P. Gleditsch (ed.), *Conflict and the Environment* (Dordrecht: Kluwer Academic Publishers, 1997), pp. 403–16; A. Swain, 'Constructing Water Institutions: Appropriate Management of International River Water', *Cambridge Review of International Affairs*, 12, 2 (1999), pp. 214–25; A. Swain, 'Long-Term Sustainability of Bilateral River Agreements', in *Water Security for Multinational Water Systems – Opportunity for Development* (Stockholm: Stockholm International Water Institute Report 8, 2000), pp. 137–42; A. Swain and J. Riviere, *Management of Transboundary Freshwater Resources: A Case for EC Conflict Prevention* (Berlin: SWP-CPN Report, 2001).
2. In the World Forum series, the first was in Marrakesh in 1997, the second in The Hague in 2000 and the third in Kyoto in 2003.
3. The UN General Assembly Resolution No. 2669 (XIV) of 8 December 1970. The recommendation was for laws on non-navigational uses only, because the navigational uses of international water had already been codified by the international community in 1815 at the Congress of Vienna.
4. D. Goldberg, 'Legal Aspects of World Bank Policy on Projects on International Waterways', *International Journal of Water Resources Development*, 7 (1991), pp. 225–9.
5. *International Rivers and Lakes*, 20 (1993).
6. Some minor changes were made to the ILC's text at the time of UN negotiations. Though the UN working group made a number of drafting changes, the essence of the ILC's draft remained unchanged.
7. M. Falkenmark, 'Living at the Mercy of the Water Cycle', in *Water Resources in the Next Century* (Stockholm: Proceedings of the Stockholm Water Symposium, Publication No. 1, 1991), pp. 11–29.
8. H. Hill, 'Strategic Planning and Policy Framework Development: Elements, Priorities and Action Plans', in M. A. Abu Zeid and A. K. Biswas (eds), *River Basin Planning and Management* (Calcutta: Oxford University Press, 1996), p. 16.
9. J. D. Priscoli, 'Conflict Resolution, Collaboration and Management in International and Regional Water Resources Issues', Paper delivered at the VIIIth Congress of the International Water Resources Association (IWRA), Cairo, Egypt, November 1994.
10. See E. Ostrom, *Governing the Commons. The Evolution of Institutions for Collective Action* (Cambridge: Cambridge University Press, 1990).
11. D. G. LeMarcquand, *International Rivers: The Politics of Cooperation* (Waterloo: University of British Columbia Press, 1977).
12. R. Mandel, 'Sources of International River Basin', Paper presented at the Annual Meeting of the International Studies Association, Vancouver, BC, Canada, March 1991.
13. For a detailed discussion on 'virtual water', see J. A. Allan, *Water, Peace and the Middle East: Negotiating Resources in the Middle East* (London: Tauris Academic Publications, 1996).

14. J. Lundqvist and P. Gleick, *Sustaining Our Waters into the 21st Century* (Stockholm: Stockholm Environment Institute, 1997).
15. S. Kirmani and R. Rangeley, *International Inland Waters: Concept for a More Active World Bank Role* (Washington DC: World Bank Technical Paper No. 239, 1994).
16. Priscoli, 'Conflict Resolution, Collaboration and Management in International and Regional Water Resources Issues'.
17. L. R. Brown, G. Gardner and B. Halweil, *Beyond Malthus: Nineteen Dimensions of the Population Challenge* (New York: W.W. Norton & Co., 1999).
18. *PECS News*, 8 (2003).
19. C. L. Kukk and D. A. Deese, 'At the Water's Edge: Regional Conflict and Cooperation over Fresh Water', *UCLA Journal of International Law & Foreign Affairs*, 21 (1996).
20. R. E. Just and S. Netanyahu, 'International Water Resource Conflicts: Experience and Potential', in R. Just and E. Netanyahu (eds), *Conflict and Cooperation on Transboundary Water Resources* (Boston MA: Kluwer Academic Publishers, 1998).

Appendix

Convention on the Law of the Non-Navigational Uses of International Watercourses, 1997

The Parties to the present Convention,

Conscious of the importance of international watercourses and the non-navigational uses thereof in many regions of the world,

Having in mind Article 13, paragraph 1 (a), of the Charter of the United Nations, which provides that the General Assembly shall initiate studies and make recommendations for the purpose of encouraging the progressive development of international law and its codification,

Considering that successful codification and progressive development of rules of international law regarding non-navigational uses of international watercourses would assist in promoting and implementing the purposes and principles set forth in Articles 1 and 2 of the Charter of the United Nations,

Taking into account the problems affecting many international watercourses resulting from, among other things, increasing demands and pollution,

Expressing the conviction that a framework convention will ensure the utilization, development, conservation, management and protection of international watercourses and the promotion of the optimal and sustainable utilization thereof for present and future generations,

Affirming the importance of international cooperation and good-neighbourliness in this field,

Aware of the special situation and needs of developing countries,

Recalling the principles and recommendations adopted by the United Nations Conference on Environment and Development of 1992 in the Rio Declaration and Agenda 21,

Recalling also the existing bilateral and multilateral agreements regarding the non-navigational uses of international watercourses,

Mindful of the valuable contribution of international organizations, both governmental and non-governmental, to the codification and progressive development of international law in this field,

Appreciative of the work carried out by the International Law Commission on the law of the non-navigational uses of international watercourses,

Bearing in mind United Nations General Assembly resolution 49/52 of 9 December 1994,

Have agreed as follows:

PART I
INTRODUCTION

Article 1
Scope of the present Convention

1. The present Convention applies to uses of international watercourses and of their waters for purposes other than navigation and to measures of protection, preservation and management related to the uses of those watercourses and their waters.

2. The uses of international watercourses for navigation is not within the scope of the present Convention except insofar as other uses affect navigation or are affected by navigation.

Article 2
Use of terms

For the purposes of the present Convention:

(a) 'Watercourse' means a system of surface waters and groundwaters constituting by virtue of their physical relationship a unitary whole and normally flowing into a common terminus;

(b) 'International watercourse' means a watercourse, parts of which are situated in different States;

(c) 'Watercourse State' means a State Party to the present Convention in whose territory part of an international watercourse is situated, or a Party that is a regional economic integration organization, in the territory of one or more of whose member states part of an international watercourse is situated;

(d) 'Regional economic integration organization' means an organization constituted by sovereign States of a given region, to which its member States have transferred competence in respect of matters governed by this Convention and which has been duly authorized in accordance with its internal procedures, to sign, ratify, accept, approve or accede to it.

Article 3
Watercourse agreements

1. In the absence of an agreement to the contrary, nothing in the present Convention shall affect the rights or obligations of a watercourse State arising from agreements in force for it on the date on which it became a party to the present Convention.

2. Notwithstanding the provisions of paragraph 1, parties to agreements referred to in paragraph 1 may, where necessary, consider harmonizing such agreements with the basic principles of the present Convention.

3. Watercourse States may enter into one or more agreements, hereinafter referred to as 'watercourse agreements', which apply and adjust the provisions of the present Convention to the characteristics and uses of a particular international watercourse or part thereof.

4. Where a watercourse agreement is concluded between two or more watercourse States, it shall define the waters to which it applies. Such an agreement may be entered into with respect to an entire international watercourse or any part thereof or a particular project, programme or use except insofar as the agreement adversely affects, to a significant extent, the use by one or more other watercourse States of the waters of the watercourse, without their express consent.

5. Where a watercourse State considers that adjustment and application of the provisions of the present Convention is required because of the characteristics and uses of a particular international watercourse, watercourse States shall consult with a view to negotiating in good faith for the purpose of concluding a watercourse agreement or agreements.

6. Where some but not all watercourse States to a particular international watercourse are parties to an agreement, nothing in such agreement shall affect the rights or obligations under the present Convention of watercourse States that are not parties to such an agreement.

Article 4
Parties to watercourse agreements

1. Every watercourse State is entitled to participate in the negotiation of and to become a party to any watercourse agreement that applies to the entire international watercourse, as well as to participate in any relevant consultations.

2. A watercourse State whose use of an international watercourse may be affected to a significant extent by the implementation of a proposed watercourse agreement that applies only to a part of the watercourse or to a particular project, programme or use is entitled to participate in consultations on such an agreement and, where appropriate, in the negotiation thereof in good faith with a view to becoming a party thereto, to the extent that its use is thereby affected.

PART II
GENERAL PRINCIPLES

Article 5
Equitable and reasonable utilization and participation

1. Watercourse States shall in their respective territories utilize an international watercourse in an equitable and reasonable manner. In particular, an international watercourse shall be used and developed by watercourse States with a view to attaining optimal and sustainable utilization thereof and benefits therefrom, taking into account the interests of the watercourse States concerned, consistent with adequate protection of the watercourse.

2. Watercourse States shall participate in the use, development and protection of an international watercourse in an equitable and reasonable manner. Such participation includes both the right to utilize the watercourse and the duty to cooperate in the protection and development thereof, as provided in the present Convention.

Article 6
Factors relevant to equitable and reasonable utilization

1. Utilization of an international watercourse in an equitable and reasonable manner within the meaning of article 5 requires taking into account all relevant factors and circumstances, including:

(a) Geographic, hydrographic, hydrological, climatic, ecological and other factors of a natural character;

(b) The social and economic needs of the watercourse States concerned;

(c) The population dependent on the watercourse in each watercourse State;

(d) The effects of the use or uses of the watercourses in one watercourse State on other watercourse States;

(e) Existing and potential uses of the watercourse;

(f) Conservation, protection, development and economy of use of the water resources of the watercourse and the costs of measures taken to that effect;

(g) The availability of alternatives, of comparable value, to a particular planned or existing use.

2. In the application of article 5 or paragraph 1 of this article, watercourse States concerned shall, when the need arises, enter into consultations in a spirit of cooperation.

3. The weight to be given to each factor is to be determined by its importance in comparison with that of other relevant factors. In determining what is a reasonable and equitable use, all relevant factors are to be considered together and a conclusion reached on the basis of the whole.

Article 7
Obligation not to cause significant harm
1. Watercourse States shall, in utilizing an international watercourse in their territories, take all appropriate measures to prevent the causing of significant harm to other watercourse States.
2. Where significant harm nevertheless is caused to another watercourse State, the States whose use causes such harm shall, in the absence of agreement to such use, take all appropriate measures, having due regard for the provisions of articles 5 and 6, in consultation with the affected State, to eliminate or mitigate such harm and, where appropriate, to discuss the question of compensation.

Article 8
General obligation to cooperate
1. Watercourse States shall cooperate on the basis of sovereign equality, territorial integrity, mutual benefit and good faith in order to attain optimal utilization and adequate protection of an international watercourse.
2. In determining the manner of such cooperation, watercourse States may consider the establishment of joint mechanisms or commissions, as deemed necessary by them, to facilitate cooperation on relevant measures and procedures in the light of experience gained through cooperation in existing joint mechanisms and commissions in various regions.

Article 9
Regular exchange of data and information
1. Pursuant to article 8, watercourse States shall on a regular basis exchange readily available data and information on the condition of the watercourse, in particular that of a hydrological, meteorological, hydro-geological and ecological nature and related to the water quality as well as related forecasts.
2. If a watercourse State is requested by another watercourse State to provide data or information that is not readily available, it shall employ its best efforts to comply with the request but may condition its compliance upon payment by the requesting State of the reasonable costs of collecting and, where appropriate, processing such data or information.
3. Watercourse States shall employ their best efforts to collect and, where appropriate, to process data and information in a manner which facilitates its utilization by the other watercourse States to which it is communicated.

Article 10
Relationship between different kinds of uses
1. In the absence of agreement or custom to the contrary, no use of an international watercourse enjoys inherent priority over other uses.

2. In the event of a conflict between uses of an international watercourse, it shall be resolved with reference to articles 5 to 7, with special regard being given to the requirements of vital human needs.

PART III
PLANNED MEASURES

Article 11
Information concerning planned measures
Watercourse States shall exchange information and consult each other and, if necessary, negotiate on the possible effects of planned measures on the condition of an international watercourse.

Article 12
Notification concerning planned measures with possible adverse effects
Before a watercourse State implements or permits the implementation of planned measures which may have a significant adverse effect upon other watercourse States, it shall provide those States with timely notification thereof. Such notification shall be accompanied by available technical data and information, including the results of any environmental impact assessment, in order to enable the notified States to evaluate the possible effects of the planned measures.

Article 13
Period for reply to notification
Unless otherwise agreed:
(a) A watercourse State providing a notification under article 12 shall allow the notified States a period of six months within which to study and evaluate the possible effects of the planned measures and to communicate the findings to it;
(b) This period shall, at the request of a notified State for which the evaluation of the planned measures poses special difficulty, be extended for a period of six months.

Article 14
Obligations of the notifying State during the period for reply
During the period referred to in article 13, the notifying State:
(a) Shall cooperate with the notified States by providing them, on request, with any additional data and information that is available and necessary for an accurate evaluation; and
(b) Shall not implement or permit the implementation of the planned measures without the consent of the notified States.

Article 15
Reply to notification
The notified States shall communicate their findings to the notifying State as early as possible within the period applicable pursuant to article 13. If a notified State finds that implementation of the planned measures would be inconsistent with the provisions of articles 5 or 7, it shall attach to its finding a documented explanation setting forth the reasons for the finding.

Article 16
Absence of reply to notification
1. If, within the period applicable pursuant to article 13, the notifying State receives no communication under article 15, it may, subject to its obligations under articles 5 and 7, proceed with the implementation of the planned measures, in accordance with the notification and any other data and information provided to the notified States.
2. Any claim to compensation by a notified State which has failed to reply within the period applicable pursuant to article 13 may be offset by the costs incurred by the notifying State for action undertaken after the expiration of the time for a reply which would not have been undertaken if the notified State had objected within that period.

Article 17
Consultations and negotiations concerning planned measures
1. If a communication is made under article 15 that implementation of the planned measures would be inconsistent with the provisions of articles 5 or 7, the notifying State and the State making the communication shall enter into consultations and, if necessary, negotiations with a view to arriving at an equitable resolution of the situation.
2. The consultations and negotiations shall be conducted on the basis that each State must in good faith pay reasonable regard to the rights and legitimate interests of the other State.
3. During the course of the consultations and negotiations, the notifying State shall, if so requested by the notified State at the time it makes the communication, refrain from implementing or permitting the implementation of the planned measures for a period of six months unless otherwise agreed.

Article 18
Procedures in the absence of notification
1. If a watercourse State has reasonable grounds to believe that another watercourse State is planning measures that may have a significant adverse effect upon it, the former State may request the latter to apply the provisions of article 12. The request shall be accompanied by a documented explanation setting forth its grounds.

2. In the event that the State planning the measures nevertheless finds that it is not under an obligation to provide a notification under article 12, it shall so inform the other State, providing a documented explanation setting forth the reasons for such finding. If this finding does not satisfy the other State, the two States shall, at the request of that other State, promptly enter into consultations and negotiations in the manner indicated in paragraphs 1 and 2 of article 17.

3. During the course of the consultations and negotiations, the State planning the measures shall, if so requested by the other State at the time it requests the initiation of consultations and negotiations, refrain from implementing or permitting the implementation of those measures for a period of six months unless otherwise agreed.

Article 19
Urgent implementation of planned measures

1. In the event that the implementation of planned measures is of the utmost urgency in order to protect public health, public safety or other equally important interests, the State planning the measures may, subject to articles 5 and 7, immediately proceed to implementation, notwithstanding the provisions of article 14 and paragraph 3 of article 17.

2. In such case, a formal declaration of the urgency of the measures shall be communicated without delay to the other watercourse States referred to in article 12 together with the relevant data and information.

3. The State planning the measures shall, at the request of any of the States referred to in paragraph 2, promptly enter into consultations and negotiations with it in the manner indicated in paragraphs 1 and 2 of article 17.

PART IV
PROTECTION, PRESERVATION AND MANAGEMENT

Article 20
Protection and preservation of ecosystems

Watercourse States shall, individually and, where appropriate, jointly, protect and preserve the ecosystems of international watercourses.

Article 21
Prevention, reduction and control of pollution

1. For the purpose of this article, 'pollution of an international watercourse' means any detrimental alteration in the composition or quality of the waters of an international watercourse which results directly or indirectly from human conduct.

2. Watercourse States shall, individually and, where appropriate, jointly, prevent, reduce and control the pollution of an international watercourse that may cause significant harm to other watercourse States or to their environment, including harm to human health or safety, to the use of the waters for any beneficial purpose or to the living resources of the watercourse. Watercourse States shall take steps to harmonize their policies in this connection.

3. Watercourse States shall, at the request of any of them, consult with a view to arriving at mutually agreeable measures and methods to prevent, reduce and control pollution of an international watercourse, such as:

(a) Setting joint water quality objectives and criteria;

(b) Establishing techniques and practices to address pollution from point and non-point sources;

(c) Establishing lists of substances the introduction of which into the waters of an international watercourse is to be prohibited, limited, investigated or monitored.

Article 22
Introduction of alien or new species
Watercourse States shall take all measures necessary to prevent the introduction of species, alien or new, into an international watercourse which may have effects detrimental to the ecosystem of the watercourse resulting in significant harm to other watercourse States.

Article 23
Protection and preservation of the marine environment
Watercourse States shall, individually and, where appropriate, in cooperation with other States, take all measures with respect to an international watercourse that are necessary to protect and preserve the marine environment, including estuaries, taking into account generally accepted international rules and standards.

Article 24
Management
1. Watercourse States shall, at the request of any of them, enter into consultations concerning the management of an international watercourse, which may include the establishment of a joint management mechanism.

2. For the purposes of this article, 'management' refers, in particular, to:

(a) Planning the sustainable development of an international watercourse and providing for the implementation of any plans adopted; and

(b) Otherwise promoting the rational and optimal utilization, protection and control of the watercourse.

Article 25
Regulation
1. Watercourse States shall cooperate, where appropriate, to respond to needs or opportunities for regulation of the flow of the waters of an international watercourse.
2. Unless otherwise agreed, watercourse States shall participate on an equitable basis in the construction and maintenance or defrayal of the costs of such regulation works as they may have agreed to undertake.
3. For the purposes of this article, 'regulation' means the use of hydraulic works or any other continuing measure to alter, vary or otherwise control the flow of the waters of an international watercourse.

Article 26
Installations
1. Watercourse States shall, within their respective territories, employ their best efforts to maintain and protect installations, facilities and other works related to an international watercourse.
2. Watercourse States shall, at the request of any of them which has reasonable grounds to believe that it may suffer significant adverse effects, enter into consultations with regard to:
(a) The safe operation and maintenance of installations, facilities or other works related to an international watercourse; and
(b) The protection of installations, facilities or other works from wilful or negligent acts or the forces of nature.

PART V
HARMFUL CONDITIONS AND EMERGENCY SITUATIONS

Article 27
Prevention and mitigation of harmful conditions
Watercourse States shall, individually and, where appropriate, jointly, take all appropriate measures to prevent or mitigate conditions related to an international watercourse that may be harmful to other watercourse States, whether resulting from natural causes or human conduct, such as flood or ice conditions, water-borne diseases, siltation, erosion, saltwater intrusion, drought or desertification.

Article 28
Emergency situations
1. For the purposes of this article, 'emergency' means a situation that causes, or poses an imminent threat of causing, serious harm to watercourse States or other States and that results suddenly from natural causes, such as floods, the breaking up of ice, landslides or earthquakes, or from human conduct, such as industrial accidents.

2. A watercourse State shall, without delay and by the most expeditious means available, notify other potentially affected States and competent international organizations of any emergency originating within its territory.

3. A watercourse State within whose territory an emergency originates shall, in cooperation with potentially affected States and, where appropriate, competent international organizations, immediately take all practicable measures necessitated by the circumstances to prevent, mitigate and eliminate harmful effects of the emergency.

4. When necessary, watercourse States shall jointly develop contingency plans for responding to emergencies, in cooperation, where appropriate, with other potentially affected States and competent international organizations.

PART VI
MISCELLANEOUS PROVISIONS

Article 29
International watercourses and installations in time of armed conflict
International watercourses and related installations, facilities and other works shall enjoy the protection accorded by the principles and rules of international law applicable in international and non-international armed conflict and shall not be used in violation of those principles and rules.

Article 30
Indirect procedures
In cases where there are serious obstacles to direct contacts between watercourse States, the States concerned shall fulfil their obligations of cooperation provided for in the present Convention, including exchange of data and information, notification, communication, consultations and negotiations, through any indirect procedure accepted by them.

Article 31
Data and information vital to national defence or security
Nothing in the present Convention obliges a watercourse State to provide data or information vital to its national defence or security. Nevertheless, that State shall cooperate in good faith with the other watercourse States with a view to providing as much information as possible under the circumstances.

Article 32
Non-discrimination
Unless the watercourse States concerned have agreed otherwise for the

protection of the interests of persons, natural or juridical, who have suffered or are under a serious threat of suffering significant transboundary harm as a result of activities related to an international watercourse, a watercourse State shall not discriminate on the basis of nationality or residence or place where the injury occurred, in granting to such persons, in accordance with its legal system, access to judicial or other procedures, or a right to claim compensation or other relief in respect of significant harm caused by such activities carried on in its territory.

Article 33
Settlement of disputes

1. In the event of a dispute between two or more Parties concerning the interpretation or application of the present Convention, the Parties concerned shall, in the absence of an applicable agreement between them, seek a settlement of the dispute by peaceful means in accordance with the following provisions.

2. If the Parties concerned cannot reach agreement by negotiation requested by one of them, they may jointly seek the good offices of, or request mediation or conciliation by, a third party, or make use, as appropriate, of any joint watercourse institutions that may have been established by them or agree to submit the dispute to arbitration or to the International Court of Justice.

3. Subject to the operation of paragraph 10, if after six months from the time of the request for negotiations referred to in paragraph 2, the Parties concerned have not been able to settle their dispute through negotiation or any other means referred to in paragraph 2, the dispute shall be submitted, at the request of any of the parties to the dispute, to impartial fact-finding in accordance with paragraphs 4 to 9, unless the Parties otherwise agree.

4. A Fact-finding Commission shall be established, composed of one member nominated by each Party concerned and in addition a member not having the nationality of any of the Parties concerned chosen by the nominated members who shall serve as Chairman.

5. If the members nominated by the Parties are unable to agree on a Chairman within three months of the request for the establishment of the Commission, any Party concerned may request the Secretary-General of the United Nations to appoint the Chairman who shall not have the nationality of any of the parties to the dispute or of any riparian State of the watercourse concerned. If one of the Parties fails to nominate a member within three months of the initial request pursuant to paragraph 3, any other Party concerned may request the Secretary-General of the United Nations to appoint a person who shall not have the nationality of any of the Parties to the dispute or of any riparian

State of the watercourse concerned. The person so appointed shall constitute a single-member Commission.

6. The Commission shall determine its own procedure.

7. The Parties concerned have the obligation to provide the Commission with such information as it may require and, on request, to permit the Commission to have access to their respective territory and to inspect any facilities, plant, equipment, construction or natural feature relevant for the purpose of its inquiry.

8. The Commission shall adopt its report by a majority vote, unless it is a single-member Commission, and shall submit that report to the Parties concerned setting forth its findings and the reasons therefore and such recommendations as it deems appropriate for an equitable solution of the dispute, which the Parties concerned shall consider in good faith.

9. The expenses of the Commission shall be borne equally by the Parties concerned.

10. When ratifying, accepting, approving or acceding to the present Convention, or at any time thereafter, a Party which is not a regional economic integration organization may declare in a written instrument submitted to the Depositary that, in respect of any dispute not resolved in accordance with paragraph 2, it recognizes as compulsory ipso facto and without special agreement in relation to any Party accepting the same obligation:

(a) Submission of the dispute to the International Court of Justice; and/or

(b) Arbitration by an arbitral tribunal established and operating, unless the parties to the dispute otherwise agreed, in accordance with the procedure laid down in the annex to the present Convention.

A Party which is a regional economic integration organization may make a declaration with like effect in relation to arbitration in accordance with subparagraph (b).

PART VII
FINAL CLAUSES

Article 34
Signature
The present Convention shall be open for signature by all States and by regional economic integration organizations from 21 May 1997 until 20 May 2000 at United Nations Headquarters in New York.

Article 35
Ratification, acceptance, approval or accession
1. The present Convention is subject to ratification, acceptance, approval or accession by States and by regional economic integration

organizations. The instruments of ratification, acceptance, approval or accession shall be deposited with the Secretary-General of the United Nations.

2. Any regional economic integration organization which becomes a Party to this Convention without any of its member States being a Party shall be bound by all the obligations under the Convention. In the case of such organizations, one or more of whose member States is a Party to this Convention, the organization and its member States shall decide on their respective responsibilities for the performance of their obligations under the Convention. In such cases, the organization and the member States shall not be entitled to exercise rights under the Convention concurrently.

3. In their instruments of ratification, acceptance, approval or accession, the regional economic integration organizations shall declare the extent of their competence with respect to the matters governed by the Convention. These organizations shall also inform the Secretary-General of the United Nations of any substantial modification in the extent of their competence.

Article 36
Entry into force

1. The present Convention shall enter into force on the ninetieth day following the date of deposit of the thirty-fifth instrument of ratification, acceptance, approval or accession with the Secretary-General of the United Nations.

2. For each State or regional economic integration organization that ratifies, accepts or approves the Convention or accedes thereto after the deposit of the thirty-fifth instrument of ratification, acceptance, approval or accession, the Convention shall enter into force on the ninetieth day after the deposit by such State or regional economic integration organization of its instrument of ratification, acceptance, approval or accession.

3. For the purposes of paragraphs 1 and 2, any instrument deposited by a regional economic integration organization shall not be counted as additional to those deposited by States.

Article 37
Authentic texts

The original of the present Convention, of which the Arabic, Chinese, English, French, Russian and Spanish texts are equally authentic, shall be deposited with the Secretary-General of the United Nations.

ANNEX
ARBITRATION

Article 1

Unless the parties to the dispute otherwise agree, the arbitration pursuant to article 33 of the Convention shall take place in accordance with articles 2 to 14 of the present annex.

Article 2

The claimant party shall notify the respondent party that it is referring a dispute to arbitration pursuant to article 33 of the Convention. The notification shall state the subject matter of arbitration and include, in particular, the articles of the Convention, the interpretation or application of which are at issue. If the parties do not agree on the subject matter of the dispute, the arbitral tribunal shall determine the subject matter.

Article 3

1. In disputes between two parties, the arbitral tribunal shall consist of three members. Each of the parties to the dispute shall appoint an arbitrator and the two arbitrators so appointed shall designate by common agreement the third arbitrator, who shall be the Chairman of the tribunal. The latter shall not be a national of one of the Parties to the dispute or of any riparian State of the watercourse concerned, nor have his or her usual place of residence in the territory of one of these Parties or such riparian State, nor have dealt with the case in any other capacity.
2. In disputes between more than two parties, parties in the same interest shall appoint one arbitrator jointly by agreement.
3. Any vacancy shall be filled in the manner prescribed for the initial appointment.

Article 4

1. If the Chairman of the arbitral tribunal has not been designated within two months of the appointment of the second arbitrator, the President of the International Court of Justice shall, at the request of a party, designate the Chairman within a further two-month period.
2. If one of the parties to the dispute does not appoint an arbitrator within two months of receipt of the request, the other party may inform the President of the International Court of Justice, who shall make the designation within a further two-month period.

Article 5

The arbitral tribunal shall render its decisions in accordance with the provisions of this Convention and international law.

Article 6

Unless the parties to the dispute otherwise agree, the arbitral tribunal shall determine its own rules of procedure.

Article 7

The arbitral tribunal may, at the request of one of the Parties, recommend essential interim measures of protection.

Article 8

1. The parties to the dispute shall facilitate the work of the arbitral tribunal and, in particular, using all means at their disposal, shall:

(a) Provide it with all relevant documents, information and facilities; and

(b) Enable it, when necessary, to call witnesses or experts and receive their evidence.

2. The parties and the arbitrators are under an obligation to protect the confidentiality of any information they receive in confidence during the proceedings of the arbitral tribunal.

Article 9

Unless the arbitral tribunal determines otherwise because of the particular circumstances of the case, the costs of the tribunal shall be borne by the parties to the dispute in equal shares. The tribunal shall keep a record of all its costs, and shall furnish a final statement thereof to the parties.

Article 10

Any Party that has an interest of a legal nature in the subject matter of the dispute which may be affected by the decision in the case, may intervene in the proceedings with the consent of the tribunal.

Article 11

The tribunal may hear and determine counterclaims arising directly out of the subject matter of the dispute.

Article 12

Decisions both on procedure and substance of the arbitral tribunal shall be taken by a majority vote of its members.

Article 13

If one of the parties to the dispute does not appear before the arbitral tribunal or fails to defend its case, the other party may request the tribunal to continue the proceedings and to make its award. Absence of a party or a failure of a party to defend its case shall not constitute a bar to the proceedings. Before rendering its final decision, the arbitral tribunal must satisfy itself that the claim is well founded in fact and law.

Article 14
1. The tribunal shall render its final decision within five months of the date on which it is fully constituted unless it finds it necessary to extend the time limit for a period which should not exceed five more months.
2. The final decision of the arbitral tribunal shall be confined to the subject matter of the dispute and shall state the reasons on which it is based. It shall contain the names of the members who have participated and the date of the final decision. Any member of the tribunal may attach a separate or dissenting opinion to the final decision.
3. The award shall be binding on the Parties to the dispute. It shall be without appeal unless the parties to the dispute have agreed in advance to an appellate procedure.
4. Any controversy which may arise between the Parties to the dispute as regards the interpretation or manner of implementation of the final decision may be submitted by either party for decision to the arbitral tribunal which rendered it.
Adopted by the UN General Assembly in resolution 51/229 of 21 May 1997.

Bibliography

Aasand, F. I., Kammerud, T. A. and Trolldalen, J. M., *Challenges in Management of Shared Water Basins – Zambezi River Basin in Southern Africa and Implementation of ZACPLAN* (Oslo: CESAR, 1996).

Abbas A T, B. M., *The Ganges Water Dispute* (Dhaka: University Press Ltd, 1982).

Abraham, K., *Ethiopia from Bullets to the Ballot Box: The Bumpy Road to Democracy and the Political Economy of Transition* (Lawrenceville, NJ: The Read Sea Press, Inc., 1994).

Abu Zeid, M. A., 'The River Nile and Its Contribution to the Mediterranean Environment', Paper presented at the Stockholm Water Symposium, 10–14 August 1992, Stockholm, Sweden.

Adhana, H., 'The Roots of Organised Internal Armed Conflicts in Ethiopia, 1960-1991', in Trevdt, T. (ed.), *Conflict in the Horn of Africa: Human and Ecological Consequence of Warfare* (Uppsala: EPOS, 1993).

Ahmed, S., 'Principles and Precedents in International Law Governing the Sharing of Nile Water', in Howell, P. P. and Allan, J. A. (eds), *The Nile: Sharing a Scarce Resource* (Cambridge: Cambridge University Press, 1994).

Akerfeldt, K., *Transboundary Water Sharing: Cooperation and Conflict in Managing Freshwater Resources in Southern Africa* (Uppsala: Uppsala University Programme of International Studies, Masters Thesis, 2001).

Alam, U., 'Water Rationality: Mediating the Indus Waters Treaty' (University of Durham: Unpublished PhD dissertation, 1998).

Allan, J. A., 'Nile Basin Water Management Strategies' in Howell, P. P. and Allan, J. A. (eds), *The Nile: Sharing Scarce Resource* (Cambridge: Cambridge University Press, 1994).

Allan, J. A., *Water, Peace and the Middle East: Negotiating Resources in the Middle East* (London: Tauris Academic Publications, 1996).

Allan, J. A., 'Hydro-Peace in the Middle East: Why no Water Wars? A Case Study of the Jordan River Basin', *SAIS Review*, 22, 2 (2002).

Arlosoroff, S., 'The Water Sector in the Middle-East: Potential Conflict Resolutions', in Chatterji, M., Arlosoroff, S. and Guha, G. (eds), *Conflict Management of Water Resources* (Aldershot: Ashgate Publishers, 2002).

Ashton, P. J., 'Potential Environmental Impacts Associated with the Abstraction of Water from the Okavango River in Namibia', Paper presented at the Annual Conference of the Southern African Association of Aquatic Scientists, Swakopmund, Namibia, 23–26 June 1999.

Ashton, P. J., 'Water Security for Multinational River Basin States: The Special Case of the Okavango River Basin', Paper presented at the SIWI Seminar on Water Scarcity for Multinational Water Systems – Opportunities for Development, Stockholm, 14–17 August 2000.

Ashton, P. J., 'The Search for an Equitable Basis for Water Sharing in the Okavango River Basin', in Nakayama, M. (ed.), *International Waters in South Africa* (Tokyo: UNU Press, 2003).

Badenoch, N., *Transboundary Environmental Governance* (Washington DC: World Resources Institute, 2002).

Banerjee, B. N., *Can the Ganga be Cleaned?* (Delhi: B.R. Publishing Corporation, 1989).

Basson, M. S., van Niekerk, P. H. and van Rooyen, J. A., *Overview of Water Resources Availability and Utilization in South Africa* (Pretoria: Department of Water Affairs and Forestry, 1997).

Beach, H. L., Hamner, J., Hewitt, J. J., Kaufman, E., Kurki, A., Oppenheimer, J. A. and Wolf, A. T., *Transboundary Freshwater Dispute Resolution: Theory, Practice, and Annotated References* (Tokyo: UNU Press, 2000).

Beaumont, P., *Environmental Management and Development in Drylands* (London: Routledge, 1989).

Begum, K., *Tension Over the Farakka Barrage: A Techno-Political Tangle in South-Asia* (Dhaka: University Press Limited, 1987).

Behera, N. C., 'State Formation Processes Weak States and Sustainable Development in South Asia', in Khanna, D. D. (ed.), *Sustainable Development Environmental, Security and Disarmament Interface in South Asia* (New Delhi: Macmillan, 1997).

Bertocci, P. J., 'Bangladesh in 1985: Resolute Against the Storms', *Asian Survey*, 26, 2 (1986).

Beschorner, N., 'Water and Instability in the Middle East', *Adelphi Papers*, 273 (1992/93).

Bilen, Ö, 'Prospects for Technical Cooperation in the Euphrates-Tigris Basin', in Biswas, A. K., (ed.), *International Waters of the Middle East: From Euphrates-Tigris to Nile* (Bombay: Oxford University Press, 1994).

Bindra, S. S., *Indo-Bangladesh Relations* (New Delhi: Deep & Deep Publications, 1982).

Biswas, A. K., 'Environmental Impact Assessment for Groundwater Management', *Water Resource Development*, 8, 2 (1992).

Biswas, A. K., 'Indus Water Treaty: The Negotiating Process', *Water International*, 17 (1992).

Biswas, A. K., 'Management of International Waters: Problems and Perspective', *Water Resource Development*, 9 (1993).

Biswas, A. K., 'Sustainable Water Development from the Perspective of the South: Issues and Constraints', in Abu-Zeid, M. A. and Biswas, A. K. (eds), *River Basin Planning and Management* (Calcutta: Oxford University Press, 1996).

Biswas, A. K., 'Water for the Urban Areas of the Developing World in the Twenty-first Century' in Uitto, J. I. and Biswas, A. K. (eds), *Water for Urban Areas: Challenges and Perspectives* (Tokyo: UNU Press, 2000).

Biswas, A. K. and Uitto, J. I. (eds), *Sustainable Development of the Ganges-Brahmaputra-Meghna Basins* (Tokyo: UNU Press, 2001).

Blyn, G., *Agriculture Trends in India, 1891-1957: Output, Availability, and Productivity* (Philadelphia PA: University of Pennsylvania Press, 1966).

Bölükbasi, S., 'Turkey Challenges Iraq and Syria: The Euphrates Dispute', *Journal of South Asian and Middle Eastern Studies*, 16, 4, (1993).

Bos, E., Vu, M. T., Massiah, E. and Bulatao, R. A., *World Population Projection, 1994-1995* (Baltimore, MD: Johns Hopkins University Press, 1994).

Botrall, A., 'Fits and Misfits Over Time and Space: Technologies and Institutions of Water Development for South Asian Agriculture', *Contemporary South Asia*, 1, 2, (1992).

Brichieri-Colombi, J. S. A. and Bradnock, R. W., 'Geopolitics, Water and Development in South Asia: Cooperative Development on the Ganges-Brahmaputra Delta', *The Geographical Journal*, 169, 1 (2003).

Brown, L. R. and Halweil, B., *China's Water Shortage* (Washington DC: Worldwatch Institute Press Release, 22 April 1998).

Brown, L. R., Gardner, G. and Halweil, B., *Beyond Malthus: Nineteen Dimensions of the Population Challenge* (New York: W.W. Norton & Co., 1999).

Brown, L. R., Renner, M. and Halweil, B., *Vital Signs 1999* (New York: W.W. Norton & Co., 1999).

Bulloch, J. and Darwish, A., *Water Wars: Coming Conflicts in the Middle East* (London: Victor Gollancz, 1993).

Burchi, S., 'National Regulations for Groundwater: Options, Issues and Best Practices', in Salman, S. M. A. (ed.), *Ground Water: Legal and Policy Perspectives* (Washington DC: World Bank Technical Paper No. 456, 1999).

Caponera, D. A., 'International Water Resources Law in the Indus Basin', Paper presented at the Regional Symposium on *Water Resources Policy in Agro-Socio-Economic Development*, 4–8 August 1985, Dhaka, Bangladesh.

Caponera, D. A., 'Ownership and Transfer of Water and Land in Islam', in Faruqui, N. I., Biswas, A. K. and Bino, M. J. (eds), *Water Management in Islam* (Tokyo: UNU Press, 2001).

CGWB, *Background Note: Colloquium on Strategy for Ground Water Development* (New Delhi: Central Ground Water Board, 1996).

Chapman, G. B. and Thompson, M. (eds), *Water and the Quest for Sustainable Development in the Ganges Valley* (London: Cassell, 1995).

Chee, A. M., *Political Structure and Public Policy Conflict Management: A Comparative Study of Thailand and Malaysia* (Uppsala: Uppsala University Programme of International Studies Masters Thesis, 2003).

Chenje, M. and Johnson, P. (eds), *Water in Southern Africa* (Harare: SADC/IUCN/SARDC, 1996).

Chenje, M. (ed.), *State of the Environment Zambezi Basin 2000* (Maseru/Harare/Lusaka: SADC/IUCN/ZRA/SARDC, 2000).

Chiuta, T. M., 'Shared Water Resources and Conflicts: the Case of the Zambezi River Basin', in Tevera, D. and Moyo, S. (eds), *Environmental Security in Southern Africa* (Harare: SARIP, 2000).

Christiansen, S., 'Shared Benefits, Shared Problems', in Lodgaard, S. and af Ornäs, A. H. (eds), *The Environment and International Security* (Oslo: PRIO Report No. 3, 1992).

Clarke, R., *Water: The International Crisis* (London: Earthscan, 1991).

Clarke, R. et al., *Groundwater: A Threatened Resource* (Nairobi: UNEP Environment Library No. 15, 1996).

Collins, R. O., *The Waters of the Nile: Hydropolitics of the Jonglei Canal, 1900-1988* (Oxford: Clarendon Press, 1990).

Conca, K. and Wu, F., 'Is there a Global River Regime', Paper presented at the 43rd Annual Meeting of the International Studies Association, New Orleans, 23–27 March 2002.

Cooper, J., *Reconstructing History from Ancient Inscriptions: The Lagash-Umma Border Conflict* (Malibu, CA: Undena, 1983).

Copaken, N. S., 'The Perception of Water as Part of Territory in Israeli and Arab Ideologies between 1964 and 1993: Toward a Further Understanding of the Arab-Jewish Conflict' (University of Haifa, Working Paper No. 8, May 1996).

Cowell, A., 'Now, a Little Steam. Later, Maybe a Water War', *New York Times*, 7 February 1990.

Crow, B. and Lindquist, A., *Development of the Rivers Ganges and Brahmaputra: The Difficulty of Negotiating a New Line* (Milton Keynes: Development Policy and Practice Research Group, 1990).

Crow, B., *Sharing the Ganges: The Politics and Technology of River Development* (New Delhi: Sage Publications, 1995).

Dagne, N., Mulugeta, D. B. and Kaihara, K., 'Towards a Cooperative Use of the Nile: A Legal Perspective', *Cambridge Review of International Affairs* 12, 2 (1999).

Dinar, A. and Wolf, A., 'International Markets for Water and the Potential for Regional Cooperation: Economic and Political Perspectives in the Western Middle East', *Economic Development and Cultural Change*, 43, 1 (1994).

D'Monte, D., 'Filthy Flows the Ganga', *People & the Planet*, 5, 3 (1996).

Elmusa, S. S., *Negotiating Water: Israel and the Palestinians* (Washington DC: Institute for Palestine Studies, 1996).

Engelman, R. and LeRoy, P., *Sustaining Water: Population and the Future of Renewable Water Supplies* (Washington DC: Population and Environment Program, Population Action International, 1993).

Ezzat, M. N., Mohamadien, M. A. and Attia, B. B., Arab Republic of Egypt's Country Paper, 'Integrated Approach to Water Resources Development', *The Nile 2002 Conference*, Kampala, Uganda, February 1996.

Faisal, I. M., 'Managing Common Waters in the Ganges-Brahmaputra-Meghna Region', *SAIS Review*, 22, 2 (2002).

Falkenmark, M., 'Global Water Issues Confronting Humanity', *Journal of Peace Research*, 27, 2 (1990).

Falkenmark, M., 'Living at the Mercy of the Water Cycle' in *Water Resources in the Next Century* (Stockholm: Proceedings of the Stockholm Water Symposium, Publication no. 1, 1991).

Falkenmark, M., 'Water Scarcity: Time for Realism', 20 (1993), pp. 11–12.

FAO, 'Food Production: The Critical Role of Water', in *Technical Background Documents 6–11: Vol. 2* (Rome: FAO, 1996).

FAO, 'Irrigation Potential in Africa: A Basin Approach', *FAO Land and Water Bulletin*, 4 (1997).

FAOSTAT, *FAOSTAT Statistics Database* (Rome: FAO, 1997).

Feitelson, E., 'The Ebb and Flow of Arab-Israeli Water Conflicts: Are Past Confrontations likely to Resurface?', *Water Policy*, 2 (2000).

Fernades, W., 'The Price of Development', *Seminar*, 412 (1993).

Foster, S., 'Ground for Concern', *Our Planet*, 8, 3 (1996).

Foster, S., 'Essential Concepts for Ground Water Regulators', in Salman,

S. M. A. (ed.), *Ground Water: Legal and Policy Perspectives* (Washington DC: World Bank Technical Paper No. 456, 1999).

Frey, F. W., 'The Political Context of Conflict and Cooperation over International River Basins', *Water International*, 18, 1 (1993).

Gardner-Outlaw, T. and Engelman, R., *Sustaining Water, Easing Scarcity: A Second Update* (Washington DC: Population Action International, 1997).

Gillani, S. N. A. and Azam, M., 'Indus River: Past, Present and Future', in Shady, A. M. et al. (eds), *Management and Development of Major Rivers* (Calcutta: Oxford University Press, 1996).

Gleditsch, N. P. and Hamner, J., 'Shared Rivers, Conflict, and Cooperation', Paper presented at the 42nd Annual Meeting of the International Studies Association, Chicago, IL, 21–24 February 2001.

Gleick, P. H. (ed.), *Water in Crisis: A Guide to the World's Fresh Water Resources* (New York: Oxford University Press, 1993).

Gleick, P. H., 'Water and Conflict', *International Security*, 18, 1 (1993).

Gleick, P. H., 'Water, War, and Peace in the Middle East', *Environment*, 36, 3 (1994).

Gleick, P. H., 'Basic Water Requirements for Human Activities: Meeting Basic Needs', *Water International*, 21, 2 (1996).

Gleick, P. H., 'The Human Right to Water', *Water Policy*, 1 (1998).

Gleick, P. H., *The World's Water: The Biennial Report on Freshwater Resources 1998–1999* (Washington DC: Island Press, 1998).

Goldberg, D., 'Legal Aspects of World Bank Policy on Projects on International Waterways', *International Journal of Water Resources Development*, 7 (1991).

Goudie, A., *The Human Impact on the Natural Environment* (Oxford: Basil Blackwell, 3rd edn, 1990).

Green Cross International, *National Sovereignty and International Watercourses* (Geneva: Green Cross International, 2000).

Gulati, C. J., *Bangladesh: Liberation to Fundamentalism: A Study of Volatile Indo-Bangladesh Relations* (New Delhi: Commonwealth Publishers, 1988).

Guner, S., 'The Turkish-Syrian War of Attrition', *Studies in Conflict & Terrorism*, 20, 1 (1997).

Guner, S., 'Water Alliances in the Euphrates-Tigris Basin' (Paper presented at the NATO Advanced Research Workshop, 9–12 October, 1997, Budapest, Hungary).

Gyawali, D., 'Energizing Development and Sustaining the Environment – A Nepali's View', *Development*, 1 (1991).

Haddadin, M. J., 'Water Issues in the Middle East Challenges and Opportunities', *Water Policy*, 4 (2002).

Haftendorn, H., 'Water and International Conflict', *Third World Quarterly*, 21, 1 (2000).

Hamner, J., 'Weapons Won't Get You Water: State Power and Distribution of Benefits', Paper presented at the 43rd Annual Meeting of the International Studies Association, New Orleans, 23–27 March 2002.

Hanneberg, P., *Our Struggle for Water* (Stockholm: SIWI, 2000).

Hansen, A. H., *The Process of Planning: A Study of India's Five Year Plans 1950–1964* (Oxford: Oxford University Press, 1966).

Heggelund, G., *China's Environmental Crisis: The Battle of Sanxia* (Oslo: NUPI Research Report No. 170, 1993).

Hill, H., 'Strategic Planning and Policy Framework Development: Elements, Priorities and Action Plans', in Abu Zeid, M. A. and Biswas, A. K. (eds), *River Basin Planning and Management* (Calcutta: Oxford University Press, 1996).

Hinrichsen, D. and Tacio, H., 'The Coming Freshwater Crisis is Already Here', in *Finding the Source: The Linkage Between Population and Water* (Washington DC: Woodrow Wilson International Centre for Scholars, ECSP Publication, 2002).

Hirji, R. and Grey, D., 'Managing International Waters in Africa: Process and Progress', in Salman, S. M. A. and de Chazournes, L. B. (eds), *International Watercourses: Enhancing Cooperation and Managing Conflict* (Washington DC: World Bank Technical Paper No. 414, 1998).

Holsti, K. J., *Peace and War: Armed Conflicts and International Order 1649–1989* (Cambridge: Cambridge University Press, 1991).

Holtsberg, P., *Sustainability in Water Management: Conflict and Cooperation in the Mekong River Basin* (Uppsala: The Uppsala University Programme of International Studies Masters Thesis, 2002).

Homer-Dixon, T. F., 'Environmental Scarcities and Violent Conflict: Evidence from Cases', *International Security*, 19, 1 (1994).

Homer-Dixon, T. and Percival, V., *Environmental Scarcity and Violent Conflict: Briefing Book* (The Project on Environment, Population and Security, American Association for the Advancement of Science & University College, University of Toronto, 1996).

Homer-Dixon, T. F., *Environment, Scarcity, and Violence* (Princeton, NJ: Princeton University Press, 1999).

Hori, H., *The Mekong: Environment and Development* (Tokyo: The UNU Press, 2000).

Horta, K., 'The Mountain Kingdom's White Oil: The Lesotho Highlands Water Project', *The Ecologist*, 25, 6 (1995).

Horta, K. and Coverdale, S., 'Dams & Distress for Kingdom in the Sky', *People & the Planet*, 5, 3 (1996).

Howell, P. P., Lock, J. M. and Cobb, S. M. (eds), *The Jonglei Canal: Impact and Opportunity* (Cambridge: Cambridge University Press, 1988).

Huth, P. K., *Standing your Ground: Territorial Disputes and International Conflict* (Ann Arbor, MI: University of Michigan Press, 1996).

Islam, M. R., *Ganges Water Dispute: Its International Legal Aspects* (Dhaka: University Press Limited, 1987).

IWMI, *Water Supply and Demand in 2025* (Colombo: International Water Management Institute, 2000).

Jensen, J. G., *MRC Programme for Fisheries Management and Development Cooperation, Annual Report, April 2000–March 2001* (Phnom Penh: Mekong River Commission, 2001).

Just, R. E. and Netanyahu, S. (eds), *Conflict and Cooperation on Transboundary Water Resources* (Boston MA: Kluwer Academic Publishers, 1998).

Kelly, K. and Homer-Dixon, T., *Environmental Scarcity and Violent Conflict: The Case of Gaza* (Toronto: AAAS and University of Toronto, the Project on Environment, Population and Security, 1995).

Kendie, D., 'Egypt and the Hydro-Politics of the Blue Nile River', *Northeast African Studies* 6, 1 (1999).

Khan, A. R., *India, Pakistan and Bangladesh: Conflict or Cooperation?* (Dacca: Sindabad, 1976).

Khosa, M. M. and Mupimpila, C., 'On Global Security: A Suggested Interpretation for Southern Africa', in Whitman, J. (ed.), *The Sustainability Challenge for Southern Africa* (London: Macmillan, 2000).

Kirmani, S. and Rangeley, R., *International Inland Waters: Concept for a More Active World Bank Role* (Washington DC: World Bank Technical Paper No. 239, 1994).

Klein, M., 'Water Balance of the Upper Jordan River Basin', *Water International*, 23 (1998).

Kliot, N., Shmueli, D. and Shamir, U., 'Institutions for Management of Transboundary Water Resources: Their Nature, Characteristics and Shortcomings', *Water Policy*, 3 (2001).

Kolars, J. and Mitchell, W. A., *The Euphrates River and the Southeast Anatolia Development Project* (Carbondale: Southern Illinois University Press, 1991).

Kolars, J., 'Problems of International River Management: The Case of the Euphrates', in Biswas, A. K. (ed.), *International Waters of the Middle East: From Euphrates-Tigris to Nile* (Bombay: Oxford University Press, 1994).

Korzoun, V. I. and Sokolov, A. A., 'World Water Balance and Water Resources of the Earth', in United Nations, *Water Development and Management Proceedings of the United Nations Water Conference* (London: Pergamon Press, 1978).

Krishna, R., 'The Legal Regime of the Nile River Basin', in Starr, J. and Stoll, D. C. (eds), *The Politics of Scarcity: Water in the Middle East* (Boulder, CO: Westview Press, 1988).

Kukk, C. L. and Deese, D. A., 'At the Water's Edge: Regional Conflict and Cooperation over Fresh Water', *UCLA Journal of International Law & Foreign Affairs*, 21 (1996).

Külz, H. R., 'Further Water Disputes Between India and Pakistan', *The International and Comparative Law Quarterly*, 18 (1969), p. 721.

LeMarcquand, D. G., *International Rivers: The Politics of Cooperation* (Waterloo: University of British Columbia Press, 1977).

Lemma, S., 'Cooperating on the Nile: Not a Zero-sum Game', *United Nations Chronicle*, 3 (2001).

Libiszewski, S., *Water Disputes in the Jordan Basin Region and their Role in the Resolution of the Arab-Israeli Conflict* (Zurich: Centre for Security Studies and Conflict Research Occasional Paper No. 13, 1995).

Lonergan, S., *Climate Warning, Water Resources and Geopolitical Conflict: A Study of Nations Dependent on the Nile, Litani and Jordan River System* (Ottawa: Operational Research and Analysis Establishment (ORAE) Extra-Mural Paper No. 55, 1991).

Lonergan, S., 'Water Resources and Conflict: Examples from the Middle East', Paper presented in the Conflict and the Environment, NATO Advanced Research Workshop, Bolkesjo, Norway, 12-16 June 1996.

Lonergan, S., 'Water Resources and Conflict: Examples from the Middle East', in Gleditsch, N. P. (ed.), *Conflict and the Environment* (Dordrecht: Kluwer Academic, 1997).

Lowi, M. R., 'Bridging the Divide: Transboundary Resource Disputes and the Case of West Bank Water', *International Security*, 18, 1 (1993).

Lowi, M., 'Rivers of Conflict, Rivers of Peace', *Journal of International Affairs*, 49 (1995).

Lundqvist, J., 'Water Scarcity in Abundance: Management and Policy Challenges', *Ecodecision*, 6 (1992).

Lundqvist, J. and Gleick, P., *Sustaining Our Waters into the 21st Century* (Stockholm: Stockholm Environment Institute, 1997).

Lundqvist, J., 'Avert Looming Hydrocide', *Ambio*, 27, 6 (1998).

Mageed, Y. L., 'The Nile Basin: Lessons from the Past', in Biswas, A. K. (ed.), *International Waters of the Middle East: From Euphrates-Tigris to Nile* (Bombay: Oxford University Press, 1994).

Majumder, M. K., 'Bangladesh Keeps Priming the Pumps', *Panscope*, 31 (1992).

Mandel, R., 'Sources of International River Basin', Paper presented at the Annual Meeting of the International Studies Association, Vancouver: BC, Canada, March 1991.

Matlosa, K., 'The Lesotho Highlands Water Project: Socio-Economic Impacts', in Tevera, D. and Moyo, S. (eds), *Environmental Security in Southern Africa* (Harare: SARIP, 2000).

McCaffrey, S. C., 'Water Politics and International Law' in Gleick, P. H., (ed.), *Water in Crisis: A Guide to the World's Fresh Water Resources* (New York: Oxford University Press, 1993).

Mehta, J. S., 'The Indus Water Treaty: A Case Study in the Resolution of an International River Basin Conflict', *Natural Resources Forum*, 12, 1 (1988).

Misra, K. P., 'The Farakka Accord', *The World Today*, 34, 2 (1978).

Mitchell, R. J. and Leys, M. D. R., *A History of London Life* (London: Penguin, 1963).

Mochebelele, R. T., 'Good Governance and the Avoidance of Conflicts: The Lesotho Highlands Water Project Experience', in Green Cross International, *Water for Peace in the Middle East and Southern Africa* (Geneva: Green Cross International, 2000).

Mohamed, A. E., 'Joint Development and Cooperation of International Water Resources' in Nakayama, M. (ed.), *International Waters in South Africa* (Tokyo: UNU Press, 2003).

Mohammed, N. A. L., 'Environmental Conflicts in Africa', Paper presented at the NATO Advanced Research Workshop on Conflict and the Environment, at Bolkesjø, Norway, 12–16 June 1996.

Mohile, A. D., 'Brahmaputra: Issues in Development', in Biswas, A. K. and Uitto, J. I. (eds), *Sustainable Development of the Ganges-Brahmaputra-Meghna Basins* (Tokyo: UNU Press, 2001).

Moris, M. E., 'Water and Conflict in the Middle East: Threat and Opportunities', *Studies in Conflict and Terrorism*, 20, 1 (1997).

MRC, *Local Knowledge in the Study of River Fish Biology: Experience from the Mekong* (Phnom Penh: Mekong River Commission, Mekong Development Series No. 1, 2001).

MRC, *Fisheries in the Lower Mekong Basin: Status and Perspectives* (Phnom Penh: Mekong River Commission, MRC Technical Paper No. 6, 2002).

Mutembwa, A., 'Towards a Sustainable Water Management Strategy for Southern Africa', in Whitman, J. (ed.), *The Sustainability Challenge for Southern Africa* (London: Macmillan, 2000).

Nachmani, A., 'Water Jitters in the Middle East', *Studies in Conflict & Terrorism*, 20, 1 (1997).

Nakayama, M., 'Mekong Spirit as an Applicable Concept for

International River Systems', in *Water Security for Multinational Water Systems – Opportunity for Development* (Stockholm: SIWI Report 8, 2000).

NEDECO, *Mekong Delta Master Plan, Working Paper No. 4: Agriculture* (Mekong Secretariat, 1991).

Nhamo, G., 'SADC Region Committed to Sharing Water', *The Zambezi*, 1, 1 (1998).

Nishat, A., 'Development and Management of Water Resources in Bangladesh: Post-1996 Treaty Opportunities', in Biswas, A. K. and Uitto, J. I. (eds), *Sustainable Development of the Ganges-Brahmaputra-Meghna Basins* (Tokyo: UNU Press, 2001).

Öjendal, J. and Torell, E., *The Mighty Mekong Mystery – A Study on the Problems and Possibilities of Natural Resources Utilization in the Mekong River Basin* (Stockholm: Sida, 1997).

Öjendal, J., *Sharing the Good: Models of Managing Water Resources in the Lower Mekong River Basin* (Gothenburg: Department of Peace and Development Research, 2000).

Okidi, C. O., 'History of the Nile and Lake Victoria Basins through Treaties', in Howell, P. P. and Allan, J. A. (eds), *The Nile: Resources Evaluation, Resource Management and Hydropolicies and Legal Issues* (London: School of Oriental and African Studies, University of London and the Royal Geographical Society, 1990).

Okidi, C. O., 'Legal and Policy Considerations for Regional Cooperation on Lake Victoria and Nile River', *The Nile 2002 Conference*, Kampala, Uganda, February 1996.

Onta, I. R., 'Harnessing the Himalayan Waters of Nepal: A Case for Partnership for the Ganges Basin', in Biswas, A. K. and Uitto, J. I. (eds), *Sustainable Development of the Ganges-Brahmaputra-Meghna Basins* (Tokyo: UNU Press, 2001).

Opie, R., 'Germany's Double Bill', *World Water and Environmental Engineer*, April (1991).

Osborne, M., *The Mekong* (Sydney: Allen & Unwin, 2001).

Ostrom, E., *Governing the Commons. The Evolution of Institutions for Collective Action* (Cambridge: Cambridge University Press, 1990).

Pallett, J. (ed.), *Sharing Water in Southern Africa* (Windhoek: DRFN, 1997).

Pankhurst, A., *Resettlement and Famine in Ethiopia: The Villagers' Experience* (Manchester: Manchester University Press, 1992).

Pantalu, V. R., 'The Mekong River System', in Davies, B. R. and Walker, K. F. (eds), *The Ecology of River Systems, Monographiae Biologicae*, 60 (Dordrecht: Dr W. Junk Publishers).

Pearce, F., 'Africa at a Watershed', *New Scientist*, 23 (1991), pp. 34–41.

Pearce, F., 'Tide of Opinion Turns Against Superdams', *Panscope*, 33 (1992).

Pitman, G. T. K., 'The Role of the World Bank in Enhancing Cooperation and Resolving Conflict on International Watercourses: The Case of the Indus Basin', in Salman, S. M. A. and de Chazournes, L. B. (eds), *International Watercourses: Enhancing Cooperation and Managing Conflict* (Washington DC: World Bank Technical Paper No. 414, 1998).

Postel, S., *Conserving Water: The Untapped Alternative* (Washington DC: Worldwatch Institute Paper 67, 1985).

Postel, S., *Last Oasis: Facing Water Scarcity* (New York: W.W. Norton & Co., 1992).

Postel, S., 'Where Have All the Rivers Gone?', *World Watch*, 8, 3 (1995).

Postel, S., 'Dividing the Waters: Food Security, Ecosystem Health, and the New Politics of Scarcity', *Worldwatch Paper*, 132 (1996).

Priscoli, J. D., 'Conflict Resolution, Collaboration and Management in International and Regional Water Resources Issues', Paper delivered at the VIIIth Congress of the International Water Resources Association (IWRA), Cairo, Egypt, November 1994.

Rangeley, R., Thiam, B. M., Andersen, R. A. and Lyle, C. A., *International River Basin Organizations in Sub-Saharan Africa* (Washington DC: World Bank Technical Paper No. 250, 1994).

Rashiduzzaman, M., 'Bangladesh in 1977: Dilemmas of the Military Rulers', *Asian Survey*, 18, 2 (1978).

Raskin, P., Hansen, E. and Morgolis, R., *Water and Sustainability: A Global Outlook* (Stockholm: Stockholm Environment Institute, Polestar Series Report No. 4, 1995).

Reisner, M., *Cadillac Desert: The American West and its Disappearing Water* (New York: Penguin Books, 1986).

Rogers, P., Bouhia, H. and Kalbermatten, J., 'Water for Big Cities: Big Problems, Easy Solutions?', in Rosan, C., Ruble, B. A. and Tulchin, J. S. (eds), *Urbanization, Population, Environment and Security: A Report of the Comparative Urban Studies Project* (Washington DC: Woodrow Wilson International Centre for Scholars, 2000).

Rosegrant, M. and Ringler, C., 'Impact on Food Security and Rural Development of Transferring Water out of Agriculture', *Water Policy*, 1 (1998).

Sadoff, C. W. and Grey, D., 'Beyond the River: The Benefits of Cooperation on International Rivers', *Water Policy*, 4, 5 (2002).

Saliba, S. N., *The Jordan River Dispute* (The Hague: Martin Nijhoff, 1968).

Salman, S. M. A. and Uprety, K. 'Hydro-Politics in South Asia: A Comparative Analysis of the Mahakali and the Ganges Treaties', *Natural Resources Journal*, 39, 2 (1999).

Satterthwaite, D., 'Securing Water for the Cities', *People & the Planet*, 2, 2 (1993).

Schweizer, P., 'The Spigot Strategy', *New York Times*, 11 November 1990.

Seckler, D., Amarasinghe, U., Mollen, D., de Silva, R. and Baker, R., *World Water Demand and Supply, 1990 to 2025: Scenarios and Issues* (Colombo: IWMI Research Report 19, 1998).

Sehmi, N., 'The Enigmatic Nile', *World Meteorological Organization Bulletin*, 45, 3 (1996).

Sen, S. R., *The Strategy for Agricultural Development and Other Essays on Economic Policy and Planning* (New York: Asia Publishing House, 1962).

Sherman, M., 'The Hydro-Political Implications of the Oslo Agreements: An Israeli Perspective', in Chatterji, M., Arlosoroff, S. and Guha, G. (eds), *Conflict Management of Water Resources* (Aldershot: Ashgate Publishers, 2002).

Shiklomanov, I. A., 'World Fresh Water Resources', in Gleick, P. H. (ed.), *Water in Crisis: A Guide to the World's Fresh Water Resources* (New York: Oxford University Press, 1993).

Shiklomanov, I. A., *Assessment of Water Resources and Water Availability in the World* (Stockholm: Stockholm Environment Institute, 1997).

Shmueli, D. F. and Shamir, U., 'Application of International Law of Water Quality to Recent Middle East Water Agreements', *Water Policy*, 3 (2001).

Singh, I. J., 'Agricultural Situation in India and Pakistan', *Economic and Political Weekly*, 32, 26 (1997).

SIWI, *Water and Development: A Commissioned Study* (Stockholm: Stockholm International Water Institute for the European Parliament, 2000).

Smith, D. R., 'Environmental Security and Shared Water Resources in Post-Soviet Central Asia', *Post-Soviet Geography*, 36 (1995).

Smith, S. E., 'General Impact of Aswan High Dam', *Journal of Water Resources Planning and Management*, 112, 4 (1986).

Smith, S. E. and Al-Rawahy, H. M., 'The Blue Nile: Potential for Conflict and Alternatives for Meeting Future Demands', *Water International*, 15, 4 (1990).

Soffer, A., *Rivers of Fire: The Conflict over Water in the Middle East* (Lanham: Rowman and Littlefield Publishers, 1999).

Son, D. K., 'Development of Agricultural Production Systems in the Mekong Delta', in Xuan, V. T. and Matsui, S. (eds), *Development of Farming Systems in the Mekong Delta* (Ho Chi Minh City: JIRCAS & CLRRI, 1998).

Starr, J. R., 'Water Wars', *Foreign Policy*, 82 (1991).

Starr, J. S., *Covenant over Middle Eastern Waters: Key to World Survival* (New York: Henry Holt, 1995).

Suliman, M., *Civil War in Sudan: The Impact of Ecological Degradation* (Zürich & Bern: Environment and Conflict Project Occasional Paper No. 4, 1992).

Sutcliffe, J. V. and Parks, Y. P., 'Environmental Aspects of the Jonglei Canal', in Abu Zeid, M. A. and Biswas, A. K. (eds), *River Basin Planning and Management* (Calcutta: Oxford University Press, 1996).

Swain, A., 'Conflicts over Water: The Ganges Water Dispute', *Security Dialogue*, 24, 4 (1993).

Swain, A., *Environment and Conflict: Analysing the Developing World* (Uppsala: Department of Peace and Conflict Research, Report No. 37, 1993).

Swain, A., 'Displacing the Conflict: Environmental Destruction in Bangladesh and Ethnic Conflict in India', *Journal of Peace Research*, 33, 2 (1996).

Swain, A., *The Environmental Trap: The Ganges River Diversion, Bangladeshi Migration and Conflicts in India* (Uppsala: Department of Peace and Conflict Research, 1996).

Swain, A., 'Water Scarcity: A Threat to Global Security', *Environment & Security*, 1, 1 (1996).

Swain, A., 'Democratic Consolidation: Environmental Movements in India', *Asian Survey*, 37, 9 (1997).

Swain, A., 'Sharing International Rivers: A Regional Approach', in Gleditsch, N. P. (ed.), *Conflict and the Environment* (Dordrecht: Kluwer Academic Publishers, 1997).

Swain, A., 'The Nile River Dispute: Ethiopia, the Sudan, and Egypt', *The Journal of Modern African Studies*, 35, 4 (1997).

Swain, A., 'A New Challenge: Water Scarcity in the Arab World', *Arab Studies Quarterly*, 20, 1 (1998).

Swain, A., 'Fight for the Last Drop: Inter-state River Disputes in India', *Contemporary South Asia*, 7, 2 (1998).

Swain, A., 'Reconciling Disputes and Treaties: Water Development and Management in Ganga Basin', *Water Nepal*, 6, 1 (1998).

Swain, A., 'Sharing the Ganges: Ugly Conflict over Holy Water', in Abbaszadegan, F. and Wennberg, F. (eds), *Hydrpolitik och Demokrati* (Uppsala: Asiatic Society, 1998).

Swain, A., 'Constructing Water Institutions: Appropriate Management of International River Water', *Cambridge Review of International Affairs*, 12, 2 (1999).

Swain, A., 'Long-Term Sustainability of Bilateral River Agreements' in *Water Security for Multinational Water Systems – Opportunity for Development* (Stockholm: Stockholm International Water Institute Report 8, 2000).

Swain, A. and Stalgren, P., 'Managing the Zambezi: The Need to Build Water Institutions', in Tevera, D. and Moyo, S. (eds), *Environmental Security in Southern Africa* (Harare: SARIP, 2000).

Swain, A., 'Water Scarcity as a Source of Crises', in Nafziger, E. W., Stewart, F. and Väyrynen, R. (eds), *War, Hunger and Displacement: The Origins of Humanitarian Emergencies* (Oxford: Oxford University Press, 2000).

Swain, A. and Riviere, J., *Management of Transboundary Freshwater Resources: A Case for EC Conflict Prevention* (Berlin: SWP-CPN Report, 2001).

Swain, A., 'Water Wars: Fact or Fiction', *Futurers*, 33, 8, 9 (2001).

Swain, A., 'Environmental Cooperation in South Asia', in Conca, K and Dabelko, G. D. (eds), *Environmental Peacemaking* (Baltimore: Johns Hopkins University Press, 2002).

Swain, A., 'Managing the Nile River: The Role of Sub-Basin Cooperation', in Chatterji, M., Arlosoroff, S. and Guha, G. (eds), *Conflict Management of Water Resources* (Aldershot: Ashgate Publishers, 2002).

Swain, A., 'The Nile Basin Initiative: Too Many Cooks, Too Little Broth', *SAIS Review*, 22, 2 (2002).

Swatuk, L., 'Environmental Cooperation for Regional Peace and Security in Southern Africa', Draft Chapter Prepared for the Project on Environmental Cooperation and Regional Peace (Washington DC: The Woodrow Wilson Centre, 1999).

Swatuk, L., 'The New Water Architecture in Southern Africa: Reflections on Current Trends in the Light of Rio + 10', *International Affairs*, 78, 3 (2002).

Thompson, L. G., Tao, Y., Mosley-Thompson, E., Davis, M. E., Henderson, K. A. and Lin, P. N., 'A High-Resolution Millennial Record of the South Asian Monsoon from Himalayan Ice Cores', *Science*, 289 (2000).

Timberlake, L. and Tinker, J., *Environment and Conflict: Links Between Ecological Decay, Environmental Bankruptcy and Political and Military Instability* (London: Earthscan Briefing Document 40, November 1984).

Toset, H. P., Gleditsch, N. P. and Hegre, H., 'Shared Rivers and Interstate Conflict', *Political Geography*, 19 (2000).

Turton, A., 'Precipitation, People, Pipelines and Power: Towards a Political Ecology Discourse of Water in Southern Africa', in Scott, P. and Sulivan, S. (eds), *Political Ecology: Science, Myth and Power* (London: Edward Arnold, 2000).

Turton, A., 'An Overview of the Hydropolitical Dynamics of the Orange River Basin', in Nakayama, M. (ed.), *International Waters in South Africa* (Tokyo: UNU Press, 2003).

UNCHS, *An Urbanizing World: Global Report on Human Settlements 1996* (Oxford: Oxford University Press, 1996).

UNDP, *Human Development Report 1994* (UNDP & Oxford University Press, 1994).

UNEP, *Technical Annexes to the State of the Marine Environment* (Nairobi: UNEP Regional Seas Reports and Studies No. 114, 1990).

UNEP, *Freshwater Pollution* (Nairobi: UNEP/GEMS Environment Library No. 6, 1991).

UNEP, *Global Environmental Outlook 2000* (London: Earthscan, 1999).

Upreti, B. C., *Politics of Himalayan River Waters: An Analysis of the River Water Issues of Nepal, India and Bangladesh* (Jaipur: Nirala, 1993).

Usher, A. D., 'Damming the Theun River, Nordic Companies in Laos', *The Ecologist*, 26, 3 (1996).

Vakil, C. N. and Rao, G. R., *Economic Relations between India and Pakistan* (Bombay: 1966).

Vale, P. and Matlosa, K., 'Beyond the Nation State: Rebuilding South Africa from Below', *Harvard International Review*, 17, 4 (1995).

Vasquez, J. A., *The War Puzzle* (Cambridge: Cambridge University Press, 1993).

Veltrop, J. A., 'Importance of Dams for Water Supply and Hydropower', in Biswas, A. K. et al. (eds), *Water for Sustainable Development in the Twenty-first Century*. (Delhi: Oxford University Press, 1993).

Verghese, B. G., *Waters of Hope: Himalaya-Ganga Development and Cooperation of Billion People* (Oxford/New Delhi: IBH Publishing, 1990).

Verghese, B. G. and Iyer, R. R. (eds), *Harnessing the Eastern Himalayan Rivers: Regional Cooperation in South Asia* (New Delhi: Konark Publishers, 1993).

Verghese, B. G. and Iyer, R. R. (eds), *Converting Water into Wealth* (New Delhi: Konark Publishers, 1994).

Verghese, B. G., 'From Dispute to Dialogue to Doing', in Biswas, A. K. and Uitto, J. I. (eds), *Sustainable Development of the Ganges-Brahmaputra-Meghna Basins* (Tokyo: UNU Press, 2001).

Vesilind, P. J., 'Middle East Water: Critical Resource', *National Geographic*, 183, 5 (1993).

Wallensteen, P. (ed.), *Peace Research: Achievements and Challenges* (Boulder, COL: Westview Press, 1988).

Wallensteen, P. and Swain, A., *International Fresh Water Resources: Source of Conflict or Cooperation* (Stockholm: Stockholm Environment Institute, 1997).

Warburg, G. R., *Egypt and the Sudan: Studies in History and Politics* (London: Frank Cass, 1985).

214

Warburg, G. R., 'The Nile in Egyptian-Sudanese Relations', *Orient*, 32, 4 (1991).

Ward, D. R., *Water Wars: Drought, Flood, Folly, and the Politics of Thirst* (New York: Riverhead Books, 2002).

Waterbury, J., *Hydropolitics of the Nile Valley* (Syracuse: Syracuse University Press, 1979).

Waterbury, J., *Riverains and Lacustrines: Toward International Cooperation in the Nile Basin* (Princeton University Research Programme in Development Studies, Discussion Paper No. 107, September 1982).

WCD, *Dams and Development: A New Framework for Decision Making* (The Report of the World Commission on Dams, 16 November 2000).

Weatherbee, D. E., 'Cooperation and Conflict in the Mekong River Basin', *Studies in Conflict & Terrorism*, 20, 2 (1997).

WHO, *Our Planet, Our Health: Report of the WHO Commission on Health and the Environment* (Geneva: World Health Organization, 1992).

WHO, *Health and Environment in Sustainable Development: Five Years after the Earth Summit* (Geneva: World Health Organization, 1997).

WMO et al., *Comprehensive Assessment of Freshwater Resources of the World* (Geneva: WMO, 1997).

Wolf, A. T., *Hydropolitics Along the Jordan River: Scarce Water and its Impact on the Arab-Israeli Conflict* (Tokyo: UNU Press, 1995).

Wolf, A. T., 'International Water Conflict Resolution: Lessons from Comparative Analysis', *International Journal of Water Resources Development*, 13, 3 (1997).

Wolf, A. T., 'Conflict and Cooperation along International Waterways, *Water Policy*, 1, 2 (1998).

Wolf, A. T., Natharius, J. A., Danielson, J. J., Ward, B. S. and Pender, J. K., 'International River Basins of the World', *International Journal of Water Resources Development*, 15, 4 (1999).

Wolf, A. T., Yoffe, S. B. and Giordano, M., 'International Waters: Identifying Basins at Risk', *Water Policy*, 5 (2003).

Wolfensohn, J., 'Rich Nations Can Remove World Poverty as a Source of Conflict', *International Herald Tribune*, 6 October 2001.

World Bank, *World Development Report 1992: Development and the Environment* (New York: Oxford University Press, 1992).

World Bank, *From Scarcity to Security: Averting a Water Crisis in the Middle East and North Africa* (Washington DC: World Bank, 1998).

World Bank, *Water Resource Management* (Washington DC: World Bank Policy Paper, 1993).

World Resource Institute, *World Resources 1990-91* (New York: Oxford University Press, 1991).

World Resource Institute, *World Resources, 1991-92* (New York: Oxford University Press, 1992).

World Resource Institute, *World Resources, 2000-01* (Washington DC: World Resource Institute, 2001).

WSCU, *Regional Strategic Action Plan for Integrated Water Resources Development and Management in the SADC Countries 1999-2004* (Maseru, Lesotho: Water Sector Coordinating Unit Summary Report, 1998).

Yetim, M., 'Governing International Common Pool Resources: The International Water Courses of the Middle East', *Water Policy*, 4 (2002).

Yoffe, S. B. and Wolf, A. T., 'Water, Conflict and Cooperation: Geographical Perspectives,' *Cambridge Review of International Affairs*, 12, 2 (1999).

Zhou, P. P., *Issues Paper on Shared Water Resources* (Regional Centre for Southern Africa, RAPID Paper, 1997).

Zich, A., 'Before the Flood: China's Three Gorges', *National Geographic*, 192, 3 (1997).

Index

Abbud, General Ibrahim 96
'absolute water scarcity' 4
Africa: dam building 21; Nile
    River see Nile River; North see
    Middle East/North Africa;
    population growth 3; runoff 2;
    South see South Africa;
    urbanization 11; water
    diversion schemes 15; water
    usage 7
agriculture: Ethiopia 104; Nile
    basin countries 94; South
    Africa/Zimbabwe 141 151;
    South Asia/Thailand 44, 132–3;
    and water scarcity 3–4; water
    use pattern/priorities 9, 15–16
Akasombo Dam (Ghana) 13, 21
Allahabad (Hindu city) 56
Allan, J. A. 85, 109
Amazon River 2, 14
Andhra Pradesh, water dispute 23,
    72
Angat basin (Philippines), water
    dispute 23
Anglo-Egyptian Agreements (1929
    and 1953) 95–6
Anglo-Egyptian Condominium on
    Sudanese affairs 95
Angola 149; civil war in, 147
Arab-Israeli conflict 83, 84
Arizona, Colorado River dispute
    (California) 22

Arun Dam (Nepal) 21
ASEAN association 128, 130
Asia: Mekong River see Mekong
    River; population growth, 3;
    South see South Asia;
    urbanization, 11; water
    diversion schemes, 15; water
    usage, 7
Asian Development Bank 160,
    177
'Assembly of the Poor' (Mekong
    River) 122
Aswan High Dam 95, 96, 97, 98,
    99, 159
Ataturk Dam (Turkey) 21, 24, 87,
    90
Atbara River (Kashm el Girba
    Dam) 95, 101, 102
Athi Dam (Kenya) 21
Athi River, water dispute 23
Awami League Government
    (Bangladesh) 70
Ayub Khan, Muhammad
    (President of Pakistan) 48
al-Azhari, Ismail (Sudanese Prime
    Minister) 96

Badrinath (Hindu city) 56
Baglihar hydroelectric dam
    (Chenab River) 49
Baisaltan (Gandak Barrage) 51
Bangladesh: Awami League

Government 70; dam
construction 21; Ganges River,
long-term solutions 63–8;
groundwater withdrawal 18;
India, relations with 56–7,
62–8, 71; Indo-Bangladesh
Joint River Commission 26;
water conflict 22 see also Indo-
Bangladesh Agreements (1975
and 1977); Indo-Bangladesh
Joint River Commission (JRC);
Indo-Bangladesh Task Force of
Experts
Bangladesh National Party (BNP)
70
Barisal coastal area (Pakistan) 59
Baro-Akobo (Nile Basin) 93
Basic Water Requirement (BWR),
failure to meet 7, 8–9
basin-based strategy 171–7;
institutions, building 174–7;
international river as single unit
172–3; rational use of water
173–4
Basu, Jyoti 68
Batang Ai Dam (Indonesia) 21
Batoka Gorge hydroelectric
project (Zambezi River) 152
Bay of Bengal 62, 71
Beas River (Punjab) 21, 48
Begin, Menachem (Israeli Prime
Minister) 100
Berlin Summit (1884) 95
Beschomer, Natasha 90
Bhabani River, water dispute 23
Bhagirathi-Hooghly distributary
55, 56, 57–8, 59, 63, 72
Bhakra Nangal project 48–9
Bharatiyn Janata Party (BJP) 69,
70
Bhasani, Maulana 60
Bhimnagar (Kosi Barrage) 51

BJP (Bharatiyn Janata Party) 69,
70
Black, Eugene 47
BNP (Bangladesh National Party)
70
Bor River (Nile area) 99
BOT (build-operation-transfer)
investment mechanism 133
Botswana: dam construction 145;
Namibia, conflict with 29, 30,
148, 152; and Okavango River
147; water abstraction projects
151; water use 141
Brahmaputra River 54–5, 62, 63,
see also Ganges-Brahmaputra
mega-basin
Brazil 14, 21
Brokopondo Dam (Suriname) 21
Buddhists, importance of water to
1
Burma, Mekong River
cooperation, exclusion from
118, 129, 135, 136
Bush, President George W 15,
179
BWR (Basic Water Requirement),
failure to meet 7, 8–9

Calcutta port 57–8, 71
California 10–11, 22
Cambodia: hydropower 120, 133;
Khmer Rouge, victory in 121;
and Mekong River 119, 120,
121, 126, 127, 131, 133, 137;
National Mekong Committee
133; Paris Peace Agreement
(1991) 127; Phnom Penh 118,
131; Tonle Saep Lake 116, 126
Camp David meeting (2000) 85,
98–9, 103
Canada 9, 10
Caponera, D. A. 1
Caracol Dam (Mexico) 21

Cauvery River dispute
(Karnataka/Tamil Nadu) 22
Central Intelligence Agency (CIA)
79
Centre for Natural Resources,
Energy and Transport
(CNRET) 26
Chad (Middle East) 81
Chao Praya River (Southeast Asia)
133
Chenab River (Punjab) 44, 49
Cherapunji (India), seasonal water
scarcity, 6
Chiang Rai (Thai city) 124, 125
Chieng Khan (Mekong tributary)
133
China: dam construction 13, 21,
32, 135; and Indo-Bangladesh
relations 63; industrial water
use 10; and Mekong River
107–8, 118, 123, 124, 129,
130, 135–6, 137; 'reservoir
resettlers' 14; South China Sea
123, 124; Three Gorges Dam
project 13, 21, 32, 135; water
diversion systems 15; Xiaowan
Dam 135; Yellow River 136,
179, *see also* Yunnan Province
(China)
Chisapani Dam (Karnali Project)
51
Chittagong port (Bangladesh) 69
Chobe River (Southern Africa)
146, 147, 148
Chon Buri (Thailand) 124
Christians, importance of water to
1
CIA (Central Intelligence Agency)
79
CNRET (Centre for Natural
Resources, Energy and
Transport) 26
Cold War 160

Colombia, dam construction 21
Colombo (International Water
Management Institute) 25
Colorado River 22, 35
Commercial Navigation
Agreement (Upper Mekong
basin) 2002 124
Committee for the Coordination
of Investigations of Lower
Mekong basin (Mekong
Committee) *see* Mekong
Committee
Communist Party, Nepal (UML)
53
Community of Interest/Optimum
Development approach 163
Comprehensive Development in
Indochina Forum 128
conflict, water 19–33; aid factor
32–3; armed, risk of 25, 33;
increasing demand for water
20; internal 20–4; international
24–5; risk factor 31–2; rivers,
international 25–31; time
factor 31;
'upstream/downstream'
conflicts 27
Congo, Independent State of 95
Congo/Zaire river basin 142, 143;
runoff 2, 36
Congress Party (India) 44, 61, 64,
69, 70
Congress Party (Nepal) 53
Convention on the Law of Non-
navigational Uses of
International Watercourses
(1997) 154, 162, 165–7
cooperation 158–81; institutions
34–5; international rivers
33–6; Mekong River 127–32;
Middle East/North Africa
105–7; South Africa (Zambezi

River) 33, 152–3; South Asia 72–3

Cooperation for Sustainable Development of Mekong River basin (1995 Agreement) 128, 129–30, 131, 132, 160; and Burma 136; and China 135, 136

Council of Ministers of Water Affairs of Nile Basin (Nile-COM) 33, 106

Covenant of Dayr-es-Sultan (Jerusalem) 109

CPI (M) 69

Crow, Ben 60, 61

dam construction: benefits/drawbacks 13–14; China 13, 21, 32, 135; Laos 21, 119, 120, 133; mega dams 13, 21; Mekong River countries 119–23, 133; North America 12; safety factors 14; water scarcity 12–14 *see also* *specific dams, e.g. High Aswan Dam*

dams, destruction in war 24

Danube River, Gabcikovo/Nagymaros dam project 29

DDT 9

Dehli Agreement (1949) 47

Desai, Shri Morarji Ranchhodji (Indian Prime Minister) 61–2

Donor Consultative Group (Mekong Commission) 129

Drakensberg Mountains (Southern Africa) 144

Earth Summit, Agenda 21, 7

earth, use of water 1–2

East Gohr Canal (Jordan) 84

Eastern National Water Carrier (ENWC) 147–8

Eastern Nile (EN-SAP) 106

ECAFE (Economic Commission for Asia and the Far East) 120

Egypt: Anglo-Egyptian Agreements (1929 and 1953) 95–6; Anglo-Egyptian Condominium on Sudanese affairs 95; Copts, status of 109; and Ethiopia 109; growing water scarcity 101, 102; and Nile River 94, 95–6; Sudan, relations with 98–9, 100, 159, *see also* Nile River Agreement (Egypt-Sudan, 1959)

EIA (Environmental Impact Assessment) 125

Eisenhower, President Dwight 83

Elephants (Transvaal) River (Southern Africa) 145

ELMS (Environment and Land Management Sector Unit) 153

Environmental Impact Assessment (EIA) 125

ENWC (Eastern National Water Carrier) 147–8

Equatorial Lakes Region (Nile) 91, 93, 106

'equitable utilization' principle 163–4, 165, 178

Eritrea-Ethiopia war (1998–2000) 30

Ershad, President Hussain Mohammed 65, 66

Ethiopia: as Africa's 'Hidden Empire', 103; and Egypt, 109; Eritrea-Ethiopia war (1998–2000), 30; and Nile River, 93, 94, 95, 98, 103–5, 160; as socialist republic, 103; as threat to Egypt's water

supply, 29; Welo famine (1972–74), 103, 104
Euphrates River Agreement (1987) 36
Euphrates-Tigris rivers 86–91; dam construction, 14; Joint Technical Committee, 33, 87; physical features, 86; and Syria, 31, 86, 87, 160; Treaties, 87; and Turkey, 86–90, 160, *see also* Tigris River
Europe: dam construction 12; EUWFD (EU Water Framework Directive) 2000, 169–70; industrial water use, 10

Falkenmark, Malin 2, 4
FAO (Food and Agricultural Organization) 162
Farakka Barrage 58, 59, 60
Farakka Peace March 60–1
fertilizers 7, 9
Finland 9, 164
fish resources, Mekong River 126
flood control, Mekong River 126–7
Food and Agricultural Organization (FAO) 162
Foreign Ministers' Conference (Istanbul) 1976 60
Foster, Stephen 18
France, water shortage 10

Gabcikovo/Nagymaros dam project (Danube River) 29
Galana River, water dispute 23
Gandak Barrage (Baisaltan) 51
Gandak River (Nepal) 49, 54
Gandhi, Indira 60, 61
Gandhi, Rajiv 65, 66
Ganga see Ganges River
'Ganga Mai' (Mother Ganges) 56

Ganga-Kobadak Scheme (Pakistan) 58
Ganges River 54–68, *55*; cooperation 33; long-term solutions, proposals for (1978) 62–8; physical features 43, 54; religious significance 55–6; runoff 2, 57; water pollution, 10
Ganges River Water Sharing Agreement (1996) 36, 68–72, 73, 161; obstacles to lasting solution 71–2
Ganges Water: Crisis in Bangladesh (Explanatory Memorandum) 61
Ganges-Brahmaputra mega-basin 2, 26, 43, 70, 72, *see also* Brahmaputra River
GAP Project (Turkey) 15, 29, 32, 87, 88–9, 160
Garden of Eden 1
GEF (Global Environmental Facility) 148, 162
GEMS (Global Monitoring System) 11–12
Germany: dams, damage to (1943) 24, *see also* West Germany
Ghana, dam construction, 13, 21
Girjapur Barrage (India), 54
Gleditsch, N. P., 25, 28, 33
Gleick, Peter, 6, 7, 30, 175
Global Environmental Facility (GEF), 148, 162
Global Monitoring System (GEMS), 11–12
Global Water Partnership (GWP), 162
Godavari River, 72
Golan Heights, 82, 84, 85
Golden Triangle (Mekong River), 116

Gorbachov, Mikhail Sergeevich, 15

Gouri Madhumati beach, 58

Grey, D., 28, 33

groundwater, exploitation of, 16–19; Middle East, 80–1

Gujarat (India) 17

Gujral, I. K. (Indian Prime Minister) 53

Gulf War (1990–91), 24, 30, 90, 100

Gwembe Valley (Zambia) 151

GWP (Global Water Partnership) 162

Habitat Conference, Istanbul (1996) 28

Haditha Dam (Euphrates) 89

Haldia, port facility at 71–2

Hamner, J. 28

Han River, dam construction 29

Hanson, Victor D. 10–11

Hardinge Bridge 69

Hardwar (Indian city) 56

Hasina, Sheikh 68

Hegre, H. 25, 33

Helsinki Rules for International Watercourses 164

Herodotus (Greek historian) 94

High Aswan Dam 95, 96, 97, 98, 159

Himalayas, ice in 43

Hindus: Ganges River, significance to 55–6; importance of water to 1

Homer-Dixon, T. F. 91

Hoover Dam 13

Huran Plain 82

Hussein, Saddam 31, 100

Hydromet Project (1967) 105

hydropower: Cambodia 120, 133; Laos, 21, 119, 120, 133; Mekong River, 119, 120, 132–5; Neelam-Jhelum River (Kishenganga), 49

ICCON (International Consortium for Cooperation on the Nile) 106

ICJ (International Court of Justice) 29, 49, 148

ILA (International Law Association) 163–4

ILC (International Law Commission) 164–5

Ilisu Dam (Tigris) 88

India: Bangladesh, relations with 56–7, 62–8, 71; Congress Party, 44, 61, 64, 69, 70; dam construction, 13, 14, 21; Five Year Plans, 44–5; Ganges River, long-term solutions, 62–3; groundwater withdrawal, 17, 18; Indus River see Indus River; Krishna River dispute, 22; Mahakali River see Mahakali River; Narmada Projects, 21, 32; National Hydro Power Corporation (NHPC), 51; national integration, 45; Nepal, relations with, 50, 161; Pakistan, relations with, 46–7, 49, 50, 159; population of, 45; United Front Government, 70; water development, large-scale, 45; water scarcity (Cherapunji), 6; Yamuna River dispute, 23; see also Dehli Agreement (1949); Ganges River; Indo-Bangladesh Agreements (1975 and 1977); Indo-Bangladesh Joint River Commission (JRC); Indo-Bangladesh Task Force of Experts; Inter-Dominion Accord (India/Pakistan, 1948);

'Standstill Agreement'
(India/Pakistan, 1947)
India-Pakistan conflict (1965 and
1999), 30, 58
Indicative Basin Plan (Mekong
Committee), 120–1
Indira Ghandhi Canal Project, 48–9
Indo-Bangladesh Agreements
(1975 and 1977) 59–60, 61,
62, 64, 69
Indo-Bangladesh Joint River
Commission (JRC) 26, 59, 62,
64, 67, 68, 71
Indo-Bangladesh Task Force of
Experts 66
Indochina War (1960s/1970s),
120
Indonesia, dam construction 21
Indus Basin Development Fund
48, 159
Indus River 21, 43–4, 46–9;
irrigation system 46; Permanent
Indus Commission 48; water
dispute 22
Indus River Treaty (1960) 36, 48,
49, 159
industrial sector, water use
pattern/priorities 9–10, 15–16
Inga rapids 36
insecticides 9
Inter-Dominion Accord
(India/Pakistan, 1948) 46–7
Interim Mekong Committee
(1978) 121
'international basins', meaning 27
International Consortium for
Cooperation on the Nile
(ICCON) 106
International Court of Justice
(ICJ) 29, 49, 148
International Drinking Water
Supply and Sanitation Decade
(UN) 7

International Law Association
(ILA) 163–4
International Law Commission
(ILC) 164–5
international rivers see rivers,
international
International Water Court,
proposals for 178
international water law 163–7
International Water Management
Institute (Colombo) 25
International Water for Peace
Conference (Washington) 1967
58
International Water Resources
Association 162
Iran-Iraq war (1980–88), dam
destruction 24
Iraq: dam construction 89;
Euphrates-Tigris Rivers 86;
Gulf War see Gulf War
(1990–91); and Syria 88, 160;
Treaty of Friendship and Good
Neighbourliness (Ankara,
1946) 87; and Turkey 90–1
irrigation: food security 3–4;
Indus River 46; Mekong River
132–5; Nepal 50; Punjab
province 44
Islam, importance of water to 1
Islamic Foreign Ministers'
Conference (Istanbul) 1976 60
Israel 79–81; Coastal Aquifer 80;
Covenant of Dayr-es-Sultan
(Jerusalem) 109; Gaza area 80,
81; groundwater supplies
17–18; Jordan River system,
82–3; National Water Carrier
84; Six-Day War (1967) 84;
unilateral initiatives 84; War of
Independence 83; Water
Commissioner of 80–1; West
Bank, Mountain Aquifer 80

Israel-Jordan Peace Agreement (1995) 85
Itaipu Dam (Parana River) 13
Italy, and Nile River 95
Itaparica Dam (Brazil) 21
Ivory Coast, Kossou Dam 21

Jammu, Indus River Treaty 49
Japan, urbanization 11
JCE (Joint Committee of Experts) 65, 66, 71
Jhelum River (Indus) 44, 48, 49
Jinghong Dam, and China 135–6
Johnston, Eric 83
Johnston Plan (Middle East) 83
Joint Committee of Experts (JCE) 65, 66, 71
Joint Permanent Technical Commission (JPTC)m South Africa/Lesotho 144
Joint Permanent Water Commission (Botswana/Namibia) 148
Jonglei Canal Project 36, 99–100
Jordan, Israel-Jordan Peace Agreement (1995) 85
Jordan River 82–6; cooperation 33, 161; physical features 82; water conflict 29, 83
JPTC (Joint Permanent Technical Commission), South Africa/Lesotho 144
JRC (Indo-Bangladesh Joint River Commission) 26, 59, 62, 64, 67, 68, 71
Just, R. E. 108

Kafue Dam (Zambezi River basin) 151
Kainji Dam (Nigeria) 21
Kalabagh, dam construction (Indus) 48
Kali River (Nepal) 49

Kanba Dam (South Africa) 13
Kaptai Dam and Lake hydroelectric project (Bangladesh) 21,22
Kariba Dam (Zambezi River basin) 13, 151
Karnali River (Nepal) 49, 54; Karnali Project (Chisapani Dam) 51
Karnataka, water dispute 22, 23
Kashm el Girba Dam (Atbara River) 95, 101, 102
Kashmir, Indus River Treaty 49, 159
Kasikili/Sedudu island dispute 148
Katse Dam (Southern Africa) 144
Keban Dam (Euphrates) 21, 87
Kedarnath (Hindu city) 56
Kedong Ombo Dam (Indonesia), 21
Khmer Rouge (Cambodia) 121
Khone Falls, and Mekong River 123–4
Khruschev, Nikita Sergeevich 97
Khulna coastal area (Pakistan) 59
King Talal Dam (Zarqa River) 84
Kishenganga hydropower project (Neelam-Jhelum River) 49
Koran 1
Korat Plateau (Thailand) 116, 132
Korean War (1950–53) 24, 29
Kosi Barrage/high dam project 51
Kossou Dam (Ivory Coast) 21
Krishna River 72; dispute 23
Kumbh Mela (Hindu festival) 56
Kuthi-Yankti River (Nepal) 49

Laem Chabong (Thai Port) 124
Lake Assad 87
Lake Mead 13
Lake Nasser 13, 97, 98, 99, 101, 109, 159
Lake Tana 95, 103, 109

Lake Tiberias (Sea of Galilee) 82
Lake Victoria, 91, 108
Lam Pao Dam (Thailand), 21
Lancang River (Upper Mekong),
    135
Laos: dam construction 21,
    119,120, 133; Luang Prabang
    124; and Mekong River 118,
    119, 120, 121, 122, 124, 131,
    133, 137; Nam Theun II
    Dam/Nam Theun tributary
    121–2; STEA (Science,
    Technology and Environment
    Agency) 122; Vientiane 131
Latin America: population growth
    3; urbanization 11; water
    diversion schemes 15; water
    usage 7
Lausanne Treaty (1923) 87
Law of Non-Navigational Uses of
    International Watercourses
    (ILC), Draft Report 164–5
LBPTC (Limpopo Basin
    Permanent Technical
    Committee) 146
Lebanon, Jordan River system 82,
    83
Letsibogo Dam (South Africa) 145
LHWP (Lesotho Highlands Water
    Project) 143–4
Libya 81
Lilienthal, David 47
Limpopo Basin Permanent
    Technical Committee (LBPTC)
    146
Limpopo River 142, 145–6
Lindquist, A. 61
Litani River, water conflict 29
Lower Manair Dam (India) 21
Lower Mekong Basin Initiative
    107, 108
Lowi, M. 83
Luang Prabang (Laos) 124

Lundqvist, J. 175

Madur Oya dam (Sri Lanka) 21
Mahabharata (Indian epic) 56
Mahakali Irrigation Project
    (Nepal) 51, 53, 54
Mahakali River 43, 49–54, 72;
    cooperation 33, 161; Treaty on
    Integrated Development (1996)
    53, 54, 73
Mahakali River Commission 54
Mahaveli Project, Sri Lanka 21,
    22
Malawi: agriculture share in 141;
    Mozambique, conflict with
    152; water abstraction projects
    151; Zambezi River, areas of
    conflict 149–50
Malaysia, Singapore, conflict with
    29–30
Mali (Manantali Dam) 21
Manantali Dam (Mali) 21
Mangla Dam (Pakistan) 21, 48
Mashai Dam (Southern Africa),
    construction plans 144
Matabeleland Zambezi Water
    Project 151
Mekong Committee 118, 127,
    135; Indicative Basin Plan
    120–1
Mekong delta 127, 133–4
Mekong River 107–8, 116–39;
    and China 107–8, 135–6;
    cooperation 33, 127–32; dam
    building 119–23; dredging for
    navigation 123–6; fish
    resources 126; flood control
    126–7; future challenges 137;
    hydropower/irrigation, demand
    for 119, 120, 132–5; Lower
    Mekong basin 118, 119, 120,
    124, 126, 128, 134, 136, 137;
    managing (recent years)

127–32; map of, *117*;
'Perspectives for Mekong
Development' (document) 121;
physical features 116; riparian
states sharing 116, 118; runoff,
2; Sambor rapids 125–6; Upper
Mekong basin 116, 118, 124,
125, 135, *see also* Cambodia;
Cooperation for Sustainable
Development of Mekong River
basin (1995 Agreement);
Interim Mekong Committee
(1978); Laos; Mekong
Committee; Mekong delta;
Mekong River Commission;
Thailand; Vietnam
Mekong River Commission
(MRC), 108, 128–32, 133,
160; achievements 131; Burma,
exclusion from 136; China,
exclusion from 136; Council
128, 129; Donor Consultative
Group 129; drawbacks, 131–2;
Joint Committee 128–9, 130;
National Mekong Committees
(NMCs), 129; procedure, 130;
Secretariat, 128, 131
'Mekong Spirit' 130
Mengistu, Haile Mariam
(Ethiopian statesman) 103, 104
Menlik II (Ethiopia) 95
Mexico 21, 35
Middle East/North Africa 79–115;
basin-wide development
107–10; Camp David meeting
(2000) 85, 98–9, 103;
cooperative arrangements,
establishing 105–7; Egypt and
Sudan, growing water scarcity
101–5; Euphrates-Tigris rivers
86–91; groundwater supplies
18; Jordan River system 82–6;
Nile River 91–110, 92; Sinai

New Lands 103; water war 32,
see also Egypt; Ethiopia; Israel;
Sudan; Turkey
Mohale Dam (Southern Africa)
144
monsoons, 6, 43–4; Mekong
River 116
Mopipi Dam (Okavango River
basin) 147
MoU (Tanakpur Agreement) 1991
52, 53
Mount Hermon (Syria) 82
Mount Meru 1
Mozambique 141, 152
MRC (Mekong River
Commission) *see* Mekong River
Commission (MRC)
Mubarak, Hosni 100, 102
multi-lateral water basins 179
Murchison Falls, Uganda 99
Murray River, water dispute 23

NAFTA (North American Free
Trade Association) 170
Nagarjunsagar Project (India) 21
Nam Ngum Dam (Laos) 21, 119
Nam Pong Dam (Thailand) 21
Nam Theun 2 Dam/Nam Theun
tributary (Laos) 121–2, 133
Namibia: Botswana, conflict with
29, 30, 148, 152; East Caprivi
region 152; and Okavango
River 147–8; water abstraction
projects, 151
Nanela Dam (Pakistan) 21
Narmada Projects (India) 21, 32
Nasser, Gamal Abdel (Egyptian
President) 96
National Hydro Power
Corporation (NHPC) 51
National Mekong Committees
(NMCs) 129, 133

Natural Water Flow Approach 163

NAWAPA (North American Water and Power Alliance) 15

NBI (Nile Basin Initiative) 33, 106, 107, 109–10, 160

Neelam-Jhelum River Kishenganga hydropower project 49

Nehru, Jawaharlal (Indian Prime Minister) 48

NEL-SAP (Nile Equatorial Lakes Region) 91, 93, 106

Nepal: Communist Party (UML) 53; Congress Party 53; dam construction 21; East-West Highway 52; Indo-Nepalese relations 50, 161; JCE delegation 65–6; Mahakali Irrigation Project, 51; Sarada Treaty, UK (1920) 50–1, 53; Tanakpur Agreement (Memorandum of Understanding) 1991, 52, 53

Nepali Congress Party 53

Netanyahu, S. 108

Netzahualcoyotl Dam (Mexico) 21

NHPC (National Hydro Power Corporation) 51

Niger Dam (Nigeria) 21

Nile Basin Initiative (NBI) 33, 106, 107, 109–10, 160

Nile River 91–110, 92, 93, 179; Anglo-Egyptian Agreements (1929 and 1953) 95–6; basin-wide development 107–10; Blue Nile 91–2, 95, 96, 97, 98, 109; cooperation initiatives 105–7; Egypt/Sudan, sharing by 29; and Ethiopia 93, 94, 95, 98, 103–5; as God Hapi 94; High Aswan Dam 95, 96, 97, 98; history 94–5; and Italy 95; Jonglei Canal Project 99–100; Lake Nasser 97, 98; physical features 91; riparian agreements 94–7; runoff, 2; and South Africa 142–3; and Sudan 94, 95, 96–7, 99; TECCONILE (Technical Committee for the Promotion of the Development and Environmental Protection of the Nile Basin) 106; Tripoli Charter (1969) 98; and United Kingdom 95; violent conflict, risk of 32; White Nile, 91, 98, 109 see also Nile Basin Initiative (NBI)

Nile River Agreement (Egypt-Sudan, 1959) 36, 96–7, 98, 99, 102

Nile-COM (Council of Ministers of Water Affairs of Nile Basin) 33, 106

Nile-SEC (Secretariat) 106

Nile-TAC (Technical Advisory Committee) 106

NMCs (National Mekong Committees) 129, 133

'no-harm principle' 165, 178

Non-aligned Movement Summit 60

North Africa see Middle East/North Africa

North America, industrial water use 10

North American Water and Power Alliance (NAWAPA) 15

Ntoahae Reservoir (Southern Africa), construction plans 144

al-Numayri, Jafar 98, 99, 100

OKACOM (Permanent Water

Commission on Okavango River) 148
Okavango River and Delta 30, 142, 146–9; Southern Okavango Integrated Water Development Projects 147
ORACOM (Orange-Senqu River Commission), Southern Africa 144
Orange River 142, 143–5
Orapa Diamond Mine (Southern Africa) 147
organochlorine insecticides 9
Orontes River, water conflict 29
Oslo Agreements 80; Oslo Accord (1995) 85
Ottoman Empire, fall of (eighteenth century) 94–5

Pa Mong Dam (Mekong River) 121
Padma see Ganges River
Pak Moon River and Dam (Thailand) 122
Pakistan: dam construction 21; groundwater withdrawal 18; India, relations with 46–7, 49, 50, 159; India-Pakistan conflicts (1965 and 1999) 30, 58; Indus River *see* Indus River; separatist movement, 21–2; *see also* Dehli Agreement (1949); Inter-Dominion Accord (India/Pakistan, 1948); 'Standstill Agreement' (India/Pakistan, 1947)
Palestine, division of (1947) 83
Pancheswar Project (Mahakali Irrigation Project) 51, 53, 54
Paradip, port facility at 72
Parana River, Itaipu Dam, 13
Paris Peace Agreement (1991), Cambodia 127

Permanent Water Commission: on Okavango River (OKACOM) 148; Southern Africa/Namibia 144
Peruca Dam, damage to (1993) 24
pesticides 7, 9
Philippines, dam construction 21
Phnom Penh (Cambodia) 118, 131
Pirzada, Sharifudin 58
PKK (Kurdish group) 87, 90
Plan 2010 (Brazil) 14
Poland 9, 10
pollution, water 7–12
Pong Dam (India) 21
population growth: Middle East 86; South Asia 43, 44; Sudan 101; urban populations 11; water scarcity 3, 4
Prasad Koirala, Girija (Nepalese Prime Minister) 52
'principle of equitability' 163–4, 165, 178
Protocol on Shared Watercourse System, 153
Punjab province: Chenab River *see* Chenab River (Punjab); colonial water development scheme 44; groundwater withdrawal 18; irrigation 44; Jhelum River *see* Jhelum River (Punjab); Pakistani part 22; Ravi River *see* Ravi River (Punjab); secessionist movement 21; Sutlej River *see* Sutlej River (Punjab)
Punjub province, Beas River *see* Beas River (Punjab)
PWC (Permanent Water Commission): Okavango River (OKACOM) 148; Southern Africa/Namibia 144

Quadrangle Economic
  Cooperation (Mekong River)
  127–8

Rahman, President Ziaur 61, 69
Ramsar Site, Okavango Delta as
  148
Rao, Narasimha (Indian Prime
  Minister) 52, 67
Ravi River (Punjab) 21, 48;
  irrigation canals 44; Madhopur
  irrigation headwork 46; Thein
  Dam 49
RBO (River Basin Organization)
  178
Reagan, Ronald 22
Red Sea 109
Redcliffe, Sir Cyril 46
Rehman, Mujibur 60, 68
Rhine, pollution in: Action Plan
  (1987) 11; Agreement (1976),
  chloride contamination 35
Rigveda (Hindu holy text) 55
Rio de la Plata river basin (South
  America), dam construction 14
Rishikesh (Hindu city) 56
River Basin Organization (RBO)
  178
river systems, diversion, 15–16
rivers, international: cooperation,
  33–6; external support to
  manage, 177–9; regional
  distribution, 27; in South
  Africa, 141–2; water conflict,
  25–31
Rogun Dam (Ukraine) 53
Roseires Dam (Blue Nile) 96, 97,
  101
runoff: Congo/Zaire river basin 2,
  36; Ganges 2, 57
Russia: water shortage 10, see also
  Soviet Union (former)
Ruwenzori Mountain 91

SAARC (South Asian Association
  for Regional Cooperation)
  66–7
Sadat, Anwar (Egyptian President)
  98, 103–4; assassination, 100
SADC (Southern African
  Development Community)
  155, 161, 170; guidelines 152;
  international rivers in, 142;
  Pretoria meeting 154; Protocol
  on Shared Watercourse System
  (1995) 153–4; rainfall 140;
  Water Sector within 154
Saddam Dam (Tigris) 89
Sadoff, C. W. 28, 33
Saivites (followers of Shiva) 55–6
Salman, S. M. A. 53–4
Sambor Dam/rapids (Mekong
  River) 125–6, 133
Samis (Arctic Circle), water
  conflict 21
Sanmenxia dam (China) 21
Sanxia (Three Gorges Dam
  project, China) 13, 21, 32; and
  Xiaowan Dam 135
Saptakoshi River (Nepal) 49
Sarada Barrage/Canal Project 51
Sarada Treaty (Nepal/UK, 1920)
  50–1, 53
Saudi Arabia 81
Savajina Dam (Colombia) 21
Save River (South Africa) 142,
  146
Scandinavia, industrial water use
  9–10
scarcity of water see water scarcity
Science, Technology and
  Environment Agency (STEA),
  Laos 122
Sea of Galilee, 82
SEARIN (South East Asia Rivers
  Network) 125
Sector Coordinator for Soil and

Water Conservation and Land Utilization (SWCLU) 153
Sedudu/Kasikili island dispute 148
Selassie, Haile (of Ethiopia) 103, 104
Sennar Dam (Blue Nile) 101
September 11 2001 attacks 30–1
Sergeldin, Ismail 28
Shamir, Uri 33
Shashe Dam (South Africa) 145
Shatt al-Arab 86
Shiklomanov, Igor A 1–2
Shire River (Zambezi basin) 152
Sikh Party (Akali Dal), Punjab 21
Simao Port (Yunnan Province) 123, 124
Sind province, water dispute 22
Singapore, Malaysia, conflict with 29–30
Six-Day War (1967) 84
Soan River (Indus) 48
South Africa 140–57; apartheid regime 143; Congo/Zaire river basin 142, 143; dam construction 13; international rivers 141–2; Limpopo River 142, 145–6; Okavango River and Delta 30, 142, 146–9; Orange River 142, 143–5; regional approach, finding 153–5; shared river basins 142; water scarcity 140–1, 151, 154; Zambezi River see Zambezi River, see also SADC (Southern African Development Community)
South Anatolia Project (Turkey) 31
South Asia 43–78; cooperation 72–3; Ganges Agreement (1996) 68–72; Ganges River 54–68; groundwater withdrawal 17; Indus River (India/Pakistan) 46–9; Mahakali River (India/Nepal) 49–54; population growth 43, 44; Punjab see Punjab province, see also Bangladesh; India; Pakistan; Punjab province
South Asian Association for Regional Cooperation (SAARC) 66–7
South East Asia Rivers Network (SEARIN) 125
South Korea, dam construction 13
Southern African Development Community (SADC) see SADC (Southern African Development Community)
Soviet Union (former): water diversion systems 15, see also Russia
SPLA (Sudanese People's Liberation Army) 100
Sri Lanka 21, 22
Srisailam Project (India) 21
'Standstill Agreement' (India/Pakistan) 1947, 46
STEA (Science, Technology and Environment Agency) Laos, 122
Stockholm Water Symposium 162
Subarnarekha Project (India) 21
Sudan: Egypt, relations with 98–9, 100, 159; growing water scarcity 101–2; and Nile River 94, 95, 96–7, 99; SPLA (Sudanese People's Liberation Army) 100, see also Nile River Agreement (Egypt-Sudan, 1959)
Sudd region (Nile area) 99
Suriname, Brokopondo Dam 21
Sutlej River (Punjab) 21, 44, 46, 48, 49
Sutlej Valley Project Region 48

Sutlej-Yamuna Link Canal 49
SWCLU (Sector Coordinator for Soil and Water Conservation and Land Utilization) 153
Sweden 9–10, 21
Syria: Euphrates-Tigris Rivers 31, 86, 87; and Iraq 88, 160; Jordan River system 82, 83, 85; and Turkey 88, 90, 160

Tabqa Dam (Euphrates) 87
Takakpur project 51, 52
Taliban 31
Tamil Nadu, water dispute 22, 23
Tana Dam (Kenya) 21
Tana River, water dispute 23
Tanakpur Barrage project 53, 54
Tanakpur MoU (1991) 52, 53
Tanzania 142–3
Tarbela Dam (Indus) 21, 48
Teban basin 26
TECCONILE (Technical Committee for the Promotion of the Development and Environmental Protection of the Nile Basin) 106
Technical Committee for the Promotion of the Development and Environmental Protection of the Nile Basin (TECCONILE) 106
Tehri Dam (India) 21
Tekezze 93
Terai plains (Nepal) 50
Territorial Sovereignty Doctrine 163
terrorism 30–1
Thailand: Chiang Rai city 124, 125; dam construction 21, 120; Korat Plateau 116, 132; Laem Chabong port 124; and Mekong River 118–19, 120, 122–3, 124, 125, 128, 132,

134, 137; Pak Moon River/Dam 122; and Quadrangle Cooperation 128; and Vietnam 134
Thames River, pollution 11
Thein Dam (Ravi River) 49
Theun Hinbaoun dam 133
Three Gorges Dam project (China) 13, 21, 32; and Xiaowan Dam 135
Tigris River 30, 87, 88, see also Euphrates-Tigris river basin
Tokyo 11
Tonle Saep Lake (Cambodia) 116, 126
Toset, H. P. 25, 33
Transboundary Freshwater Database Project (Oregon State University) 26
Transvaal (Elephants) River, Southern Africa 145
Treaty of Friendship and Good Neighbourliness (Ankara, 1946) 87
Tripoli Charter (1969) 98
Tsoelike Reservoir (Southern Africa), construction plans 144
Tucurul Dam (Brazil) 21
Tugela River (Southern Africa) 145
Tulbul Navigation Project 49
Turkey: Ataturk Dam, use in international conflict 24; dam construction 13, 14, 21; Euphrates-Tigris Rivers 86–90; GAP Project 15, 29, 32, 87, 88–9, 160; Habitat Conference (1996), Istanbul 28; and Iraq 90–1; Islamic Foreign Ministers' Conference (Istanbul, 1976) 60; Lausanne Treaty (1923) 87; population growth 86; South Anatolia

Project 31; and Syria 88, 90, 160; Treaty of Friendship and Good Neighbourliness (Ankara, 1946) 87; water diversion systems 15, *see also* Ataturk Dam (Turkey)

Uganda, Murchison Falls 99
UK *see* United Kingdom
Ukai Reservoir Project (India) 21
Ukraine, Rogun Dam 53
UML (Communist Party) Nepal, 53
Umzimvabu River (Southern Africa) 145
UN *see* United Nations
UNDP (United Nations Development Program) 105, 160, 162, 177
UNESCO (United Nations Educational, Scientific and Cultural Organization) 148, 162
Unified Plan (Middle East) 83
United Front Government (India) 70
United Kingdom: Anglo-Egyptian Agreement (1929) 95–6; Anglo-Egyptian Agreement (1953) 96; Anglo-Egyptian Condominium on Sudanese affairs 95; and Nile River, 95–6; Sarada Treaty, Nepal (1920) 50–1, 53; South Asia, colonial rule 44; Thames River, pollution 11
United Nations: Charter of 129; Convention on the Law of Non-navigational Uses of International Watercourses (1997) 154, 162, 165–7; Dakar inter-regional seminar (1981), 169; Development Program

(UNDP) 105, 160, 162, 177; International Drinking Water Supply and Sanitation Decade 7; Map Library 26; UNESCO (United Nations Educational, Scientific and Cultural Organization) 148, 162; Water Conference (Mar del Plata, 1977) 103
United States of America: dam construction (North America) 12; Mexico, Agreement with (1972) 35; terrorism 30–1; Transboundary Freshwater Database Project (Oregon State University) 26; water diversion systems 15; water shortage 10–11; water use patterns 9, *see also* California; Latin America; North America
Upper Atbara Dam (Sudan) 101
Upper Krishna Projects (India) 21
Upper Pampanga Dam (Philippines) 21
Uprety, K. 53–4
urbanization 11, 15–16, 19
USA *see* United States of America

Vaal tributary (Orange River) 143, 144, 145
Vaishnavites (followers of Vishnu) 55–6
Varanasi (Hindu city) 56
Vientiane (Laos), 131
Vietnam: and Mkong River 119–20, 121, 134, 137; and Thailand 134; unification, 121; war, and dam destruction 24
'virtual water', meaning 173
Volga River 26

water agreements 158–81; availability of water, regional

variation 167–70; basin-based strategy, 171–7; exploitation, 159–61; future issues, 179–80; international organizations 161, 162; international water law, 155–9; legal principles 161, 163–7; quantity allocation 151

water availability, and regional variation 167–70

water barrier concept 4, 6

water crisis 2

water diversion systems 15–16

water scarcity 1–42; absolute 4; availability, and regional variation 167–70; conflict, water 19–33; countries affected 5–6; Egypt/Sudan 101–5; Euphrates-Tigris Rivers 86–7; future challenges 36–7; growing problem 3–7; human survival, and 6–7; pollution 7–12; seasonal 6; Southern Africa 140–1, 151, 154; strategies 12–19

water stress 4

water war (2500 BC) 30

Waterbury, John 101

Weser basin 26

West Bank 80, 84

West Germany, industrial water use 10

Wheeler, Raymond/Wheeler Commission 120

WHO (World Health Organization) minimum water requirements, 7

Windhoek (Namibia) 147

WMO (World Meteorological Organization) 105, 162

Wolf, Aaron 30, 32, 33

Wolfensohn, James (World Bank President) 106

World Bank: and Gap Project 88–9; India/Pakistan negotiations 47; Indus Basin Development Fund 48, 159; International Consortium for Cooperation on the Nile (ICCON) 106; minimum water requirements, 7; policy change (1994) 32

World Commission on Dams 14

World Commission for Water in the Twenty-first Century 162

World Meteorological Organization (WMO) 105, 162

World Summit on Sustainable Development (2002) 162

Worldwatch Institute 179

Wular Barrage 49

WWC (World Water Council) 162

Xiaowan Dam (China) 135

Yamuna Link Canal, Sutlej River (Punjab) 49

Yamuna River (India) 10, 23

Yangtze River (China) 13, 15, 23

Yarmuk River 29, 82, 84

Yellow River (China) 136, 179

Yemen 81

Yoffe S. B., 33

Yohnnes IV (of Ethiopia) 95

Yunnan Province (China) 118, 135; Simao Port, 123, 124

ZACPLAN (Zambezi Action Plan) 152, 153

ZACPROs (ZACPLAN projects) 152, 153

Zambezi Aqueduct 151

Zambezi River 36, 142, 149–53; conflict areas 149–52; cooperation 33, 152–3, 160–1

Zambezi River Authority (ZRA)
151, 152
Zambia 140, 151
ZAMCOM river basin
commission 153

Zarqa River (King Talal Dam) 84
Zia, Begum Khaleda 67, 69, 71
Zimbabwe 145, 149–50, 151
ZRA (Zambezi River Authority)
151, 152